Source Readings in Music History

I. ANTIQUITY AND THE
MIDDLE AGES

II. THE RENAISSANCE

III. THE BAROQUE ERA

IV. THE CLASSIC ERA

V. THE ROMANTIC ERA

SOURCE READINGS IN MUSIC HISTORY

The Baroque Era

Selected and Annotated by
OLIVER STRUNK
PRINCETON UNIVERSITY

W · W · NORTON & COMPANY · INC · New York

Published simultaneously in Canada by
George J. McLeod Limited, Toronto

Musical examples by Gordon Mapes

SBN 393 09682 3

PRINTED IN THE UNITED STATES OF AMERICA
67890

To the Memory of
CARL ENGEL
1883–1944

ACKNOWLEDGMENTS

THE EDITOR wishes to acknowledge with thanks the co-operation of the Oxford University Press which has granted permission to reprint the translation, by F. T. Arnold, of Viadana's preface to the *Cento concerti ecclesiastici*, first published in Arnold's *The Art of Accompaniment from a Thorough-Bass*, a work in which it holds the copyright.

Throughout the book, small letters refer to notes by the authors of the individual selections, arabic numerals to editor's notes. The abbreviation "S.R." followed by a Roman numeral refers to another volume in the *Source Readings in Music History*.

Contents

I

"SECONDA PRATICA" AND "STILE RAPPRESENTATIVO"

1. Pietro de' Bardi — Letter to G. B. Doni   3
2. Ottavio Rinuccini — Euridice — *Dedication*   7
3. Giulio Caccini — Euridice — *Dedication*   10
4. Jacopo Peri — Euridice — *Foreword*   13
5. Giulio Caccini — Le nuove musiche — *Foreword*   17
6. G. M. Artusi — *From* L'Artusi, ovvero, Delle imperfezioni della moderna musica   33
7. Claudio Monteverdi — Il quinto libro de' madrigali — *Foreword with the "Declaration" of His Brother G. C. Monteverdi*   45
8. Claudio Monteverdi — Madrigali guerrieri ed amorosi — *Foreword*   53

II

MUSICAL PRACTICE IN THE BAROQUE AGE

9. Lodovico Grossi da Viadana — Cento concerti ecclesiastici — *Preface*   59
10. Agostino Agazzari — Del sonare sopra il basso   64
11. Heinrich Schütz — Symphoniae sacrae — *Dedications and forewords*   72
12. Georg Muffat — Florilegia *and* Auserlesene Instrumental-Music — *Forewords*   82
13. F. E. Niedt — Musikalische Handleitung — *Foreword*   93

III

OPERATIC RIVALRY IN FRANCE: PRO AND CONTRA LULLY

14. François Raguenet — Parallèle des Italiens et des Français   113

15. Le Cerf de La Viéville, Seigneur de Freneuse — *From the* Comparaison de la musique italienne et de la musique française   129

IV

CRITICAL VIEWS OF ITALIAN OPERA: ADDISON AND MARCELLO

16. Joseph Addison — *From* The Spectator   151
17. Benedetto Marcello — *From* Il teatro alla moda   158

V

THE REFORMULATION OF THE THEORY OF HARMONY AND COUNTERPOINT

18. J. J. Fux — *From the* Gradus ad Parnassum   175
19. J. P. Rameau — *From the* Traité de l'harmonie   204
     Index   215

Preface to the Five-Volume Edition

My *Source Readings in Music History*, a music-historical companion running to more than 900 pages and extending from classical antiquity through the romantic era, was originally published in 1950. That it is now being reissued in parts is due to a recognition, shared by the publishers and myself, that the usefulness of the book would be considerably enhanced if the readings for the single periods were also available separately and in a handier form. From the first, the aim had been to do justice to every age without giving to any a disproportionate share of the space. Thus the book has lent itself naturally to a division into parts, approximately equal in length, each part complete in itself. For use in the classroom, the advantages of the present edition are sufficiently obvious. For the casual reader, whose interest in the history of music is not likely to be all-inclusive, it will have other advantages, equally obvious. In the meantime, the original edition in one volume will remain in print and will be preferred by those who wish to have the whole between two covers, to be able to refer readily from one part of the book to another, and to be able to consult a single index.

In reprinting here the foreword to the edition of 1950, I have retained only those paragraphs that apply in some measure to all parts of the whole.

O. S.

Rome, 1965

Foreword

THIS BOOK began as an attempt to carry out a suggestion made in 1929 by Carl Engel in his *Views and Reviews*—to fulfil his wish for "a living record of musical personalities, events, conditions, tastes . . . a history of music faithfully and entirely carved from contemporary accounts." It owes something, too, to the well-known compilations of Kinsky and Schering and rather more, perhaps, to Andrea della Corte's *Antologia della storia della musica* and to an evaluation of this, its first model, by Alfred Einstein.

In its present form, however, it is neither the book that Engel asked for nor a literary anthology precisely comparable to the pictorial and musical ones of Kinsky and Schering, still less an English version of its Italian predecessor, with which it no longer has much in common. It departs from Engel's ideal scheme in that it has, at bottom, a practical purpose—to make conveniently accessible to the teacher or student of the history of music those things which he must eventually read. Historical documents being what they are, it inevitably lacks the seemingly unbroken continuity of Kinsky and Schering; at the same time, and for the same reason, it contains far more that is unique and irreplaceable than either of these. Unlike della Corte's book it restricts itself to historical documents as such, excluding the writing of present-day historians; aside from this, it naturally includes more translations, fewer original documents, and while recognizing that the somewhat limited scope of the *Antologia* was wholly appropriate in a book on music addressed to Italian readers, it seeks to take a broader view.

That, at certain moments in its development, music has been a subject of widespread and lively contemporary interest, calling forth a flood of documentation, while at other moments, perhaps not less critical, the records are either silent or unrevealing—this is in no way remarkable, for it is inherent in the very nature of music, of letters, and of history. The beginnings of the classical symphony and string quartet passed virtually unnoticed as developments without interest for the literary man; the beginnings of the opera and cantata, developments which concerned him immediately and deeply, were heralded and reviewed in documents so numerous that, even in a book of this size, it has been possible to include only the most significant. Thus, as already suggested, a documentary history of music cannot properly exhibit even the degree of continuity that is possible for an iconographic one or a collection of musical monuments, still less the degree expected of an interpretation. For this reason, too, I have rejected the simple chronological arrangement as inappropriate and misleading and have preferred to allow the documents to arrange themselves naturally under the various topics chronologically ordered in the Table of Contents and the book itself, some of these admirably precise, others perhaps rather too inclusive. As Engel shrewdly anticipated, the frieze has turned out to be incomplete, and I have left the gaps unfilled, as he wished.

For much the same reason, I have not sought to give the book a spurious unity by imposing upon it a particular point of view. At one time it is the musician himself who has the most revealing thing to say; at another time he lets someone else do the talking for him. And even when the musician speaks it is not always the composer who speaks most clearly; sometimes it is the theorist, at other times the performer. If this means that few readers will find the book uniformly interesting, it ought also to mean that "the changing patterns of life," as Engel called them, will be the more fully and the more faithfully reflected.

It was never my intention to compile a musical Bartlett, and I have accordingly sought, wherever possible, to include the complete text of the selection chosen, or—failing this—the complete text of a continuous, self-contained, and independently intelligible passage or series of passages, with or without regard for the chapter divisions of the original. But in a few cases I have made cuts to eliminate digressions or to avoid needless repetitions of things equally well said by earlier writers; in other cases the excessive length and involved construction of the original has forced me to abridge, reducing the scale of the whole while retaining the essential continuity of the argument. All cuts are clearly indicated, either by a row of dots or in annotations.

Without the lively encouragement and patient sympathy of the late William Warder Norton my work on this book would never have been begun. Nor is it at all likely that I would ever have finished it without the active collaboration of my father, William Strunk, Jr., Emeritus Professor of English at Cornell University, whose expert assistance and sound advice were constantly at my disposal during the earlier stages of its preparation and who continued to follow my work on it with the keenest interest until 1946, the year of his death. A considerable number of the translations now published for the first time are largely his work and there are few to which he did not make some improving contribution.

My warmest thanks are due to Professor Otto Kinkeldey, of Cornell University, and to Professor Alfred Einstein, of Smith College, for their extraordinary kindness in consenting to read the entire book in proof and for the many indispensable corrections and suggestions that they have sent me; again to Alfred Einstein, and to Paul Hindemith, for a number of constructive recommendations which grew out of their experiments with sections of the manuscript in connection with their teaching; likewise to my old friends Paul Lang, Arthur Mendel, and Erich Hertzmann, who have always been ready to listen and to advise.

Acknowledgment is due, also, to Dr. Dragan Plamenac, who prepared the greater number of the brief biographical notes which accompany the single readings; to two of my students—Philip Keppler, Jr., who relieved me of some part of the proofreading and J. W. Kerman, who prepared the index; to Gordon Mapes, for his careful work on the autographing of the musical examples; and to Miss Katherine Barnard, Miss Florence Williams, and the entire staff of W. W. Norton & Co., Inc., for their unflagging interest and innumerable kindnesses.

OLIVER STRUNK

The American Academy in Rome

I

"Seconda pratica" and "stile rappresentativo"

1. Pietro de' Bardi

The letter reproduced below was addressed by Pietro de' Bardi—the son of Giovanni, the patron and promoter of the first Florentine "Camerata"—to G. B. Doni (1594–1647), who had asked for information about the first attempts at realizing the new "representative" style which Pietro had witnessed as a youth in his father's home.

Letter to G. B. Doni [1]
[*1634*]

To MY very illustrious and revered patron, the Most Honored Signor Giovan Battista Doni:

My father, Signor Giovanni, who took great delight in music and was in his day a composer of some reputation, always had about him the most celebrated men of the city, learned in this profession, and inviting them to his house, he formed a sort of delightful and continual academy from which vice and in particular every kind of gaming were absent. To this the noble youth of Florence were attracted with great profit to themselves, passing their time not only in pursuit of music, but also in discussing and receiving instruction in poetry, astrology, and other sciences which by turns lent value to this pleasant converse.

Vincenzo Galilei, the father of the present famous astronomer, a man of a certain repute in those days, was so taken with this distinguished assembly that, adding to practical music, in which he was highly regarded, the study of musical theory, he endeavored, with the help of these virtuosi and of his own frequent vigils, to extract the essence of the Greek, the

---

1 Text: Angelo Solerti, *Le origini del melo-dramma* (Turin, 1903), pp. 143–147. Doni makes extensive use of this letter in Chapter 9 of his "Trattato della musica scenica," published posthumously in his collected works (Florence, 1763).

3

Latin, and the more modern writers, and by this means became a thorough master of the theory of every sort of music.

This great intellect recognized that, besides restoring ancient music in so far as so obscure a subject permitted, one of the chief aims of the academy was to improve modern music and to raise it in some degree from the wretched state to which it had been reduced, chiefly by the Goths, after the loss of the ancient music and of the other liberal arts and sciences. Thus he was the first to let us hear singing in *stile rappresenta- tivo*, in which arduous undertaking, then considered almost ridiculous, he was chiefly encouraged and assisted by my father, who toiled for en- tire nights and incurred great expense for the sake of this noble discovery, as the said Vincenzo gratefully acknowledges to my father in his learned book on ancient and modern music.[2] Accordingly he let us hear the lament of Count Ugolino, from Dante,[3] intelligibly sung by a good tenor and precisely accompanied by a consort of viols. This novelty, al- though it aroused considerable envy among the professional musicians, was pleasing to the true lovers of the art. Continuing with this under- taking, Galilei set to music a part of the Lamentations and Responds of Holy Week, and these were sung in devout company in the same man- ner.

Giulio Caccini, considered a rare singer and a man of taste, although very young, was at this time in my father's "Camerata," and feeling himself inclined toward this new music, he began, entirely under my father's instructions, to sing ariettas, sonnets, and other poems suitable for reading aloud, to a single instrument and in a manner that astonished his hearers.

Also in Florence at this time was Jacopo Peri, who, as the first pupil of Cristofano Malvezzi, received high praise as a player of the organ and the keyboard instruments and as a composer of counterpoint and was rightly regarded as second to none of the singers in that city. This man, in competition with Giulio, brought the enterprise of the *stile rappresenta- tivo* to light, and avoiding a certain roughness and excessive antiquity which had been felt in the compositions of Galilei, he sweetened this style, together with Giulio, and made it capable of moving the passions in a rare manner, as in the course of time was done by them both.

By so doing, these men acquired the title of the first singers and in- ventors of this manner of composing and singing. Peri had more science, and having found a way of imitating familiar speech by using few sounds

---

2 See *S.R.* II, 113, note 5.   8 *Inferno*, xxxiii, 4-75.

and by meticulous exactness in other respects, he won great fame. Giulio's inventions had more elegance.

The first poem to be sung on the stage in *stile rappresentativo* was the story of *Dafne*, by Signor Ottavio Rinuccini, set to music by Peri in few numbers and short scenes and recited and sung privately in a small room.[4] I was left speechless with amazement. It was sung to the accompaniment of a consort of instruments, an arrangement followed thereafter in the other comedies. Caccini and Peri were under great obligation to Signor Ottavio, but under still greater to Signor Jacopo Corsi,[5] who, becoming ardent and discontent with all but the superlative in this art, directed these composers with excellent ideas and marvelous doctrines, as befitted so noble an enterprise. These directions were carried out by Peri and Caccini in all their compositions of this sort and were combined by them in various manners.

After the *Dafne*, many stories were represented by Signor Ottavio himself, who, as good poet and good musician in one, was received with great applause, as was the affable Corsi, who supported the enterprise with a lavish hand. The most famous of these stories were the *Euridice* and the *Arianna;*[6] besides these, many shorter ones were set to music by Caccini and Peri. Nor was there any want of men to imitate them, and in Florence, the first home of this sort of music, and in other cities of Italy, especially in Rome, these gave and are still giving a marvelous account of themselves on the dramatic stage. Among the foremost of these it seems fitting to place Monteverdi.

I fear that I have badly carried out Your Most Reverend Lordship's command, not only because I have been slow to obey Your Lordship, but also because I have far from satisfied myself, for there are few now living who remember the music of those times. Nonetheless I believe that as I serve Your Lordship with heartfelt affection, so Your Lordship will confirm the truth of my small selection from the many things that might be said about this style of *musica rappresentativa* which is in such esteem.

But I hope that I shall in some way be excused through the kindness of Your Most Excellent Lordship, and predicting for Your Lordship

---

4 For the involved history of this work, see O. G. Sonneck's " 'Dafne,' the First Opera," *Sammelbände der Internationalen Musik-Gesellschaft,* XV (1913–14), 102–110, or his note on the libretto in the Catalogue of *Opera Librettos Printed before 1800* (Washington, 1914), I, 339–345.

5 See the further references to this influential patron and amateur by Rinuccini and Peri (pp. 8, 13 and 15 below). Corsi set at least two numbers from Rinuccini's *Dafne* to music; for a recent reprint of the second of these see Robert Haas, *Die Musik des Barock* (Potsdam, 1934), p. 23. An elegy on Corsi's death, set to music by Marco da Gagliano, was published in 1604.

6 Set to music by Monteverdi in 1608.

a most happy Christmas, I pray that God Himself, the father of all blessings, may grant Your Lordship perfect felicity.

Florence, December 14, 1634.
   Your Very Illustrious and Reverend Lordship's
      Most humble servant,
         Pietro Bardi, Conte di Vernio.

2. Ottavio Rinuccini

Ottavio Rinuccini, the librettist of the *Euridice,* was born in Florence in 1562, and if we except his brief stay in Paris following the marriage of Maria dei Medici and Henry IV of France, he remained a resident of Florence until his death in 1621. We first hear of him in a musical connection as the author of the texts for a group of madrigals performed in honor of the wedding of Virginia dei Medici and Cesare d'Este in 1587; two years later, in 1589, he provided the texts set to music by Marenzio for the intermezzo depicting Apollo's combat with the dragon, performed in honor of the wedding of Ferdinand dei Medici and Christine of Lorraine. His work for this intermezzo was later expanded in his *Dafne,* set to music by Peri and Corsi in 1594, by Marco da Gagliano in 1607, and—in a German translation by Martin Opitz—by Heinrich Schütz in 1627; it thus becomes the connecting link between the long series of Florentine intermezzi, which had begun in 1539, and the opera itself. Aside from his early wedding-pieces and his librettos for *Dafne* and *Euridice,* Rinuccini is also the author of two librettos written for Monteverdi in 1608—*Arianna* and *Il Ballo delle ingrate*—and of madrigals and canzonette set to music by Monteverdi, Marco da Gagliano, and other early monodists. His collected verses were published posthumously in 1622.

Euridice [1]

[*1600*]

Dedication

To THE most Christian Maria Medici, Queen of France and of Navarre.

It has been the opinion of many, most Christian Queen, that the ancient Greeks and Romans, in representing their tragedies upon the stage,

---

1 Text: Solerti, *op. cit.,* pp. 40–42.

sang them throughout. But until now this noble manner of recitation has been neither revived nor (to my knowledge) even attempted by anyone, and I used to believe that this was due to the imperfection of the modern music, by far inferior to the ancient. But the opinion thus formed was wholly driven from my mind by Messer Jacopo Peri, who, hearing of the intention of Signor Jacopo Corsi and myself, set to music with so much grace the fable of *Dafne* (which I had written solely to make a simple trial of what the music of our age could do) that it gave pleasure beyond belief to the few who heard it.

Taking courage from this, Signor Jacopo gave to this same fable a better form and again represented it at his house, where it was heard and commended, not only by the entire nobility of our favored state, but also by the most serene Grand Duchess and by the most illustrious cardinals Dal Monte and Montaldo.[2]

But much greater favor and fortune have been bestowed upon the *Euridice*, set to music by the aforesaid Peri with wonderful art, little used by others, for the graciousness and magnificence of the most serene Grand Duchess found it worthy of representation upon a most noble stage in the presence of Your Majesty, the Cardinal Legates, and ever so many princes and lords of Italy and France.[3]

For this reason, beginning to recognize with what favor such representations in music are received, I have wished to bring these two to light, in order that others, more skillful than myself, may employ their talents to increase the number and improve the quality of poems thus composed and cease to envy those ancients so much celebrated by noble writers.

To some I may seem to have been too bold in altering the conclusion of the fable of Orpheus,[4] but so it seemed fitting to me at a time of such great rejoicing, having as my justification the example of the Greek poets in other fables. And our own Dante ventured to declare that Ulysses was drowned on his voyage,[5] for all that Homer and the other poets had related the contrary. So likewise I have followed the authority of Sophocles in his *Ajax* [6] in introducing a change of scene, being unable to represent otherwise the prayers and lamentations of Orpheus.

May Your Majesty recognize in these my labors, small though they

---

2 Sonneck (see p. 5, note 4) argues that this later performance, in Corsi's palace, must have taken place not later than January 18, 1599.

3 The performance took place on October 6, 1600. It will be noticed that Rinuccini does not mention Caccini's connection with it.

4 In the original fable, Orpheus obtains Euryd-

ice's release only on the condition that he shall not look back at her as she follows him. When he forgets this condition, Eurydice vanishes, and Orpheus is later torn to pieces by Thracian Maenads.

5 *Inferno*, XXVI, 139–142.

6 At line 815.

be, the humble devotion of my mind to Your Majesty and live long in happiness to receive from God each day greater graces and greater favors.

Florence, October 4, 1600.
   Your Majesty's most humble servant,
      Ottavio Rinuccini.

3. Giulio Caccini

Born at Rome in 1550 and called "Romano" after his birthplace, Caccini settled in Florence in 1564. His importance in music history is twofold: on the one hand, he took an active part in the invention of the *stile rappresentativo* and the opera, and on the other, he applied the new style to the composition of vocal chamber music, i.e., monodic songs (arias, madrigals) with *basso continuo*. Primarily interested in singing, Caccini shunned dry musical recitation of the text; in his epoch-making collection of monodic songs *Le nuove musiche* (1602) he made abundant use of coloratura, and in so doing greatly influenced the music of the forthcoming monodic period. Caccini's setting of Rinuccini's *Euridice* was the first opera to be printed.

Euridice [1]

[*1600*]

Dedication

To THE most illustrious lord, Signor Giovanni Bardi, Conte di Vernio, Lieutenant-General of both companies of the Guard of Our Most Holy Father.

After composing the fable of *Euridice* in music in *stile rappresentativo* and having it printed, I felt it to be part of my duty to dedicate it to Your Illustrious Lordship, whose especial servant I have always been and to whom I find myself under innumerable obligations. In it Your Lordship will recognize that style which, as Your Lordship knows, I used on other occasions, many years ago, in the eclogue of Sannazaro, "Itene

---

1 Text: Solerti, *op. cit.*, pp. 50–52.

all'ombra degli ameni faggi," [2] and in other madrigals of mine from that time: "Perfidissimo volto," "Vedrò il mio sol," "Dovrò dunque morire," [3] and the like. This is likewise the manner which Your Lordship, in the years when Your Lordship's "Camerata" was flourishing in Florence, discussing it in company with many other noble virtuosi, declared to be that used by the ancient Greeks when introducing song into the representations of their tragedies and other fables.

Thus the harmony of the parts reciting in the present *Euridice* is supported above a *basso continuato*.[4] In this I have indicated the most necessary fourths, fifths, sixths, and sevenths, and major and minor thirds, for the rest leaving it to the judgment and art of the player to adapt the inner parts in their places; the notes of the bass I have sometimes tied in order that, in the passing of the many dissonances that occur, the note may not be struck again and the ear offended. In this manner of singing I have used a certain neglect which I deem to have an element of nobility, believing that with it I have approached that much nearer to ordinary speech. Further, when two sopranos are making passages, singing with the inner parts, I have not avoided the succession of two octaves or two fifths, thinking thereby, with their beauty and novelty, to cause a greater pleasure, especially since apart from these passages all the parts are free from such faults.

I had thought, on the present occasion, to deliver a discourse to my readers upon the noble manner of singing, in my judgment the best for others to adopt, along with some curious points relating to it and with the new manner of passages and redoubled points, invented by me, which Vittoria Archilei, a singer of that excellence to which her resounding fame bears witness,[5] has long employed in singing my works. But since this has not at present seemed best to some of my friends (to whom I cannot and must not be disloyal), I have reserved this for another occasion,[6] enjoying, for the time being, this single satisfaction of having been the first to give songs of this kind and their style and manner to the press.[7] This manner appears throughout my other compositions, composed at various times going back more than fifteen years, as I have

2 From his *Arcadia*. The line given is the beginning of the monologue of Montano in terza rima, following the "Prosa seconda." Caccini's music seems not to have been preserved.

3 *Le nuove musiche*, nos. 6, 7, and 11. A modern reprint, edited by Carlo Perinello, was published in 1919 as Vol. 4 of the *Classici della musica italiana*.

4 For examples of Caccini's *basso continuato*, see pp. 28–30 below.

5 Vittoria Archilei, who had taken part in the Florentine intermezzi of 1589, sang the role of

Eurydice at the first performance of the Peri-Caccini score (see also p. 15 below).

6 The promised "discourse" was subsequently published as a foreword to the *Nuove musiche* (see pp. 17–32 below).

7 Caccini has evidently rushed into print in order to anticipate the publication of Peri's score; his claim is that he is the first to have printed songs in the new style; Peri's claim (p. 16 below) is that his *Euridice* was performed before Caccini's was composed or printed.

never used in them any art other than the imitation of the conceit of the words, touching those chords more or less passionate which I judged most suitable for the grace which is required for good singing, which grace and which manner of singing Your Most Illustrious Lordship has many times reported to me to be universally accepted in Rome as good.

Meanwhile I pray Your Lordship to receive with favor the expression of my good will, etc., and to continue to grant me Your Lordship's protection, under which shield I hope ever to be able to take refuge, etc., and to be defended from the perils that commonly threaten things little used, knowing that Your Lordship will always be able to testify that my compositions are not unpleasing to a great prince who, having occasion to test all the good arts, can judge them supremely well. With which, kissing Your Illustrious Lordship's hand, I pray Our Lord to bestow happiness upon Your Lordship.

Florence, December 20, 1600.
Your Illustrious Lordship's
Most affectionate and beholden servant,
Giulio Caccini.

4. Jacopo Peri

Born at Rome in 1561, but of Florentine extraction, Peri occupied the position of "general music manager" to the Florentine court. He was a distinguished member of Bardi's "Camerata" and collaborated in the first attempts at realizing the *stile rappresentativo*. In contrast to Caccini, who was a gifted writer of melodies, Peri was primarily interested in drama and declamation. The score of his opera *Euridice*, on Rinuccini's text, was not printed until 1601. Peri died in Florence in 1633.

Euridice [1]

[*1601*]

Foreword

To my readers:

Before laying before you, gracious readers, these my compositions, I have thought it fitting to let you know what led me to seek out this new manner of music, for in all human operations reason should be the principle and source, and he who cannot readily give his reasons affords ground for believing that he has acted as the result of chance.

Although Signor Emilio del Cavaliere, before any other of whom I know, enabled us with marvelous invention to hear our kind of music upon the stage, nonetheless as early as 1594, it pleased the Signors Jacopo Corsi and Ottavio Rinuccini that I should employ it in another guise and should set to music the fable of *Dafne*, written by Signor Ottavio to make a simple trial of what the music of our age could do. [2]

---

1 Text: Solerti, *op. cit.*, pp. 43–49.

2 Here, as elsewhere in his foreword, Peri borrows literally from Rinuccini's dedication.

Seeing that dramatic poetry was concerned and that it was therefore necessary to imitate speech in song (and surely no one ever spoke in song), I judged that the ancient Greeks and Romans (who, in the opinion of many, sang their tragedies throughout in representing them upon the stage) had used a harmony surpassing that of ordinary speech but falling so far below the melody of song as to take an intermediate form. And this is why we find their poems admitting the iambic verse, a form less elevated than the hexameter but said to be advanced beyond the confines of familiar conversation. For this reason, discarding every other manner of singing hitherto heard, I devoted myself wholly to seeking out the kind of imitation necessary for these poems. And I considered that the kind of speech that the ancients assigned to singing and that they called "diastematica" (that is, sustained or suspended) could in part be hastened and made to take an intermediate course, lying between the slow and suspended movements of song and the swift and rapid movements of speech, and that it could be adapted to my purpose (as they adapted it in reading poems and heroic verses) and made to approach that other kind of speech which they called "continuata," a thing our moderns have already accomplished in their compositions, although perhaps for another purpose.[3]

I knew likewise that in our speech some words are so intoned that harmony can be based upon them and that in the course of speaking it passes through many others that are not so intoned until it returns to another that will bear a progression to a fresh consonance. And having in mind those inflections and accents that serve us in our grief, in our joy, and in similar states, I caused the bass to move in time to these, either more or less, following the passions, and I held it firm throughout the false and true proportions [4] until, running through various notes, the voice of the speaker came to a word that, being intoned in familiar speech, opened the way to a fresh harmony. And this not only in order that the flow of the discourse might not distress the ear (as though stumbling among the repeated notes that it encountered because of the rapid succession of the consonances) and in order that it might not seem in a way to dance to the movement of the bass (especially where the subject was sad or grave, more cheerful subjects naturally calling for more rapid movements), but also because the use of the false proportions would either diminish or offset whatever advantage it brought us, because of

---

3 Peri borrows the terms "diastematica" and "continuata" from Aristoxenian theory (cf. Cleonides, *Introduction, S.R.* I, 35).

4 The "false proportions" are the non-harmonic tones that occur in a recitative over a sustained bass.

the necessity of intoning every note, which the ancient music may perhaps have had less need of doing.

And therefore, just as I should not venture to affirm that this is the manner of singing used in the fables of the Greeks and Romans, so I have come to believe that it is the only one our music can give us to be adapted to our speech. For this reason, having imparted my opinion to the gentlemen in question, I demonstrated to them this new manner of singing, which gave the highest pleasure, not only to Signor Jacopo, who had already composed some most beautiful airs for this fable, and to Signor Pietro Strozzi, to Signor Francesco Cini, and to other most learned gentlemen (for music flourishes today among the nobility), but also to that celebrated lady whom one may call the Euterpe of our age, Signora Vittoria Archilei. This lady, who has always made my compositions seem worthy of her singing, adorns them not only with those groups and those long windings of the voice, simple and double, which the liveliness of her talent can invent at any moment (more to comply with the usage of our times than because she considers the beauty and force of our singing to lie in them), but also with those elegances and graces that cannot be written or, if written, cannot be learned from writing. One who heard and praised her was Messer Giovan Battista Jacomelli, most excellent in every part of music, who has almost changed his name to Violino, being a marvelous violinist, and who, for the three successive years in which he appeared at the carnival, was heard with the greatest delight and received with the universal applause of those who attended.

But the present *Euridice* had an even greater success, not because it was heard by these same gentlemen and other worthy men whom I have named and further by Count Alfonso Fontanella and Signor Orazio Vecchi, noble confirmers of my belief, but because it was represented before so great a queen and before so many celebrated princes of Italy and France and because it was sung by the most excellent musicians of our times. Of these, Signor Francesco Rasi, a nobleman of Arezzo, represented Amyntas; Signor Antonio Brandi, Arcetro; and Signor Melchior Palantrotti, Pluto.[5] Behind the scenes, music was played by gentlemen illustrious by noble blood and excellence in music: Signor Jacopo Corsi, whom I have so frequently named, played a gravicembalo; Signor Don Grazia Montalvo, a theorbo; Messer Giovan Battista dal Violino, a lira grande; and Messer Giovanni Lapi, a large lute.

And although until then I had composed the work exactly as it is now

---

[5] Peri mentions only the "noble" members of the cast.

published, nonetheless Giulio Caccini (called Romano), whose extreme merit is known to the world, composed the airs of Eurydice and some of those of the shepherd and of the nymphs of the chorus, also the choruses "Al canto, al ballo," "Sospirate," and "Poi che gli eterni imperi," and this because they were to be sung by persons under his direction. These airs may be seen in his *Euridice*, composed and printed only after mine was represented before Her Most Christian Majesty.

Receive it then graciously, courteous readers, and although I have not arrived, with this manner, at the goal that I had thought it possible to attain, the consideration of novelty having been a brake upon my course, give it in every way a welcome and it may be that on another occasion I may show you something more perfect than this. Meanwhile I shall consider myself to have done enough, having cleared the road for others who, by their merit, may go on in my footsteps to that glory which it has not been granted me to reach. And I hope that the use of the false proportions, played and sung without hesitation, discreetly, and precisely, being pleasing to men so numerous and so distinguished, may not offend you, especially in the more mournful and serious airs of Orpheus, Arcetro, and Dafne, the part represented with so much grace by Jacopo Giusti, a little boy from Lucca.

And live happily.
Jacopo Peri.

5. Giulio Caccini

Le nuove musiche [1]

[1602]

Foreword

To my readers:

If hitherto I have not put forth to the view of the world those fruits of my music studies employed about that noble manner of singing which I learned of my master, the famous Scipione del Palla, nor my compositions of airs, composed by me at different times, seeing them frequently practised by the most famous singers in Italy, both men and women, and by other noble lovers of this art, this has proceeded from my not esteeming them, as the said compositions have in my opinion received enough honor, indeed much more than they deserve. But seeing many of them go about maimed and spoiled; seeing ill used those long winding points, simple and double, that is redoubled or intertwined one with the other,[2] therefore devised by me to avoid that old manner of running division which has been hitherto used, being indeed more proper for wind and stringed instruments than for the voice; and seeing that there is made nowadays an indifferent and confused use of those excellent graces and ornaments to the good and true manner of singing which we call trills and groups, exclamations of increasing and abating

---

[1] Text: The basis of the present translation is the abridged version printed in later editions of John Playford's *Introduction to the Skill of Music* under the title: "A brief discourse of the Italian manner of singing, wherein is set down the use of those graces in singing, as the trill and *gruppo*, used in Italy and now in England; written some years since by an English gentleman who had lived long in Italy, and being returned, taught the same here." Arnold Dolmetsch seems to have been the first to identify this as a translation of Cac-

cini's foreword (see his *Interpretation of the Music of the XVIIth and XVIIIth Centuries* [London, 1915]). Using the 10th edition (London, 1693), I have corrected the old translation here and there and have completed it by translating those passages that it omitted. For the Italian text, cf. Solerti, *op. cit.*, pp. 55-70, or the facsimile reprint (Rome, 1934).

[2] Quei lunghi giri di voci semplici e doppi, cioè radoppiate, intrecciate l'una nell' altra.

of the voice;[3] I have found it necessary and also have been urged by my friends to have my said compositions printed, in this my first publication to explain to my readers in this discourse the reasons which led me to this manner of singing for a solo voice, and in this my discourse, since compositions of that complete grace which I can hear in my mind have been hitherto unknown in modern times (so far as I know), to leave some footprints that others may attain to this excellent manner of singing, for "a great fire follows a little spark."

Indeed, in the times when the most virtuous "Camerata" of the most illustrious Signor Giovanni Bardi, Count of Vernio, flourished in Florence, and in it were assembled not only a great part of the nobility but also the first musicians and men of talent and poets and philosophers of the city, and I too frequently attended it, I can say that I learned more from their learned discussions than I learned from descant in over thirty years; for these most understanding gentlemen always encouraged me and convinced me with the clearest reasons not to follow that old way of composition whose music, not suffering the words to be understood by the hearers, ruins the conceit and the verse, now lengthening and now shortening the syllables to match the descant, a laceration of the poetry, but to hold fast to that manner so much praised by Plato and other philosophers, who declare that music is nothing other than the fable and last and not the contrary, the rhythm and the sound,[4] in order to penetrate the perception of others and to produce those marvelous effects, admired by the writers, which cannot be produced by descant in modern musical compositions, especially in singing a solo above a stringed instrument, not a word of it being understood for the multitude of divisions made upon long and short syllables and in every sort of music, though by the vulgar such singers were cried up for famous.

It being plain, then, as I say, that such music and musicians gave no other delight than what harmony could give the ear, for, unless the words were understood, they could not move the understanding, I have endeavored in those my late compositions to bring in a kind of music by which men might, as it were, talk in harmony, using in that kind of singing, as I have said at other times,[5] a certain noble neglect of the song, passing now and then through certain dissonances, holding the bass note firm, except when I did not wish to observe the common practice, and playing the inner voices on an instrument for the expression of some passion, these being of no use for any other purpose. For which reason,

---

3 Il crescere o scemare della voce, l'esclamazioni, trilli e gruppi.

4 *Republic*, 398D (*S.R.* I, 4).

5 See the dedication of his *Euridice* (p. 11 above).

having in those times made a beginning of such songs for a single voice and believing that they had more power to delight and move than the greatest number of voices singing together, I composed in those times the madrigals "Perfidissimo volto," "Vedrò il mio sol," "Dovrò dunque morire," and the like, and in particular the air based on the eclogue of Sannazaro, "Itene a l'ombra degli ameni faggi," [6] in that very style which later served me for the fables which were represented in song at Florence.

The affectionate applause with which these madrigals and this air were received in the "Camerata" and the exhortations to pursue by this path the end I had proposed to myself led me to betake myself to Rome to make trial of them there also.[7] At Rome, when the said madrigals and air were heard in the house of Signor Nero Neri by many gentlemen accustomed to gather there, and particularly by Signor Leone Strozzi, all can testify how I was urged to continue the enterprise I had begun, all telling me that they had never before heard harmony of a single voice, accompanied by a single stringed instrument, with such power to move the passion of the mind as those madrigals, both because of their style and because, when madrigals published for several voices were sung by a single voice, as was then a common practice, the single part of the soprano, sung as a solo, could have no effect by itself, so artificial were the corresponding parts.

Returning from Rome to Florence, and having in mind that in those times there were also in use among musicians certain canzonets, for the most part with despicable words which I considered unseemly and not such as would be esteemed by men of understanding, the thought also came to me to compose from time to time for the relief of my depressed spirits some canzonets to be used as airs in a consort of several stringed instruments. I imparted this thought of mine to many gentlemen of the city and was courteously gratified by them with many canzonets in various metres, and soon afterwards Signor Gabriello Chiabrera favored me with a great abundance, very different from all the rest, and provided me with great opportunity for variety.[8] All these canzonets, which from time to time I set to various airs, were not unpleasing even to all Italy. Now everyone wishing to compose for a single voice employs this style, particularly here in Florence, where, during the thirty years that I have

6 See p. 11 above. notes 2 and 3.

7 Caccini seems to have left Florence for Rome sometime after July 30, 1593 (see the documents published by Gandolfi, *Rivista musicale italiana,* III [1896], 718).

8 Chiabrera is the author of the words of several of the *ariette* included in the *Nuove musiche* (nos. 3, 9, and 10), also of the madrigal "Deh, dove son fuggiti" (see pp. 29–30 below); he was also the librettist for the *Rapimento di Cefalo* and the author of an elegy on Caccini's death ("Belle ninfe de' prati").

received a salary from these most serene princes, whoever has so wished has, thanks to their bounty, been able to see and hear at his pleasure all that I have accomplished in these studies throughout that time.

In which, as well in the madrigals as in the airs, I endeavored the imitation of the conceit of the words, seeking out the chords more or less passionate according to the meaning of them and what had especial grace, having concealed in them so much as I could the art of descant, and passed or stayed the consonances or chords upon long syllables, avoiding the short and observing the same rule in making the passages of division by some few quavers to notes and to cadences not exceeding the value of a quarter or half a semibreve at most, chiefly on short syllables. These are allowable because they pass soon and are, not divisions, but a means of adding grace and because in special cases judgment makes every rule suffer some exception. But, as I said before, those long windings and turnings of the voice are ill used; for I have observed that divisions have been invented, not because they are necessary unto a good fashion of singing, but rather for a certain tickling of the ears of those who do not well understand what it is to sing passionately; for if they did, undoubtedly divisions would have been abhorred, there being nothing more contrary to passion than they are. I have said that these long winding points are ill used because I introduced them for use in some kind of music less passionate or affectuous, and upon long syllables, not short, and in final cadences, for the rest these long points of division needing to observe no rule concerning the vowels than that the vowel "u" produces a better effect in the soprano voice than in the tenor, the vowel "i" a better effect in the tenor than the vowel "u," the others being all in common use, though the open vowels are more sonorous than the closed, as also easier and fitter for stirring up the disposition. And again, if some short points of division should be used, let this be according to the rules observed in my works, not at all adventures, but upon the practice of the descant, to think of them first in those things that a man will sing by himself and to fashion out the manner of them, but not to promise a man's self that this descant will bear it. For to the good manner of composing and singing in this way, the understanding of this conceit and the humor of the words, imitating it and giving it its flavor as well in passionate chords as passionate expressions in singing, doth more avail than descant, I having made use of it only to accord two parts together and to avoid certain notable errors and bind certain discords for the accompanying of the passion more than to use the art. And certain it is that an air composed in this manner upon the conceit of the words by one that hath a good fashion of singing will work a better effect and delight more than another made with all the art of descant, for which no better reason can be given than experience itself. Such then were the reasons that led me to this manner of singing for a solo voice and showed me where, and on which syllables and vowels, long points of division should be used.

It now remains to say why the increasing and abating of the voice, exclamations, trills, groups, and other effects above mentioned are used indifferently, for they are now said to be used indifferently whenever anyone uses them, whether in passionate compositions where they are most required, or in canzonets for dancing where the humor or conceit of the words is not minded.

The original of which defect (if I deceive not myself) is hence occasioned because the musician doth not well possess and make himself master of that which he is to sing. For if he did so, undoubtedly he would not run into such errors as most easily he falleth into who hath framed to himself a manner of singing, for example altogether passionate, with a general rule that in increasing and abating the voice, and in exclamations, is the foundation of passion, and who doth always use them in every sort of music, not discerning whether the words require it; whereas those that well understand the conceit and meaning of the words, know our defects and can distinguish where the passion is more or less required. Which sort of people we should endeavor to please with all diligence and more to esteem their praise than the applause of the ignorant vulgar.

This art admitteth no mediocrity; and how much the more curiosities are in it, by reason of the excellence thereof, with so much the more labor and love ought we, the professors thereof, to find them out. Which love hath moved me (considering that from writings we receive the light of all science and of all art) to leave behind me this little light in the ensuing notes and discourses, it being my intention to show so much as appertaineth to him who maketh the profession of singing alone to the harmony of the theorbo or other stringed instrument, so that he be already entered into the theory of music and play sufficiently. Not that this cannot also be attained by long practise (as it is seen that many, both men and women, have done, and yet this they attain is but unto a certain degree), but because the theory of the writings conduceth unto the attaining of that degree, and because in the profession of a singer (in regard of the excellence thereof) not only particular things are of use, but they all together do better it.

Therefore, to proceed in order, thus will I say that the chiefest founda-
tions and most important grounds of this art are the tuning of the voice [9]
in all the notes, not only that it be neither too high nor too low, but that
there be a good manner of tuning it used. Which tuning being used for the
most part in two fashions, we will consider both of the one and the other,
and by the following notes will show that which to me seemeth more
proper to other effects.

There are some, therefore, that in the tuning of the first note, tune it a
third under; others tune the said first note in his proper tune, always
increasing it in loudness, saying that this is the good way of putting forth
the voice gracefully.

Concerning the first: Since it is not a general rule, because it agrees
not in many chords, although in such places as it may be used it is now
become so ordinary; that instead of being a grace (because some stay too
long in the third note under, whereas it should be but lightly touched)
it is rather tedious to the ear; and that, for beginners in particular, it
ought seldom to be used; but instead of it, as being more strange, I would
choose the second for the increasing of the voice.

Now, because I have not contained myself within ordinary terms and
such as others have used, yea rather have continually searched after
novelty so much as was possible for me, so that the novelty may fitly
serve to the better obtaining of the musician's end, that is, to delight and
move the affections of the mind, I have found it to be a more affectuous
way to tune the voice by a contrary effect to the other, that is, to tune the
first note in its proper tune, diminishing it; because exclamation is the
principal means to move the affection, and exclamation properly is no
other thing but the slacking of the voice to reinforce it somewhat more;
whereas increasing of the voice in the treble part, especially in feigned
voices,[10] doth oftentimes become harsh and insufferable to the hearing, as
upon divers occasions I have heard. Undoubtedly, therefore, as an affection more proper to move, it will work a better effect to tune the voice
diminishing it rather than increasing of it; because in the first of these ways
now mentioned, when a man increases the voice to make an exclamation,
it is needful that, in slacking of it, he increase it the more, and therefore
I have said that it showeth harsh and rough; but in the diminishing of
the voice it will work a quite contrary effect, because when the voice is
slacked, then to give it a little spirit will always make it more passionate.
Besides that also, using sometimes one, sometimes another, variety may

9 L'intonazione della voce.   10 Voci finte.

be used, which is very necessary in this art, so that it be directed to the said end.

So then, if this be the greatest part of that grace in singing which is apt to move the affection of the mind in those conceits, certainly where there is most use of such affections or passions, and if it be demonstrated with such lively reasons, a new consequence is hence inferred: that from writings of men likewise may be learned that most necessary grace which cannot be described in better manner and more clearly for the understanding thereof, and yet it may be perfectly attained unto. So that after the study of the theory and after these rules, they may be put in practice, by which a man grows more perfect in all arts, especially in the profession of a perfect singer, be it man or woman.

Of tuning, therefore, with more or less grace, and how it may be done in the aforesaid manner, trial may be made in the above-written notes, with the words under them "Cor mio, deh non languire." For in the first minim with the prick, you may tune "Cor mio," diminishing it by little and little, and in the falling of the crotchet increase the voice with a little more spirit, and it will become an exclamation passionate enough, though in a note that falls but one degree. But much more sprightful will it appear in the word "deh," by holding of a note that falls not by one degree, as likewise it will become most sweet by the taking of the greater sixth that falls by a leap. Which thing I have observed, not only to show to others what a thing exclamation is and from whence it grows, but also that there may be two kinds of it, one more passionate than the other, as well by the manner in which they are described or tuned in the one way or other, as also by imitation of the word when it shall have a signification suitable to the conceit. Besides that, exclamations may be used in all passionate musics, by one general rule in all minims and crotchets with a prick falling; and they shall be far more passionate by the following note, which runneth, than they can be in semibreves, in which it will be fitter for increasing and diminishing the voice without using the exclamations. Yet by consequence understand that in airy musics or courantes to dance, instead of these passions, there is to be used only a lively, cheerful kind of singing which is carried and ruled by the air itself. In the which, though sometimes there may be place for some exclamation, that liveliness of singing is in that place to be omitted, and not any passion to be used which savoreth of languishment. Whereupon we see how necessary a certain judgment is for a musician, which sometimes useth to prevail above art. As also we may perceive by the foregoing notes how much greater grace the four first quavers have upon the second syllable of the word "languire" (being so stayed by the second quaver with a prick) than the four last equal quavers, so printed for example.

But because there are many things which are used in a good fashion of singing which, because there is found in them a greater grace, being described in some one manner, make a contrary effect one to the other (whereupon we use to say of a man that he sings with much grace or little grace), these things will occasion me at this time: first, to demonstrate in what fashion I have described the trill and the group, and the manner used by me to teach them, to those who have been interested, in my house; and further, all other the more necessary effects, so that I leave not unexpressed any curiosity which I have observed.

Trill, or plain shake   Gruppo, or double relish

The trill described by me is upon one note only. My only reason for demonstrating it in this fashion is that in teaching it to my first wife and then to my second wife, now living, and to my daughters, I have observed no other rule than that of its description, both as trill and as group, that is to say, to begin with the first crotchet and to beat every note with the throat upon the vowel "a" unto the last breve, as likewise the *gruppo*, or double relish. Which trill and *gruppo* was exactly learned and exquisitely performed by my former wife according to the aforesaid rule, as I shall leave to the judgment of anyone who has heard her sing and as I likewise leave to the judgment of others, for this can be heard, with what exquisiteness it is performed by my second wife, now living. So that if it be true that experience is the teacher of all things, I can with some confidence affirm and say that there cannot be a better means used to teach it nor a better form to describe it, as each is so expressed. Which trill and group, because they are a step necessary unto many things that are described, and are effects of that grace which is most desired for singing well, and (as is aforesaid) being described in one or other manner do work a contrary effect to that which is requisite, I will show not only how they may be used, but also all the effects of them described in two manners with the same value of the notes, that still we may know (as is aforementioned) that by these writings, together with practice, may be learned all the curiosities of this art.

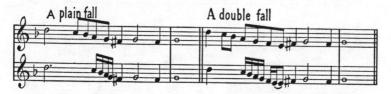

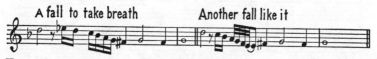

From the notes written above in two manners it is to be observed in these graces that the second hath more grace in it than the first. And for your better experience we will in this following air describe some of these graces with words under, together with the bass for the theorbo, in which air is contained the most passionate passages, by practicing which you may exercise yourself in them and attain ever greater perfection in them.

Cor   mio,   deh   non   lan-

gui — re deh   non langui- re

11   10 14 10   11   #10 14 #
      #   #   Trill

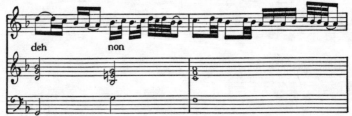

deh   non

lan-gui — — re deh   non

6   11   #10 14
          #   #

Passionate exclamation   Trill

lan-gui — re Ahi me ch'io mo — — ro

11   10 14 #   6 5 11   10 9 10
     #   #   #

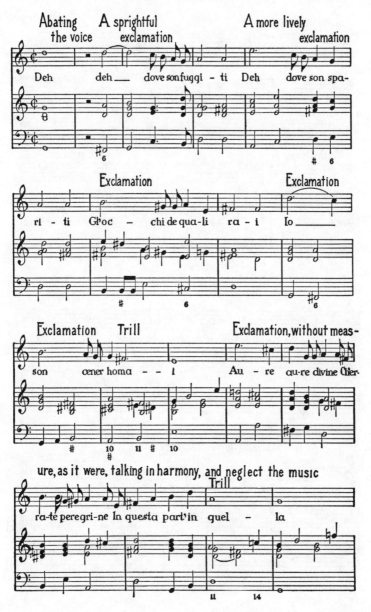

And because in the two last lines, at the words "Ahi dispietato Amor" in the *aria di romanesca* and afterwards in the madrigal "Deh, dove son fuggiti," there are contained the best passions that can be used in this noble manner of singing, I have therefore thought good to set them down; both to show where it is fit to increase and abate the voice, to make exclamations, trills, and groups, and in a word all the treasures of this art, as also not to have to demonstrate this again in all the works which will follow later, and that they may serve for example, whereby men may take notice in the music of the places where they are most necessary according to the passions of the words; although I call that the noble manner of singing which is used without tying a man's self to the ordinary measure of time, making many times the value of the notes less by half, and sometimes more, according to the conceit of the words, whence proceeds that excellent kind of singing with a graceful neglect, whereof I have spoken before.[a]

Since, then, there are so many effects to be used for the excellency of this art, there is required (for the performing of them) necessarily a good voice, as also good wind to give liberty and serve upon all occasions where is most need. It shall therefore be a profitable advertisement that the professor of this art, being to sing to a theorbo or other stringed instrument and not being compelled to fit himself to others, that he so pitch his tune as to sing his clear and natural voice, avoiding feigned tunes of notes. In which, to feign them, or at the least to enforce notes, if his wind serve him well so as he do not discover them much (because for the most part they offend the ear), yet a man must have a command of breath to give the greater spirit to the increasing and diminishing of the voice, to exclamations and other passions, as is related. Therefore let him take heed that, spending much breath upon such notes, it do not afterward fail him in such places as it is most needful; for from a feigned

---

a Our author having briefly set forth this chief or most usual grace in singing called the trill, which, as he saith very right, is by a beating in the throat on the vowel "ah," some observe that it is rather the shaking of the uvula or palate on the throat in one sound upon a note. For the attaining of this, the most surest and ready way is by imitation of those who are perfect in the same. Yet I have heard of some that have attained it after this manner: In the singing a plainsong of six notes up and six down, they have in the midst of every note beat or shaked with their finger upon their throat, which by often practice came to do the same notes exactly without. It was also my chance to be in company with some gentlemen at a musical practice which sang their parts very well and used this grace (called the trill) very exactly. I desired to know their tutor; they told me I was their tutor, for they had never

had any other but this my *Introduction*. That (I answered) could direct them but in the theory; they must needs have a better help in the practice, especially in attaining to sing the trill so well. One of them made this reply (which made me smile): I used, said he, at my first learning the trill, to imitate that breaking of a sound in the throat which men use when they lure their hawks, as *he-he-he-he-he;* which he used slow at first, and after more swift on several notes higher and lower in sound, till he became perfect therein.

The trill, being the most usual grace, is usually made in closes, cadences, and when on a long note exclamation or passion is expressed (there the trill is made in the latter part of such note), but most usually upon binding notes and such notes as precede the closing note. Those who once attain to the perfect use of the trill, other graces will become easy. [Note by Playford]

voice can come no noble manner of singing, which only proceeds from a natural voice, serving aptly for all the notes which a man can manage according to his ability, employing his wind in such a fashion as he command all the best passionate graces used in this most worthy manner of singing.

The love whereof, and generally of all music, being kindled in me by a natural inclination and by the study of so many years, shall excuse me if I have suffered myself to be carried further than perhaps was fit for him who no less esteems and desires to learn from others than to communicate to others what himself hath learned, and to be further transported in this discourse than can stand with that respect I bear to all the professors of this art. Which art, being excellent and naturally delightful, doth then become admirable and entirely wins the love of others when such as possess it, both by teaching and delighting others, do often exercise it and make it appear to be a pattern and true resemblance of those never ceasing celestial harmonies whence proceed so many good effects and benefits upon earth, raising and exciting the minds of the hearers to the contemplation of those infinite delights which Heaven affordeth.

Inasmuch as I have been accustomed, in all the compositions which have come from my pen, to indicate by figures above the bass part the major thirds and sixths where a sharp is set down and the minor ones where there is a flat, and in the same way to indicate that sevenths and other dissonances should be used in the inner voices for accompaniment, it now remains to be said that the ties in the bass part have been so used by me because after the consonance only the note indicated is to be struck again, it being the one most necessary (if I am not mistaken) for the theorbo in its special capacity and the easiest to use and put into effect, as that instrument is better fitted to accompany the voice, especially the tenor voice, than any other. For the rest, I leave to the discretion of the more intelligent the striking again, along with the bass, of those notes which may accord with their best judgment and which will best accompany the solo voice part, as it is not possible, so far as I know, to designate them more clearly without tablature.

6. G. M. Artusi

Born in 1540, Artusi was a canon of the church of San Salvatore at Bologna. He died in 1613. He was a distinguished theorist, well versed in the art of counterpoint but of a completely reactionary turn of mind. The innovations that had been introduced into polyphonic music by such great composers as Rore, Monteverdi, and Gesualdo were quite beyond his understanding. His *L'Artusi, ovvero, Delle imperfezioni della moderna musica,* shows to what lengths he could go in his fight against what he called the "imperfections" of the new music. From his limited point of view, however, as an ardent partisan of traditional polyphony, Artusi was perfectly consistent in his attacks, for the madrigal of his time had indeed begun to disintegrate.

From L'Artusi, ovvero, Delle imperfezioni della moderna musica [1]

[*1600*]

SECOND DISCOURSE

THE DAWN of the seventeenth day was breaking as Signor Luca left his house and proceeded toward the monastery of the reverend fathers of Santa Maria del Vado [2] where dwelt Signor Vario, in the service of the Most Illustrious and Reverend Signor the Cardinal Pompeo Arigoni, truly most illustrious for the many virtues, the goodness, the justice, and the piety which in that Most Illustrious and Reverend Signor universally shine in the service of persons of every quality. On his reaching the monastery, his arrival was announced to Signor Vario, who indeed was momentarily expecting him. Signor Vario immediately left his room and met Signor Luca at the head of the stairs, from whence, after

---

1 Text: The original edition (Venice, 1600), ff. 39–44, 71v. The postils of the original have been omitted.   2 The scene is laid in Ferrara.

33

due ceremonies and salutations, they went again to carry on their discussion, according to the arrangement adopted the day before, into a room sufficiently remote and conveniently free from disturbing sounds. After they had seated themselves, Signor Luca began.

(Luca) Yesterday, sir, after I had left Your Lordship and was going toward the Piazza, I was invited by some gentlemen to hear certain new madrigals. Delighted by the amiability of my friends and by the novelty of the compositions, I accompanied them to the house of Signor Antonio Goretti, a nobleman of Ferrara, a young virtuoso and as great a lover of music as any man I have ever known. I found there Signor Luzzasco and Signor Hippolito Fiorini,[3] distinguished men, with whom had assembled many noble spirits, versed in music. The madrigals were sung and repeated, but without giving the name of the author. The texture was not unpleasing. But, as Your Lordship will see, insofar as it introduced new rules, new modes, and new turns of phrase, these were harsh and little pleasing to the ear, nor could they be otherwise; for so long as they violate the good rules—in part founded upon experience, the mother of all things, in part observed in nature, and in part proved by demonstration—we must believe them deformations of the nature and propriety of true harmony, far removed from the object of music, which, as Your Lordship said yesterday, is delectation.

But, in order that you may see the whole question and give me your judgment, here are the passages, scattered here and there through the above-mentioned madrigals, which I wrote out yesterday evening for my amusement.

(Vario) Signor Luca, you bring me new things which astonish me not a little. It pleases me, at my age, to see a new method of composing, though it would please me much more if I saw that these passages were founded upon some reason which could satisfy the intellect. But as castles in the air, chimeras founded upon sand, these novelties do not please me; they deserve blame, not praise. Let us see the passages, however.[4]

(L) Indeed, in the light of what little experience I have in this art, these things do not seem to me to entitle their authors or inventors to build a four-story mansion (as the saying goes), seeing that they are contrary to what is good and beautiful in the harmonic institutions. They are

---

[3] Goretti, Luzzasco, and Fiorini were of course real persons, prominent in the musical life of Ferrara. Luzzasco, in particular, is cited by Monteverdi as one of those who "renewed" the "Second Practice" (cf. p. 48 below).

[4] See opposite page. "Passages" 8 and 9 are from the first and second parts of Claudio Monteverdi's "Anima mia perdona" (*Quarto libro a 5*), 1 to 7 from his "Cruda Amarilli" (*Quinto libro a 5*). These madrigals did not appear in print until 1603 and 1605, three to five years after the publication of Artusi's criticism. Artusi's examples differ in a few minor points from the editions later published by the composer.

harsh to the ear, rather offending than delighting it, and to the good rules left by those who have established the order and the bounds of this science they bring confusion and imperfection of no little consequence. Instead of enriching, augmenting, and ennobling harmony by various means, as so many noble spirits have done, they bring it to such estate that the beautiful and purified style is indistinguishable from the barbaric. And all the while they continue to excuse these things by various arguments in conformity with the style.

(V) You say well. But how can they excuse and palliate these imperfections, which could not possibly be more absurd?

(L) Absurd? I do not know how you can defend that opinion of yours. They call absurd the things composed in another style and would have it that theirs is the true method of composition, declaring that this novelty and new order of composing is about to produce many effects which ordinary music, full of so many and such sweet harmonies, cannot and never will produce. And they will have it that the sense, hearing such asperities, will be moved and will do marvelous things.

(V) Are you in earnest or are you mocking me?

(L) Am I in earnest? It is rather they who mock those who hold otherwise.

(V) Since I see that you are not mocking me, I will tell you what I think of them, but take note that I shall not be so ready to yield to their opinion. And, for the first argument against them, I tell you that the high is a part of the low and arises from the low and, being a part of it, must continue to be related to it, as to its beginning or as the cloud to the spring from which it is derived. That this is true, the experiment of the monochord will show you. For if two strings of equal length and thickness are stretched over one and the same equal space and tuned perfectly in unison (which is regarded by the musician as a single sound, just as two surfaces which are throughout in contact with each other are regarded by Vitello [5] as a single surface), and if you cut off a part from one of these or bring out a high sound from it by placing a bridge under it, I say that beyond doubt the high will be a part of the low. And if you would know that a part produces the high sound, strike the whole and then the part which is high with respect to the whole, and it will necessarily be related to the low, as the part to the whole or as to its beginning.

At the lowest note of the complete system, or of any composition, there may be represented an eye, sending forth various visual rays and regarding all the parts, observing in what proportion they correspond to their beginning and foundation. How then will the first, second, fourth, fifth, and other measures stand, if the higher part has no correspondence or harmonic proportion to the lower?

(L) They claim that they do observe harmonic relation, saying that the semiminim in the first measure, which is taken after the rest of the

---

5 Erasmus Vitello (Erazm Ciolek), Polish mathematician of the thirteenth century.

same value and which forms a sixteenth with the lower part, would already be dissonant if the cantus were to sing as follows:

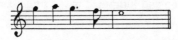

for then the tenor, singing the first semiminim an octave lower, would cause the second one, which forms the dissonance, to be heard with it above; aside from this, they say, since the third of the four semiminims is consonant, what difference can it make if we cause a little more harshness to be heard by converting two semiminims, one consonant, the other dissonant, into one minim wholly dissonant; this is as though we were to sing four semiminims, alternately consonant and dissonant, following the rule for figures of this value. In this way they make all that they do more gross.

(V) Good! I follow you perfectly, and answer that the sense of hearing does not perceive what it does not hear and, not perceiving it, cannot present it to the intellect, there being nothing in the intellect that has not first been perceived by the senses. How absurd it is to say that the tenor sustains a note in one register while the soprano, immediately afterward in a higher register, produces the effect the tenor should have produced! Especially after the rest, how much more evident it is to the ear that the soprano sings a sixteenth and then a fourteenth! It is one thing that the ear should hear a dissonance in one part after a rest, another that, when several semiminims are successively taken by step, one after another, one is perceived to be consonant, another dissonant; one thing to hear two semiminims taken by step in the natural way, another to hear a minim, and that taken by leap, in place of the dissonant semiminim. This last offends the ear; the others do not, for the movement is by step.

(L) Well said. But they say that all this is called grace and is an accented singing.

(V) I do not remember having read in any author—and countless excellent ones have written of music—that there is such a thing as accented music. I shall welcome it if you will tell me what it is, according to the pretension of these modern composers.

(L) They say that the accents in compositions have a remarkable effect and that these accents occur only when a part ascends to a higher note; for example, that when four notes ascend by step, the accent is produced on the last note and not on the others, the voice beginning a third lower than the note on which the accent is to be produced and being carried gracefully to its level. But, to produce good accord always, this demands the greatest discretion and judgment in the singer for its execution. Here is an example:

(V) I will tell you two things. First, that these words do not explain in clear terms the nature, the peculiarity, and the essence of this manner of accented singing, but seem to be a circumlocution calculated to show, not that they are disposed to regulate all things with rules founded on truth, but rather that they wish to confuse them. We must define what this accent is; then we shall see whether the parts of our definition are mutually in accord, a thing which I do not know that any serious author has so far done. Second, this manner of singing which you call accented does not assume that the composers will employ barbarisms such as are seen in the examples you show me. It requires that the composers produce good accord (a point which you must note well and above all else) and that the singer use great discretion and judgment in "carrying the voice" on such occasions. And if you tell me that the effect which the tenor produces in the seventh measure tends to demonstrate this manner of accented singing, I will reply that the singer does not know at what point, in the opinion and intent of the composers, he should, with discretion, "carry the voice." For this reason there is necessarily an error in grammar. It would be better if, when they mean that the singer should, with judgment and discretion, "carry the voice," they introduced at that point some sign indicating their wish, in order that, perceiving the need, he might produce better accord and more pleasing harmony than he produces by singing along at his own will.

(L) Such an indication would not be unprofitable if one could reasonably discover a universal sign to indicate this manner of "carrying the voice" to the singer. But, while these new inventors are exhausting themselves in new inventions to make this manifest, they go on scattering these passages through their compositions, which, when sung or sounded on different instruments by musicians accustomed to this kind of accented music, full of things left implicit, yield a not unpleasing harmony at which I marvel.

(V) This may result from two things. First, that the singers do not sing what is written, but "carry the voice," sustaining it in such a way that, when they perceive that it is about to produce some bad effect, they divert it elsewhere, carrying it to a place where they think it will not offend the ear. Second, that sensuous excess corrupts the sense, meaning simply that the ear is so taken up with the other parts that it does not fully perceive the offense committed against it (as it would if the composition were for two, three, or four voices), while reason, which knows and distinguishes the good from the bad, perceives right well that a deception is wrought on the sense, which receives the material only in a certain confused way, even though it border on truth. This manifestly is clearly seen when the organist adds to his other registers that of the twelfth; here it is reason and not the ear that discovers the many dissonances which occur among them.

(L) It is known that the ear is deceived, and to this these composers, or new inventors, apply themselves with enthusiasm. They seek only to satisfy the ear and with this aim toil night and day at their instruments to hear the effect which passages so made produce; the poor fellows do not perceive that what the instruments tell them is false and that it is one thing to search with voices and instruments for something pertaining to the harmonic faculty, another to arrive at the exact truth by means of reason seconded by the ear.

(V) I should like to give you my opinion, but I suspect that it may displease you.

(L) Give it; I shall be glad to listen.

(V) It is my belief that there is nothing but smoke in the heads of such composers and that they are so enamored of themselves as to think it within their power to corrupt, spoil, and ruin the good old rules handed down in former times by so many theorists and most excellent musicians, the very men from whom these moderns have learned to string together a few notes with little grace. But do you know what usually happens to such works as these? What Horace says in the tenth ode of his second book:

> Saepius ventis agitatur ingens
> pinus et celsae graviore casu
> decidunt turres feriuntque summos
> fulmina montis.[6]

---

[6] 'Tis oftener the tall pine that is shaken by the wind; 'tis the lofty towers that fall with the heavier crash, and 'tis the tops of the mountains that the lightning strikes. [Bennett]

In the end, since they are built without foundation, they are quickly consumed by time and cast to the ground, and the builders remain deluded and mocked at.

(L) I grant you that all this is true. But tell me if this science can be advanced by new modes of expression. Why is it that you are unwilling to augment it, or that augmenting it displeases you or does not seem good to you? The field is large; everyone is occupied with new things; musicians too should expand their art, for making all compositions after one fashion sickens and disgusts the ear.

(V) I do not deny that discovering new things is not merely good but necessary. But do you tell me first why you wish to employ these dissonances as they employ them. If you do it in order to say, "I wish them to be plainly heard, but so that the ear may not be offended," why do you not use them in the ordinary way, conformable to reason, in accordance with what Adriano,[7] Cipriano,[8] Palestrina, Porta, Claudio,[9] Gabrieli, Gastoldi, Nanino, Giovanelli, and so many, many others in this academy have written? Have they perhaps failed to cause asperities to be heard? Look at Orlando di Lasso, Philippe de Monte, and Giaches de Wert, and you will find full heaps of them. If you do not wish the ear to be so much offended by them, you will find the manner and order of their use in the same authors. Now, even if you wish dissonance to become consonant, it remains necessary that it be contrary to consonance; by nature it is always dissonant and can hence become consonant only when consonance becomes dissonant; this brings us to impossibilities, although these new composers may perhaps so exert themselves that in the course of time they will discover a new method by which dissonance will become consonance, and consonance dissonance. And it is no great matter, for lofty intelligences like these, to be doing and inventing things of this kind exclusively.

(L) Their aim is precisely to temper to some degree the harshness of dissonance in another way than that used by their predecessors, and to this they devote their efforts.

(V) If the purpose can be attained by observing the precepts and good rules handed down by the theorists and followed by all the practitioners, what reason is there to go beyond the bounds to seek out new extravagances? Do you not know that all the arts and sciences have been brought under rules by scholars of the past and that the first elements, rules, and precepts on which they are founded have been handed down to us in

---

7 Willaert.   9 Merulo.
8 Rore.

order that, so long as there is no deviation from them, one person shall
be able to understand what another says or does? And just as, to avoid
confusion, it is not permitted to every schoolmaster to change the rules
bequeathed by Guarino,[10] nor to every poet to put a long syllable in
verse in place of a short one, nor to every arithmetician to corrupt the
processes and proofs which are proper to that art, so it is not permitted
to everyone who strings notes together to deprave and corrupt music,
introducing new modes of composing with new principles founded on
sand. Horace says:

> Est modus in rebus, sunt certi denique fines
> Quos ultra citraque nequit consistere rectum.[11]

(L) The truth is that all the arts and sciences have been brought
under rules. But still, since dissonances are employed in harmonies as
nonessentials, it seems that musicians are entitled to use them at their
pleasure.

(V) I do not deny that dissonances are employed as nonessentials in
compositions, but I say none the less that, being by nature contrary to
consonance, they can by no means agree in the same way and should not
be employed in the same way. Consonances are used freely in harmonies,
by leap or by step, without distinction, but dissonances, being of another
nature, must be considered in another way; this way is demonstrated by
Artusi in his *Art of Counterpoint*,[12] but not in the manner which these
new masters follow.

(L) These musicians observe the rule that the part forming the dissonance with the lowest part has a harmonic correspondence with the
tenor, so that it accords with every other part while the lowest part also
accords with every other part. Thus they make a mixture of their
own.

(V) I see that this rule of theirs is observed in the first, fourth, fifth,
sixth, and seventh measures. But in the sixth measure the quavers have
no harmonic relation, either with the bass or with the tenor. With what
sort of rule do you think they can save themselves?

(L) I do not know how they can help themselves here. I see the observance of no rule, although I believe that the quavers are the result of
perceiving, with instruments, that they do not greatly offend the ear because of their rapid movement.

----

10 The grammatical *Regulae* of the humanist
Guarino Veronese (1374–1460), a resident of Ferrara after 1429.
11 There is a measure in all things. There are,
in short, fixed bounds, beyond and short of which
right can find no place (*Satires*, I, i, 106–107).
[Fairclough]
12 Venice, 1586–89. and later editions.

(V) Are you not reminded of what Aristoxenus says of such men as these? Yesterday I gave you the substance of his thought; now I shall give you his very words. In the second book of his *Harmonics* he says: "It is therefore a very great and altogether disgraceful sin to refer the nature of a harmonic question to an instrument." [13] As regards the point that, because of their rapid movement they do not offend the ear, the intellect, recognizing the deception wrought upon the sense, declares that since these intervals are not consonant, but dissonant and placed at random, they can in no way be in a harmonic relation; that they can therefore cause no harmony pleasing to the ear; and that their rapidity, accompanied by so many parts making noise together, is nothing else than the sensuous excess which corrupts the sense.

(L) They think only of satisfying the sense, caring little that reason should enter here to judge their compositions.

(V) If such as these had read the ninth chapter of the first book of Boethius, and the first chapter of his fifth book,[14] and the first chapter of the first book of Ptolemy,[15] they would beyond doubt be of a different mind.

(L) They do not even think of looking at the volumes of Boethius. But if you would know what they say, they are content to know how to string their notes together after their fashion and to teach the singers to sing their compositions, accompanying themselves with many movements of the body, and in the end they let themselves go to such an extent that they seem to be actually dying—this is the perfection of their music.

(V) You have said the very thing. They and their activities die together. By the general judgment of the wise and learned, ignorance, more than anything else, is considered the greatest of the many accidents which makes uncertain for every workman the road of good work which leads to immortality. Through ignorance a man is unable to distinguish which activities are better and which worse, and as a result of this inability he commonly embraces many things from which he should flee and flees from many which he should follow and embrace. Of ignorance, then, are born compositions of this sort, which, like monstrosities, pass through the hands of this man and that, and these men do not know themselves what the real nature of these compositions is. For them it is enough to create

---

13 Cf. *S.R.* I, 31. Artusi quotes Aristoxenus in the Latin translation of Antonius Gogava (Venice, 1562).
14 "Not every judgment is to be pronounced by the senses, but reason is rather to be believed: wherein of the fallibility of the senses" (I, ix); "Of the nature of harmony, and what the means of judging it are, and whether the senses are always to be believed" (V, i).
15 "Of harmonic judgments."

a tumult of sounds, a confusion of absurdities, an assemblage of imperfections, and all springs from that ignorance with which they are be-
clouded.

(L) Ignorance has always been a cause of evil, the more so when accompanied by self-love. Horace says:

Est caecus Amor sui.[16]

It does not stop to discover its own imperfections, but believes that all
it does and thinks is well done, as the drunkard thinks that he is sober
and the sober man drunk.

(V) It is too onerous to discuss scientific questions with one who is
ignorant of science. It is as when the countryman plows a field full of
stalks and thorns and other things which hinder him from tilling the
soil, instead of a field that has been well plowed before and has yielded
fruits from the seed sown upon it. Observe how harsh and uncouth is
this passage, which to their minds is exquisite. In the third measure,
after the minim rest, the lowest part clashes with the highest in a semi-
diapente which leaves the singer in doubt whether he is making an error or singing correctly. All composers have employed this interval,
but in a different way. I say "in a different way," because although they
employ it in the first and second parts of the measure, called arsis and
thesis, they do not use it in either case after a "privation" of sound; as
Artusi demonstrates in his *Art of Counterpoint*, a sixth or some other
consonance precedes it.

(L) I have never seen or heard the interval used as these composers
use it. They imply that the minim rest serves as a consonance. But, as
you have said, the ear does not judge what it does not hear. Cipriano
uses this interval in his madrigal "Non gemme, non fin'oro," [17] and
Morales in his Magnificat in the fifth mode, at the verse "Sicut locutus
est," [18] but in the manner taught by our elders, of which they left fully
a thousand examples. And it is truly marvelous that the ancients, with
their great industry and diligence, have taught the way, not to make
consonant those intervals which nature herself created dissonant, but so
to use them that they seem properly to lose some of their harshness and
to acquire sweetness. But when, by a departure from the manner taught
by the ancients, they are used and taken absolutely, they cannot have a
good effect.

---

16 Blind self-love (*Odes*, I, xviii, 14). [Ben-
nett]
17 *Primo libro a 4*, No. 22, measure 4 (*Smith
College Music Archives*, VI, 75).

18 Cf. Ambros. *Geschichte der Musik*, IV
(Leipzig, 1878), 370.

(V) This is one of those things in which experience has taught them to recognize what is good and beautiful and what is bad.

(L) Beyond doubt, much experience about many particulars, of which this is but one, shows the truth.

(V) Our ancients never taught that sevenths may be used absolutely and openly, as you see them used in the second, third, fourth, fifth, sixth, and seventh measures, for they do not give grace to the composition and, as I said a little while ago, the higher part has no correspondence to its whole, beginning, or foundation.

(L) This is a new paradox.

(V) If this new paradox were reasonably founded on some reason, it would deserve much praise and would move onward to eternal life. But it is destined to have a short life, for demonstration can only show that truth is against it.

.   .   .   .   .

(L) I remain under great obligation to Your Lordship's amiability. I believe that we shall depart tomorrow morning without fail; it remains for me to pray that you will both retain me in your favor and consider me at your command. I shall go well content, for by Your Lordship's favor I take with me things that console and content me greatly.

(V) Signor Luca, it is my duty always to serve you, just as I pray you to command me. And if any doubt occurs to you concerning our discussions, let me know, for I shall gladly do what is necessary. So I remain at your service and pray the Lord to give you a pleasant journey.

(L) Signor Vario, I kiss your hand. Farewell.

7. Claudio Monteverdi

Born at Cremona in 1567, Monteverdi studied counterpoint with Marcantonio Ingegneri and entered the service of the dukes of Gonzaga at Mantua as a viol player. He waited until 1603 to be made choirmaster at the Mantuan court. In 1613 he left for Venice, where he assumed the position of *maestro di cappella* at St. Mark's, a post he held until his death in 1643.

The Fifth Book of Monteverdi's madrigals—there are nine books in all—is introduced by a foreword in which the composer replies to the bitter attacks that had been leveled against his art by the reactionary critic Artusi. The pieces contained in this book already show a strong tendency toward the new style. In the Eighth Book (*Madrigali guerrieri ed amorosi*, 1638), the pieces no longer have anything in common with the tradition. That Monteverdi should call such pieces "Madrigali" is an indication of the level to which the madrigal had sunk by the third decade of the seventeenth century.

Il quinto libro de' madrigali

[*1605*]

Foreword with the "Declaration" of His Brother G. C. Monteverdi [1]

[*1607*]

Some months ago a letter of my brother Claudio Monteverdi was printed and given to the public. A certain person, under the fictitious name of Antonio Braccini da Todi, has been at pains to make this seem to the world a chimera and a vanity.[2] For this reason, impelled by the love I bear my brother and still

---

1 Text: The original edition, printed at the end of Claudio's *Scherzi musicali* (Venice, 1607); published in facsimile by Malipiero in his edition of Monteverdi's works, X, 69-72.

2 Artusi had continued his attack on Monteverdi in his *Seconda parte dell' Artusi* (Venice, 1603), and on the publication of Monteverdi's

Quinto libro a 5 in 1605, had replied to it in a *Discorso musicale*, publishing it in 1606 or 1607 under the pseudonym Antonio Braccini. No copy of this abusive pamphlet is known to have been preserved. Subsequently (1608), Artusi published a *Discorso secondo musicale*, replying to the "Declaration" printed here.

more by the truth contained in his letter, and seeing that he pays attention to deeds and takes little notice of the words of others, and being unable to endure that his works should be so unjustly censured, I have determined to reply to the objections raised against them, declaring in fuller detail what my brother, in his letter, compressed into little space, to the end that this person and whoever follows him may learn that the truth that it contains is very different from what he represents in his discussions. The letter says:

Do not marvel that I am giving these madrigals to the press without first replying to the objections that the Artusi [a] *has brought against some*

[a] By the Artusi is to be understood the book bearing the title, *L'Artusi; or, Of the Imperfections of Modern Music*, whose author, disregarding the civil precept of Horace, *Nec tua laudabis studia, haud aliena reprendes* [Praise not your own studies; blame not those of others], and without any cause given by him, and therefore unjustly, says the worst he can of certain musical compositions of my brother Claudio.

very minute details [b] *in them, for being in the service of His Serene*

[b] These details, called "passages" by Artusi, which are seen so lacerated by him in his Second Discourse, are part of my brother's madrigal "Cruda Amarilli," and their harmony is part of the melody of which this is composed; for this reason he has called them details and not "passages."

Highness, I have not at my disposal the time that would be required. [c]

[c] This my brother said, not only because of his responsibility for both church and chamber music, but also because of other extraordinary services, for, serving a great prince, he finds the greater part of his time taken up, now with tourneys, now with ballets, now with comedies and various concerts, and lastly with the playing of the two *viole bastarde*, a responsibility and study which is not so usual as his adversary would have understood. And my brother has bided his time and continues to bide his time, not only for the reason and valid excuse set forth, but also because he knows that *properantes omnia perverse agunt* [the hasty do all things badly], that excellence and speed are not companions in any undertaking whatsoever, and that perfect excellence requires the whole man, the more so in attempting to treat of a matter hardly touched upon by intelligent harmonic theorists, and not, like his opponent, of a matter *nota lippis atque tonsoribus* [familiar to the blear-eyed and to barbers].

Nevertheless, to show that I do not compose my works at haphazard, [d]

[d] My brother says that he does not compose his works at haphazard because, in this kind of music, it has been his intention to make the words the mistress of the harmony and not the servant, and because it is in this manner that his work is to be judged in the composition of the melody. Of this Plato speaks as follows:

"The song is composed of three things: the words, the harmony, and the rhythm"; and, a little further on: "And so of the apt and the unapt, if the rhythm and the harmony follow the words, and not the words these." Then, to give greater force to the words, he continues: "Do not the manner of the diction and the words follow and conform to the disposition of the soul?" and then: "Indeed, all the rest follows and conforms to the diction." [3] But in this case, Artusi takes certain details, or, as he calls them, "passages," from my brother's madrigal "Cruda Amarilli," paying no attention to the words, but neglecting them as though they had nothing to do with the music, later showing the said "passages" deprived of their words, of all their harmony, and of their rhythm. But if, in the "passages" noted as false, he had shown the words that went with them, then the world would have known without fail where his judgment had gone astray, and he would not have said that they were chimeras and castles in the air from their entire disregard of the rules of the First Practice. But it would truly have been a beautiful demonstration if he had also done the same with Cipriano's madrigals "Dalle belle contrade," "Se ben il duol," "Et se pur mi mantieni amor," "Poiche m'invita amore," "Crudel acerba," "Un altra volta," [4] and, to conclude, with others whose harmony obeys their words exactly and which would indeed be left bodies without soul if they were left without this most important and principal part of music, his opponent implying, by passing judgment on these "passages" without the words, that all excellence and beauty consist in the exact observance of the aforesaid rules of the First Practice, which makes the harmony mistress of the words. This my brother will make apparent, knowing for certain that in a kind of composition such as this of his, music turns on the perfection of the melody, considered from which point of view the harmony, from being the mistress, becomes the servant of the words, and the words the mistress of the harmony, to which way of thinking the Second Practice, or modern usage, tends. Taking this as a basis, he promises to show, in refutation of his opponent, that the harmony of the madrigal "Cruda Amarilli" is not composed at haphazard, but with beautiful art and excellent study, unperceived by his adversary and unknown to him.

And since my brother promises, in refutation of his opponent, to show with writings that with respect to the perfection of the melody the writings of his adversary are not based upon the truth of art, let his opponent, in refutation of my brother's madrigal, show the errors of others through the medium of the press with a comparable practical performance—with harmony observing the rules of the First Practice, that is, disregarding the perfection of the melody, considered from which point of view the harmony, from being servant, becomes mistress; for *purpura juxta purpuram dijudicanda* [the purple is to be judged

<hr />

3 *Republic*, 398D (*S.R.* I, 4 and 7). Monteverdi quotes Plato in the Latin translation of Marsilio Ficino.
4 *Quinto libro a 5* (1566), No. 2 (reprinted by Walter Wiora in *Das Chorwerk*, Heft 5); *Quarto libro a 5* (1557), No. 3 (quoted by Einstein in

The Italian Madrigal, I, 420); *Le vive fiamme* (1565), Nos. 18 and 16; *Secondo libro a 4* (1557), Nos. 9 (second part) and 1 (reprinted by Gertrude Parker Smith in *Smith College Music Archives*, VI, 127 and 90).

according to the purple]—for using only words to oppose the deeds of another is *nil agit exemplum litem quod lite resolvit* [the example that, settling one dispute by another, accomplishes nothing]. Then let him allow the world to be the judge, and if he brings forward no deeds, but only words, deeds being what commend the master, my brother will again find himself meriting the praise, and not he. For as the sick man does not pronounce the physician intelligent from hearing him prate of Hippocrates and Galen, but does so when he recovers health by his wisdom, so the world does not pronounce the musician intelligent from hearing him ply his tongue in telling of the honored harmonic theorists. For it was not in this way that Timotheus incited Alexander to war, but by singing. To such a practical performance my brother invites his opponent, not others, for he yields to them all, honors and reveres them all; his opponent he invites, once and for all, because he wishes to devote himself to music and not to writing, except as promised on this one occasion, and, following the divine Cipriano de Rore, the Signor Prencipe di Venosa, Emilio del Cavaliere, Count Alfonso Fontanella, the Count of the Camerata, the Cavalier Turchi, Pecci, and other gentlemen of that heroic school, to pay no attention to nonsense and chimeras.

I have written a reply which will appear, as soon as I have revised it, bearing the title, Seconda Pratica; [e] ovvero, Perfezioni della Moderna

[e] Because his opponent seeks to attack the modern music and to defend the old. These are indeed different from one another in their manner of employing the consonances and dissonances, as my brother will make apparent. And since this difference is unknown to the opponent, let everyone understand what the one is and what the other, in order that the truth of the matter may be more clear. Both are honored, revered, and commended by my brother. To the old music he has given the name of First Practice from its being the first practical usage, and the modern music he has called Second Practice from its being the second practical usage.

By First Practice he understands the one that turns on the perfection of the harmony, that is, the one that considers the harmony not commanded, but commanding, not the servant, but the mistress of the words, and this was founded by those first men who composed in our notation music for more than one voice, was then followed and amplified by Ockeghem, Josquin Desprez, Pierre de La Rue, Jean Mouton, Crequillon, Clemens non Papa, Gombert, and others of those times, and was finally perfected by Messer Adriano with actual composition and by the most excellent Zarlino with most judicious rules.

By Second Practice, which was first renewed in our notation by Cipriano de Rore (as my brother will make apparent), was followed and amplified, not only by the gentlemen already mentioned, but by Ingegneri, Marenzio, Giaches de Wert, Luzzasco, likewise by Jacopo Peri, Giulio Caccini, and finally by loftier spirits with a better understanding of true art, he understands the one that turns on the perfection of the melody, that is, the one that considers harmony not commanding, but commanded, and makes the words the mistress of the harmony. For reasons of this sort he has called it "second," and not "new," and he has called it "practice," and not "theory," because he understands its explanation to turn on the manner of employing the consonances and dissonances in actual composition. He has not called it "Musical Institutions" because he confesses that he is not one to undertake so great an enterprise, and he leaves the composition of such noble writings to the Cavalier Ercole Bottrigari and to the Reverend Zarlino. Zarlino used the title "Harmonic Institutions" because he wished to teach the laws and rules of harmony; my brother has used the title "Second Practice," that is, second practical usage, because he wishes to make use of the considerations of that usage, that is, of melodic considerations and their explanations, employing only so many of them as concern his defense against his opponent.

Musica.[f] *Some, not suspecting that there is any practice other than that*

[f] He will call it "Perfections of Modern Music" on the authority of Plato, who says: "Does not music also turn on the perfection of the melody?" [5]

taught by Zarlino, will wonder at this,[g] but let them be assured that,

[g] He has said "some," and not "all," to indicate only the opponent and his followers. He has said "they will wonder" because he knows for certain that these men are wanting, not only in understanding of the Second Practice, but (as he will make apparent) to a considerable extent in that of the First also. "Not suspecting that there is any practice other than that taught by Zarlino," that is, not suspecting that there is any practice other than that of Messer Adriano, for the Reverend Zarlino did not intend to treat of any other practice, as he indeed declares, saying: "It never was nor is it my intention to treat of the usage of practice according to the manner of the ancients, either Greeks or Latins, even if at times I touch upon it; my intention is solely to describe the method of those who have discovered our way of causing several parts to sound together with various modulations and various melodies, especially according to the way and manner observed by Messer Adriano." [6] Thus the Reverend Zarlino concedes that the practice taught by him is not the one and only truth. For this reason my brother intends to make use of the principles taught by Plato and practiced by the divine Cipriano and by modern usage, principles different from those taught and established by the Reverend Zarlino and practiced by Messer Adriano.

with regard to the consonances and dissonances,[h] there is still another

[h] But let the opponent and his followers be assured that, with regard to the consonances and dissonances, that is, with regard to the manner of employing the consonances and dissonances.

[5] *Gorgias,* 449D.   [6] *Sopplimenti musicali,* I, i.

way of considering them, different from the established way,[1] *which,*

[1] By the established way of considering the consonances and dissonances, which turns on the manner of their employment, my brother understands those rules of the Reverend Zarlino that are to be found in the third book of his *Institutions* and that tend to show the practical perfection of the harmony, not of the melody, as is clearly revealed by the musical examples he gives there; these show in actual music the meaning of his precepts and laws, which are seen to have no regard for the words, for they show the harmony to be the mistress and not the servant. For this reason my brother will prove to the opponent and his followers that, when the harmony is the servant of the words, the manner of employing the consonances and dissonances is not determined in the established way, for the one harmony differs from the other in this respect.

with satisfaction to the reason and to the senses,[j] *defends the modern method of composing.*

[j] "With satisfaction to the reason" because he will take his stand upon the consonances and dissonances approved by mathematics (for he has said "with regard to the manner of employing them") and because he will likewise take his stand upon the command of the words, the chief mistress of the art considered from the point of view of the perfection of the melody, as Plato affirms in the third book of his *Republic* [7] (for he has said "Second Practice"). "With satisfaction to the senses" because the combination of words commanding with rhythm and harmony obedient to them (and I say "obedient" because the combination in itself is not enough to perfect the melody) affects the disposition of mind. Here is what Plato says: "For only melody, turning the mind away from all things whatsoever that distract, reduces it to itself"; [8] not harmony alone, be it ever so perfect, as the Reverend Zarlino concedes in these words: "If we take harmony absolutely, without adding to it anything else, it will have no power to produce any extrinsic effect," adding, a little further on: "In a certain way, it intrinsically prepares for and disposes to joy or sadness, but it does not on this account lead to the expression of any extrinsic effect." [9]

I have wished to say this to you in order that the expression "Second Practice" may not be appropriated by any one else,[k] *and further, that*

[k] My brother has made known to the world that this expression is assuredly his in order that it may be known and concluded that when his adversary said, in the second book of the Artusi: "This Second Practice, which may in all truth be said to be the dregs of the First," he spoke as he did to speak evil of my brother's works. This was in the year 1603, when my brother had first decided to begin writing his defense of himself against his opponent and when the expres-

7 *Republic.* 398D (*S.R.* I, 4).
8 Marsilio Ficino, "Compendium in Timaeum," xxx.
9 *Istituzioni armoniche,* II, vii.

sion "Second Practice" had barely passed his lips, a sure indication that his adversary was desirous of defaming in the same vein my brother's words and his music as well, although they were still in manuscript. And for what reason? Let him say it who knows; let him see it who can find it on the map! But why does the adversary show so much astonishment in that discourse of his, saying further: "You show yourself as jealous of that expression as though you feared that someone would rob you of it," as though he meant to say, in his language: "You should not fear such a theft, for you are not worth imitating, let alone robbing"? I inform him that, if the matter has to be considered in this light, my brother will have not a few arguments in his favor, in particular the *canto alla francese* in the modern manner that has been a matter of marvel for the three or four years since it was published and which he has applied, now to motets, now to madrigals, now to canzonets and airs. Who before him brought this to Italy until he returned from the baths of Spa in the year 1599? Who before him began to apply it to Latin words and to words in our vulgar tongue? Has he not now composed his *Scherzi?* There would be much to say of this to his advantage, and still more (if I wished) of other things, but I pass over them in silence since, as I have said, the matter does not need to be considered in this light. I shall call it "Second Practice" with regard to the manner of its employment; with regard to its origin it might be called "First."

the ingenious may reflect meanwhile upon other secondary matters concerning harmony [1] *and believe that the modern composer builds upon*

[1] "Other matters," that is, not clinging obstinately to the belief that the whole requirement of art is to be found only in the rules of the First Practice on the ground that, in all varieties of composition, the harmony is always the same thing, having reached its limit, and that it is thus incapable of obeying the words perfectly. "Secondary matters," that is, matters concerning the Second Practice, or the perfection of the melody. "Concerning harmony," that is, concerning not merely the details or "passages" of a composition, but its fruit. For if the opponent had considered the harmony of my brother's madrigal "O Mirtillo" in this light, he would not, in that discourse of his, have uttered such extravagances with regard to its mode, although it appears that he speaks generally, his words being: "The Artusi has likewise explained and demonstrated the confusion introduced into composition by those who begin in one mode, follow this with another, and end with one wholly unrelated to the first and second ideas, which is like hearing the talk of a madman, who, as the saying goes, hits now the hoop and now the cask." Poor fellow, he does not perceive that, while he is posing before the world as preceptor ordinary, he falls into the error of denying the mixed modes. If these did not exist, would not the Hymn of the Apostles,[10] which begins in the sixth mode and ends in the fourth, strike now the hoop and now the cask; likewise the introit "Spiritus Domini replevit

---

10 "Exsultet coelum laudibus," *Ant. Rom.*, Hymni antiqui, p. 33.

orbem terrarum" [11] and especially the Te Deum laudamus? [12] Would not Josquin be an ignoramus for having begun his mass on "Faisant regrets" [13] in the sixth mode and finished it in the second? The "Nasce la pena mia" of the excellent Striggio,[14] the harmony of which composition (from the point of view of the First Practice) may well be called divine—would it not be a chimera, being built upon a mode consisting of the first, eighth, eleventh, and fourth? The madrigal "Quando signor lasciaste" of the divine Cipriano de Rore,[15] which begins in the eleventh mode, passes into the second and tenth in the middle, and ends in the first, the second part in the eighth—would not this thing of Cipriano's be a truly trifling vanity? And what would Messer Adriano be called for having begun in the first mode in "Ne projicias nos in tempore senectutis" (a motet for five voices to be found at the end of his first book), making the middle in the second mode and the end in the fourth? But let the opponent read Chapter 14 of the fourth book of the Reverend Zarlino's *Institutions* and he will learn.[16]

the foundation of truth.[m] *Farewell.*

[m] My brother, knowing that, because of the command of the words, modern composition does not and cannot observe the rules of practice and that only a method of composition that takes account of this command will be so accepted by the world that it may justly be called a usage, has said this because he cannot believe and never will believe—even if his own arguments are insufficient to sustain the truth of such a usage—that the world will be deceived, even if his opponent is. And farewell.

---

11 *Grad. Rom.*, p. 292.
12 *Ibid.*, p. 141*.
13 *Missarum Josquin liber III* (Venice, 1514), No. 2. Cf. Ambros, *Geschichte der Musik,* 3d ed., III (Leipzig, 1893), 220, and for the Osanna and Benedictus, Burney, *A General History of Music,* II (London, 1782), 499–500.

14 *Primo libro a 6* (1560), No. 3, reprinted by Charles van den Borren as an appendix to his edition of Philippe de Monte's *Missa Nasce la pena mia* (Düsseldorf, n.d.).
15 *Quarto libro a 5* (1557), No. 9.
16 "On the common or mixed modes."

8. Claudio Monteverdi

Madrigali guerrieri ed amorosi [1]

[*Venice, 1638*]

Foreword

I HAVE reflected that the principal passions or affections of our mind are three, namely, anger, moderation, and humility or supplication; so the best philosophers declare, and the very nature of our voice indicates this in having high, low, and middle registers. The art of music also points clearly to these three in its terms "agitated," "soft," and "moderate" (*concitato, molle,* and *temperato*).[2] In all the works of former composers I have indeed found examples of the "soft" and the "moderate," but never of the "agitated," a genus nevertheless described by Plato in the third book of his *Rhetoric* in these words: "Take that harmony that would fittingly imitate the utterances and the accents of a brave man who is engaged in warfare."[3] And since I was aware that it is contraries which greatly move our mind, and that this is the purpose which all good music should have—as Boethius asserts, saying, "Music is related to us, and either ennobles or corrupts the character"[4]—for this reason I have applied myself with no small diligence and toil to rediscover this genus.

After reflecting that according to all the best philosophers the fast pyrrhic measure was used for lively and warlike dances, and the slow spondaic measure for their opposites,[5] I considered the semibreve, and proposed that a single semibreve should correspond to one spondaic beat; when this was reduced to sixteen semiquavers, struck one after the other,

1 Text: The original edition (Venice, 1638). A facsimile of Monteverdi's Foreword is published in Vol. 8 of Malipiero's edition of the collected works.

2 Evidently a reference to Aristotle's threefold classification of melodies or to its reformulation by the school of Aristoxenus (*S.R.* I, 22 and 45). above).

3 *Republic*, 399A (*S.R.* I, 5).

4 *De institutione musica*, I, i (*S.R.* I, 79).

5 Plato, *Laws*, 816C.

and combined with words expressing anger and disdain, I recognized in this brief sample a resemblance to the passion which I sought, although the words did not follow metrically the rapidity of the instrument.

To obtain a better proof, I took the divine Tasso, as a poet who expresses with the greatest propriety and naturalness the qualities which he wishes to describe, and selected his description of the combat of Tancred and Clorinda [6] as an opportunity of describing in music contrary passions, namely, warfare and entreaty and death. In the year 1624 I caused this composition to be performed in the noble house of my especial patron and indulgent protector the Most Illustrious and Excellent Signor Girolamo Mocenigo, an eminent dignitary in the service of the Most Serene Republic, and it was received by the best citizens of the noble city of Venice with much applause and praise.

After the apparent success of my first attempt to depict anger, I proceeded with greater zeal to make a fuller investigation, and composed other works in that kind, both ecclesiastical and for chamber performance. Further, this genus found such favor with the composers of music that they not only praised it by word of mouth, but, to my great pleasure and honor, they showed this by written work in imitation of mine. For this reason I have thought it best to make known that the investigation and the first essay of this genus, so necessary to the art of music, came from me. It may be said with reason that until the present, music has been imperfect, having had only the two general—"soft" and "moderate."

It seemed at first to the musicians, especially to those who were called on to play the *basso continuo*, more ridiculous than praiseworthy to strum on a single string sixteen times in one measure, and for that reason they reduced this multiplicity to one stroke to the measure, sounding the spondee instead of the pyrrhic foot, and destroying the resemblance to agitated speech. Take notice, therefore, that in this kind the *basso continuo* must be played, along with its accompanying parts, in the form and manner as written. Similarly, in the other compositions, of different kind, all the other directions necessary for performance are set forth. For the manners of performance must take account of three things: text, harmony, and rhythm.[7]

My rediscovery of this warlike genus has given me occasion to write certain madrigals which I have called *Guerrieri*. And since the music played before great princes at their courts to please their delicate taste is of three kinds, according to the method of performance—theater music,

---

[6] *La Gerusalemme liberata*, xii, 52–68.   [7] Plato, *Republic*, 398D (*S.R.* I, 4).

chamber music, and dance music—I have indicated these in my present work with the titles *Guerriera, Amorosa,* and *Rappresentativa.*[8]

I know that this work will be imperfect, for I have but little skill, particularly in the warlike genus, because it is new and *omne principium est debile.* I therefore pray the benevolent reader to accept my good will, which will await from his learned pen a greater perfection in the said style, because *inventis facile est addere.* Farewell.

8 This seems to say, but cannot mean, that there is a correspondence between Monteverdi's three methods of performance and his three varieties of madrigal. Among the *Madrigali guerrieri,* for example, some are *teatrali,* some *da camera,* some *da ballo.* To put it differently, *guerriero* and *amoroso* correspond to kinds of music—*concitato* and *molle*—while *rappresentativo* corresponds to *teatrale,* a method of performance.

II

Musical Practice in the Baroque Age

9. Lodovico Grossi da Viadana

Born at Viadana near Mantua in 1564, Lodovico Grossi studied with Costanzo Porta and became in 1594 choirmaster at the Cathedral of Mantua, remaining there until 1609. About 1595 Viadana entered the Franciscan order. Later he lived at Rome, Padua, and Fano; he died near his birthplace in 1627.

Viadana published a number of volumes of sacred and secular music in the various polyphonic forms, but the work upon which his historical reputation chiefly rests is the collection *Cento concerti ecclesiastici* (for one to four voices with a bass for the organ), published at Venice in 1602. Viadana cannot be regarded as the inventor of the figured bass, as it had been advanced repeatedly before his time, but through his *Cento concerti* he exerted a lasting influence on the development of religious chamber music.

Cento concerti ecclesiastici [1]

[*1602*]

Preface

LODOVICO VIADANA to his kind readers.

There have been many reasons (courteous readers) which have induced me to compose concertos of this kind, among which the following is one of the most important: I saw that singers wishing to sing to the organ, either with three voices, or two, or to a single one by itself, were sometimes forced by the lack of compositions suitable to their purpose to take one, two, or three parts from motets in five, six, seven, or even eight; these, owing to the fact that they ought to be heard in conjunction with other

1 Text. As translated by F. T. Arnold in *The Art of Accompaniment from a Thorough-Bass* (London, Oxford University Press, 1931), pp. 3-4, 10-19. I have translated the last paragraph, omitted by Arnold, from the text printed by Max Schneider in his *Anfänge des Basso continuo* (Leipzig, 1918).

parts, as being necessary for the imitations, closes, counterpoints, and other features of the composition as a whole, are full of long and repeated pauses; closes are missing; there is a lack of melody, and, in short, very little continuity or meaning, quite apart from the interruptions of the words which are sometimes in part omitted, and sometimes separated by inconvenient breaks which render the style of performance either imperfect, or wearisome, or ugly, and far from pleasing to the listeners, not to mention the very great difficulty which the singers experience in performance.

Accordingly, having repeatedly given no little thought to these difficulties, I have tried very hard to find a way of remedying to some extent so notable a deficiency, and I believe, thank God, that I have at length found it, having, to this end, composed some of these concertos of mine for a single voice (soprano, alto, tenor, bass) and some others for the same parts in a variety of combinations, always making it my aim to give satisfaction thereby to singers of every description, combining the parts in every variety of ways, so that whoever wants a soprano with a tenor, a tenor with an alto, an alto with a cantus, a cantus with a bass, a bass with an alto, two sopranos, two altos, two tenors, two basses, will find them all, perfectly adapted to his requirements; and whoever wants other combinations of the same parts will also find them in these concertos, now for three, and now for four voices, so that there will be no singer who will not be able to find among them plenty of pieces, perfectly suited to his requirements and in accordance with his taste, wherewith to do himself credit.

You will find some others which I have composed for instruments in various ways, which makes the invention more complete and gives the concertos greater adaptability and variety.

Furthermore, I have taken particular care to avoid pauses in them, except so far as is necessitated by the character and scheme of the different pieces.

I have, to the very best of my ability, endeavored to achieve an agreeable and graceful tunefulness in all the parts by giving them a good and well-sustained melodic progression.

I have not failed to introduce, where appropriate, certain figures and cadences, and other convenient opportunities for ornaments and passage-work and for giving other proofs of the aptitude and elegant style of the singers, although, for the most part, to facilitate matters, the stock passages have been used, such as nature itself provides, but more florid.

I have taken pains that the words should be so well disposed beneath the notes that, besides insuring their proper delivery, all in complete and due sequence, it should be possible for them to be clearly understood by the hearers, provided that they are delivered distinctly by the singers.

The other less important reason (in comparison with the one aforesaid) which has also made me hasten to publish this my invention is the following: I saw that some of these *Concerti*, which I composed five or six years ago when in Rome (happening then to bethink myself of this new fashion), found such favor with many singers and musicians that they were not only found worthy to be sung again and again in many of the leading places of worship, but that some persons actually took occasion to imitate them very cleverly and to print some of these imitations; wherefore, both for the above reason and also to satisfy my friends, by whom I have frequently been most urgently requested and advised to publish my said concertos as soon as possible, I have at last made up my mind, after having completed the intended number, to print them, as I am now doing, being convinced that this work need not be altogether displeasing to discerning singers and musicians, and that even though it possess no other merit, a willing and active spirit will, at least, not have been lacking, and since it provides, along with its novelty, more than ordinary food for thought, you cannot disdain to read the following instructions, which, in practice, will be of no slight assistance.

1. Concertos of this kind must be sung with refinement, discretion, and elegance, using accents with reason and embellishments with moderation and in their proper place: above all, not adding anything beyond what is printed in them, inasmuch as there are sometimes certain singers, who, because they are favored by nature with a certain agility of the throat, never sing the songs as they are written, not realizing that nowadays their like are not acceptable, but are, on the contrary, held in very low esteem indeed, particularly in Rome, where the true school of good singing flourishes.

2. The organist is bound to play the organ part simply, and in particular with the left hand; if, however, he wants to execute some movement with the right hand, as by ornamenting the cadences, or by some appropriate embellishment, he must play in such a manner that the singer or singers are not covered or confused by too much movement.

3. It will likewise be a good thing that the organist should first cast an eye over the concerto which is to be sung, since, by understanding the nature of the music, he will always execute the accompaniments better.

4. Let the organist be warned always to make the cadences in their proper position: that is to say, if a concerto for one bass voice alone is being sung, to make a bass cadence; if it be for a tenor, to make a tenor cadence; if an alto or soprano, to make it in the place of the one or the other, since it would always have a bad effect if, while the soprano were making its cadence, the organ were to make it in the tenor, or if, while someone were singing the tenor cadence, the organ were to make it in the soprano.

5. When a concerto begins after the manner of a fugue, the organist begins also with a single note, and, on the entry of the several parts, it is at his discretion to accompany them as he pleases.

6. No tablature has been made for these concertos, not in order to escape the trouble, but to make them easier for the organist to play, since, as a matter of fact, not every one would play from a tablature at sight, and the majority would play from the partitura as being less trouble; I hope that the organists will be able to make the said tablature at their own convenience, which, to tell the truth, is much better.

7. When passages in full harmony are played on the organ, they are to be played with hands and feet, but without the further addition of stops; because the character of these soft and delicate *concerti* does not bear the great noise of the full organ, besides which, in miniature *concerti*, it has something pedantic about it.

8. Every care has been taken in assigning the accidentals where they occur, and the prudent organist will therefore see that he observes them.

9. The organ part is never under any obligation to avoid two fifths or two octaves, but those parts which are sung by the voices are.

10. If anyone should want to sing this kind of music without organ or clavier, the effect will never be good; on the contrary, for the most part, dissonances will be heard.

11. In these concertos, falsettos will have a better effect than natural sopranos; because boys, for the most part, sing carelessly, and with little grace, likewise because we have reckoned on distance to give greater charm; there is, however, no doubt that no money can pay a good natural soprano; but there are few of them.

12. When one wants to sing a concerto written in the four usual parts,[2]

---

2 For "in the four usual parts" read "for equal voices" (*à voci pari*). Viadana follows the usual practice of his time, which applies the expression *à voci pari* not only to music in a single register, high or low, but also to music in which the over-all register is relatively restricted. Then in his "O sacrum convivium" *à voci pari* (Arnold, *op. cit.*, pp. 31–33) the four clefs are alto, tenor, tenor, and bass.

the organist must never play high up, and, vice versa, when one wants to sing a concerto of high pitch, the organist must never play low down, unless it be in cadences in the octave, because it then gives charm.

Nor let anyone presume to tell me here that the said concertos are a little too difficult, for my intention has been to make them for those who understand and sing well, and not for those who abuse their craft. And be in good health.

10. Agostino Agazzari

Born of a noble family at Siena in 1578, Agazzari was teaching in 1602 as *musicae praefectus* at the Germanic College in Rome. Ultimately, however, he returned to his native city and became choirmaster at its cathedral, a post he retained until his death in 1640.

Agazzari was an intimate friend of Viadana and one of the first to adopt the figured bass and to publish instructions concerning its realization. He sets forth his views in his *Del sonare sopra il basso*, 1607, and in the second book of his *Sacrae cantiones*, 1608. His musical publications are numerous and include an early opera, *Eumelio*, performed at the Roman Seminary, the Jesuit headquarters, in 1606.

Of Playing upon a Bass with All Instruments and of Their Use in the Consort [1]

[*1607*]

HAVING NOW to speak to you of musical instruments, I must first, for the sake of the order and brevity required in all discussions, classify them according to the needs of my subject and proposed material. I shall therefore divide them into classes, namely, into instruments like a foundation and instruments like ornaments. Like a foundation are those which guide and support the whole body of the voices and instruments of the consort; such are the organ, harpsichord, etc., and similarly, when there are few voices or solo voices, the lute, theorbo, harp, etc. Like ornaments are those which, in a playful and contrapuntal fashion, make the harmony more agreeable and sonorous, namely, the lute,

---

1 Text: The facsimile reprint of the original edition of 1607 (Milan, 1933); see also Otto Kinkeldey, *Orgel und Klavier in der Musik des 16 Jahrhunderts* (Leipzig, 1910), pp. 216–221.

theorbo, harp, *lirone*, cithern, spinet, *chitarrino*, violin, pandora, and the like.

Further, some are stringed instruments, others wind instruments. Of those of this second group (excepting the organ) I shall say nothing, because they are not used in good and pleasing consorts, because of their insufficient union with the stringed instruments and because of the variation produced in them by the human breath, although they are introduced in great and noisy ones. Sometimes in small consorts, when there are *organetti* in the octave above, the trombone replaces the double bass, but it must be well and softly played. All this I say in general, for in particular cases these instruments may be played so excellently by a master hand that they adorn and beautify the harmony.

In the same way, among the stringed instruments, some have within them a perfect harmony of the parts, such as the organ, harpsichord, lute, *arpa doppia*, etc.; others have an imperfect one, such as the common cithern, *lirone*, *chitarrino*, etc.; others have little or none, such as the viol, violin, pandora, etc. For this reason I shall speak in the first place of those instruments of the first class which are the foundation and have perfect harmony and in the second place of those which serve for ornament.

Having made this division and laid down these principles, let us come to the instructions for playing upon a bass. I say, then, that he who wishes to play well should understand three things. First he must know counterpoint (or at least sing with assurance, understand proportions and tempora, and read in all the clefs) and must know how to resolve dissonances with consonances, how to distinguish the major and minor thirds and sixths, and other similar matters. Second, he must know how to play his instrument well, understanding its tablature or score, and must be very familiar with its keyboard or finger board in order not to have to search painfully for the consonances and beats during the music, knowing that his eye is busy watching the parts before him. Third, he must have a good ear in order to perceive the movements of the parts in their relation to one another. Of this I do not speak, for I could not say anything that would help those poor in it by nature.

But to come to the point, I conclude that no definite rule can be laid down for playing works where there are no signs of any sort, it being necessary to be guided in these by the intention of the composer, who is free and can, if he sees fit, place on the first half of a note a fifth or sixth, or vice versa, and this a major or a minor one, as seems more suitable to him or as may be necessitated by the words. And even though some writers who treat of counterpoint have defined the order of progression from one consonance to another as though there were but one way, they are in the wrong; they will pardon me for saying this, for they show that they have not understood that the consonances and the harmony as a whole are subject and subordinate to the words, not vice versa, and this I shall defend, if need be, with all the reasons I can. While it is perfectly true that, absolutely and in general, it is possible to lay down definite rules of progression, when there are words they must be clothed with that suitable harmony which arouses or conveys some passion.

As no definite rule can be given, the player must necessarily rely upon his ear and follow the work and its progressions. But if you would have an easy way of avoiding these obstacles and of playing the work exactly, take this one, indicating with figures above the notes of the bass the consonances and dissonances used with them by the composer; for example, if on the first half of a note there is a fifth and then a sixth, or vice versa, or a fourth and then a third, as illustrated:

Further, you must know that all consonances are either natural or accidental to the mode. When they are natural, no accidental is written at all; for example, when b is natural, the third above G (otherwise b-flat or b-natural) is naturally major; to make it minor, you must write a flat above the note G, in which case the third is accidentally minor; conversely, when b is flat, to make the third major, you must write a sharp above the note G. I say the same of the sixths, reminding you that an accidental below or near a note refers to the note itself, while one above it refers to the consonance which it serves to indicate, as in the following example:

Since all cadences, whether medial or final, require the major third, some musicians do not indicate it; to be on the safe side, however, I advise writing the accidental, especially in medial cadences.

The instruments being divided into two classes, it follows that they have different functions and are differently used. An instrument that serves as foundation must be played with great judgment and due regard for the size of the chorus; if there are many voices one should play with full harmonies, increasing the registers, while if there are few one should use few consonances, decreasing the registers and playing the work as purely and exactly as possible, using few passages and few divisions, occasionally supporting the voices with low notes and frequently avoiding the high ones which cover up the voices, especially the sopranos or falsettos. For this reason one should take the greatest possible care to avoid touching or diminishing with a division the note which the soprano sings, in order not to duplicate it or obscure the excellence of the note itself or of the passage which the good singer executes upon it; for the same reason one does well to play within a rather small compass and in a lower register.

I say the same of the lute, harp, theorbo, harpsichord, etc., when they serve as foundation with one or more voices singing above them, for in this case, to support the voice, they must maintain a solid, sonorous, sustained harmony, playing now piano, now forte, according to the quality and quantity of the voices, the place, and the work, while, to avoid interfering with the singer, they must not restrike the strings too often when he executes a passage or expresses a passion.

Finally, my purpose being to teach how to play upon a bass (not simply how to play, for this must be known beforehand), I take for granted a certain number of principles and terms; for example, that imperfect consonances progress to the nearest perfect ones; that cadences require the major third, as is for the most part true; that dissonances are resolved by the nearest consonance, the seventh by the sixth and the fourth by the third when the part containing the resolution lies above, the opposite when it lies below. But these matters I shall not discuss at length; he who does not know them must learn them. At present I shall teach the conduct of the hand on the organ.

The bass proceeds in many ways, namely, by step, by leap, with conjunct divisions, or with disjunct notes of small value. When it ascends by step, the right hand must descend by step or by leap; conversely, when the left hand ascends or descends by a leap of a third, fourth, or fifth, the right hand must proceed by step. For it is not good for both to ascend or descend together; not only is this ugly to see and to hear, but there is in it no variety at all, for it will be all octaves and fifths. When the bass ascends with a conjunct division, the right hand must remain stationary; when the progression is disjunct, with notes of small value, each note must have its own accompaniment. Here is an example of the whole:

Having now spoken sufficiently of the instruments which serve as a foundation to enable a judicious man to obtain much light from this slender ray (for saying too much makes for confusion), I shall speak briefly of those which serve as ornaments.

These instruments, which are combined with the voices in various ways, are in my opinion so combined for no other purpose than to ornament and beautify, and indeed to season the consort. For this reason, these instruments should be used in a different way than those of the first class; while those maintained the tenor and a plain harmony, these must make the melody flourishing and graceful, each according to its quality, with a variety of beautiful counterpoints. But in this the one class differs from the other; while the instruments of the first class, playing the bass before them as it stands, require no great knowledge of counterpoint in the player, those of the second class do require it, for the player must compose new parts above the bass and new and varied passages and counterpoints.

For this reason, he who plays the lute (which is the noblest instrument of them all) must play it nobly, with much invention and variety, not as is done by those who, because they have a ready hand, do nothing but play runs and make divisions from beginning to end, especially when playing with other instruments which do the same, in all of which nothing is heard but babel and confusion, displeasing and disagreeable to the listener. Sometimes, therefore, he must use gentle strokes and repercussions, sometimes slow passages, sometimes rapid and repeated ones, sometimes something played on the bass strings, sometimes beautiful vyings and conceits, repeating and bringing out these figures at different pitches and in different places; he must, in short, so weave the voices together with long groups, trills, and accents, each in its turn, that he gives grace to the consort and enjoyment and delight to the listeners, judiciously preventing these embellishments from conflicting with one another and allowing time to each, especially when there are other similar instruments, a thing to be avoided, in my opinion, unless they play at a great distance or are differently tuned or of different sizes.

And what I say of the lute, as the principal instrument, I wish understood of the others in their kind, for it would take a long time to discuss them all separately.

But since each instrument has its own peculiar limitations, the player must take advantage of them and be guided by them to produce a good result. Bowed instruments, for example, have a different style than those plucked with a quill or with the finger. The player of the *lirone* must bow with long, clear, sonorous strokes, bringing out the inner parts well, with attention to the major and minor thirds and sixths, a matter difficult but important with his instrument. The violin requires beautiful passages, distinct and long, with playful figures and little echoes and imitations repeated in several places, passionate accents, mute strokes of the bow, groups, trills, etc. The *violone*, as lowest part, proceeds with gravity, supporting the harmony of the other parts with soft resonance, dwelling as much as possible on the heavier strings, frequently touching the lowest ones. The theorbo, with its full and gentle consonances, reinforces the melody greatly, restriking and lightly passing over the bass strings, its special excellence, with trills and mute accents played with the left hand. The *arpa doppia*, which is everywhere useful, as much so in the soprano as in the bass, explores its entire range with gentle plucked notes, echoes of the two hands, trills, etc.; in short, it aims at good counterpoint. The cithern, whether the common cithern or the *ceterone*, is used with the other instruments in a playful way, making counterpoints upon the part. But all this must be done prudently; if the instruments are alone in the consort, they must lead it and do everything; if they play in company, each must regard the other, giving it room and not conflicting with it; if there are many, they must each await their turn and not, chirping all at once like sparrows, try to shout one another down. Let these few remarks serve to give some light to him who seeks to learn. He who relies on his own efforts needs no instruction at all; I do not write for him—I esteem and honor him. But if perchance some wit desires to carry the discussion further, I am at his service.

Finally, one must know how to transpose music from one step to another that has all the consonances natural and proper to the given tone.[2] No other transposition is possible without a very disagreeable sound, for, as I have sometimes observed, in transposing a first or second tone, naturally pleasing because of its many b-flats, to some step whose tone requires b-natural, it will be difficult for the player to avoid stumbling

---

2 For a full discussion of this problem cf. Arthur Mendel, "Pitch in the 16th and Early 17th Centuries," *The Musical Quarterly*, XXXIV (1948), nos. 1–4.

against some conflicting note; thus, with this crudity, the consort is spoiled and the listeners are offended, while the natural character of the given tone does not appear. Most natural and convenient of all is the transposition to the fourth or fifth, sometimes to a step higher or lower; in short, one must see which transposition is most appropriate and suitable to the given tone, not as is done by those who pretend to play every tone on every step, for if I could argue at length, I could show these their error and the impropriety of this.

Having treated thus far of playing upon a bass, it seems to me desirable to say something about the bass itself, for it has, I know, been censured by some, ignorant of its purpose or lacking the soul to play it. It is, then, for three reasons that this method has been introduced: first, because of the modern style of composing and singing recitative; second, because of its convenience; third, because of the number and variety of works which are necessary for concerted music.

As to the first reason, I shall say that, since the recent discovery of the true style of expressing the words, namely, the imitation of speech itself in the best possible manner, something which succeeds best with a single voice or with few voices, as in the modern airs of certain able men and as is now much practiced at Rome in concerted music, it is no longer necessary to make a score or tablature, but, as we have said above, a bass with its signs suffices. And if anyone objects that a bass will not suffice to play the ancient works, I shall reply that music of this kind is no longer in use, both because of the confusion and babel of the words, arising from the long and intricate imitations, and because it has no grace, for, with all the voices singing, one hears neither period nor sense, these being interfered with and covered up by imitations; indeed, at every moment, each voice has different words, a thing displeasing to men of competence and judgment. And on this account music would have come very near to being banished from Holy Church by a sovereign pontiff had not Giovanni Palestrina found the remedy, showing that the fault and error lay, not with music, but with the composers, and composing in confirmation of this the mass entitled *Missa Papae Marcelli*.[3] For this reason, although such compositions are good according to the rules of counterpoint, they are at the same time faulty according to the rules of music that is true and good, something which arises from disregarding the aim and function and good precepts of the latter, such composers wishing to stand solely on the observance of canonic treatment and imitation of the notes,

---

[3] Probably the earliest reference to the salvation of church music through the agency of the *Missa Papae Marcelli*.

not on the passion and expression of the words. Indeed, many of them wrote their music first and fitted words to it afterwards. For the moment, let this suffice, for it would not be to the purpose to discuss the matter at length in this place.

The second reason is the great convenience of the method, for with little labor the musician will have a large stock for his needs; apart from this, the learner is free from tablature, a matter difficult and burdensome to many and likewise very liable to error, the eye and mind being wholly occupied with following so many parts, especially when it is necessary to play concerted music on the spur of the moment.

The third and last reason, namely, the number of works which are necessary for concerted music, is alone sufficient ground, it seems to me, for introducing this so convenient method of playing, for if he were to put into tablature or score all the works which are sung in the course of a year in a single church in Rome, wherever concerted music is professed, the organist would need to have a larger library than a Doctor of Laws.

There was then abundant reason for the introduction of this kind of bass, with the method described above, on the ground that there is no need for the player to play the parts as written if he aims to accompany singing and not to play the work as written, a matter foreign to our subject. Accept what I have said in place of all I might have said, my desire being to satisfy in brief your courteous demands, so many times repeated, and not my natural bent, which is rather to learn from others than to teach them. Take it as it is, then, and let the shortness of the time be my excuse.

11. Heinrich Schütz

Born in Saxony in 1585, Schütz is the composer who first introduced into German music the new style that was coming to the fore in Italy at the beginning of his career. As a chorister in the service of the Landgrave Moritz of Hesse, he was sent in 1609 to Venice, where he studied under Giovanni Gabrieli. In 1612, after Gabrieli's death, Schütz returned to Cassel and was appointed organist to the Landgrave. In 1614 he exchanged this post with that of choirmaster to the Elector of Saxony at Dresden. In 1628, Schütz set out on a second visit to Venice. The artistic results of this second journey to Italy are contained in the first part of his *Symphoniae sacrae,* published in 1629. A second and third part were added in 1647 and 1650. Among Schütz's later works are his German *Passions,* which paved the way for J. S. Bach's great works in this form. Schütz died at Dresden in 1672.

Symphoniae sacrae [1]

Dedications and forewords

PRIMA PARS—OPUS II

[*Venice, 1629*]

To the Eldest Son
of the Elector of Saxony in the Holy Roman Empire, the Most
Serene Prince and Lord, Lord Johann Georg, Duke of Saxony,
Jülich, Cleves, and Berg, Landgrave of Thuringia, Margrave
of Meissen, Count of the Mark and Ravensberg,
Lord of Ravenstein, etc.,

---

1 Texts: *Sämmtliche Werke,* V (Leipzig, 1887), 3; VII (Leipzig, 1888), 3–6; X (Leipzig, 1891), 3–5.

A youth of heroic nature, the splendor of the House of Saxony, the most desired hope of his country, the author's most clement lord,

Heinrich Schütz presents his greetings.

IN MY absence, best of Princes,[2] I am not absent from you, for I still feel that by your great father's [3] orders I am accompanying you through the charming fields of music. For just as when I sailed from my port the tried benignity of him who made this possible was to me constantly as a favoring breeze (I refer to the security of my fortunes), I may stray with you with the same security, since you also are a guiding star to me. I therefore rejoice marvelously to be making my entire sojourn abroad in company with your image, as if you were sharing it. When this comes to my mind (and it does so at almost every point of my journey) it brings before me your very distinguished intellectual adornments, derived from your eminent father. It is no marvel that these, like seeds that have been sown, should grow up marvelously with you in the flower of your youth in the fertile soil of your intelligence and portend everything marvelous to the happiness of the Saxon land.

For this reason I think it good that in preparation for my return I should consider bringing something to offer as a votive gift and hang up as a tablet to my divinity. But it first occurs to me that I must present you with something from my studies that would above all find approval with you. This indeed, most fortunately, is the case.

Let your clemency incline you to listen. When I arrived at Venice, I cast anchor here where as a youth I had passed the novitiate of my art under the great Gabrieli [4]—Gabrieli, immortal gods, how great a man! If loquacious antiquity had seen him, let me say it in a word, it would have set him above Amphions, or if the Muses loved wedlock, Melpomene would have rejoiced in no other spouse, so great was he in the art of awakening the modes. This fame reports, and indeed unvarying fame. I myself am a most trustworthy witness, having derived the highest benefit from full four years' association with him. But this I pass over.

Staying in Venice as the guest of old friends, I learned that the long unchanged theory of composing melodies had set aside the ancient rhythms to tickle the ears of today with fresh devices. To this method

2 Johann Georg II (1613–1680), Elector after 1656.
3 Johann Georg I (1585–1656), Elector after 1611.
4 Schütz, writing during his second stay in Venice (1628–1629), refers here to his first stay (1609–1613) and to his studies with Giovanni Gabrieli, undertaken with the support of Landgrave Moritz of Hesse-Cassel; see also the dedication of his Opus 1, the Italian madrigals of 1611 (*Sämmtliche Werke*, IX, 3).

I directed my mind and energies, to the end that, in accordance with my purpose, I might offer you something from the store of my industry, while this labor, such as it is, is being undergone, I see myself undertaking a perilous risk for you, a young man both trained in the other virtues worthy of a highly praised prince and so skilled in this art as to have unusual expectations. With you I include your most able prefect Volrad von Watzdorff, a master of the same art, unless, I might say, it should serve him, and you as well, as a refuge from severer cares, such as befall princes like yourselves. But consider, Prince, and you, most noble Volrad, while we in sincerity offer these gifts, that even the highest divinities look upon pure hands, not full ones, upon hands, that is, which the candor of the soul, not waters of the spring, keeps free from stain. When men like you, standing next to the gods, show themselves in such light to us, why should I not have confidence? But if these things of mine should provoke some distaste, I shall appeal to your clemency and to the graciousness of the prefect, and shall urge as excuses the shortness of the time, the inconveniences of travel, and a mind perhaps aspiring, in the hope of your gratitude, to too great a task.

Farewell, renowned ornament of your house, and continue, I earnestly pray, to cherish me in the bosom of your clemency as you have begun to do.

Venice, August 19.

Secunda Pars—Opus X

[Dresden, 1647]

To the most serene all-powerful high-born Prince and Lord

Lord Christian V
Prince in Denmark, Norway, and of the Wends and Goths; Duke of
Schleswig, Holstein, Stormarn, and the Dithmarschen;
Count of Oldenburg and Delmenhorst, etc.;

My most gracious Prince and Lord.

Most serene and all-powerful Prince and gracious Lord: [5] That, now two years ago in connection with my then most humbly rendered per-

---

[5] Prince Christian (1603–1647), who died in the year of this dedication and during the lifetime of his father, King Christian IV (1577–1648), was the son-in-law of Johann Georg I.

sonal attendance in Copenhagen, Your Princely Serenity received and accepted with uncommon grace the present insignificant little musical work, composed by me and at that time extant only in manuscript copies; that, out of inborn princely inclination toward all praiseworthy arts and especially toward noble music, you caused the same to be used and performed on several occasions; and also that you gave me real and conspicuous assurance of your gracious satisfaction in that, my humble dedication; all this I call to mind in everlasting and most respectful recollection and, in consequence, find myself obliged in turn, out of bounden gratitude, to celebrate at all times and to the best of my ability your heroic nature and outstanding princely virtues and to consider at each and every opportunity how the great and unmerited favor shown to me may, through most bounden attendance, be to some extent repaid.

Moreover, since for various reasons (some of them hereinafter stated in my memorial to the reader) this little work, thoroughly revised and somewhat enlarged and improved, is now through publication to be brought to light, I have regarded it as in all respects my duty not even this time to pass by Your Princely Serenity in silence but, with this now new and public edition, also to renew my first and earlier humblest dedication, thereby above all to demonstrate and reaffirm my unceasing and most bounden devotion.

May it then please Your Princely Serenity now, with your gracious hands and eyes, to accept anew, as you did before, my repeatedly mentioned unworthy little work (the which I herewith once more present to you in deepest humility) and, with princely indulgence and graciousness, to be further inclined, so always to remain, toward my insignificant person and toward the praiseworthy profession of music, which otherwise has thus far suffered during these upset martial times great loss of its patrons.[6]

May the All-Highest, whose honor, praise, and glory the heavenly hosts continually do sing, again lend unity and good harmony on all sides and to all stations and also long preserve in health and happiness, and in all prosperity pleasing to Him, Your Princely Serenity, together with Your Princely Spouse and the whole most praiseworthy crown of Denmark, to the honor of His holy name, to the improvement of the free arts and especially of beloved music, at present greatly deteriorated, and also to the advantage of my unworthy person in particular. I faithfully

---

6 Here, as elsewhere, Schütz refers to the effects of the Thirty Years' War (1618–1648).

and humbly commend Your Princely Serenity to His fatherly care, myself then to your perpetual and gracious affection.

Dresden, on the first day of the month of May in the year 1647.
Your Princely Serenity's
Most dutiful and humble
Servant,

Heinrich Schütz

Ad benevolum lectorem.

Dear gracious reader: How, in the year 1629, when I had come for the
second time to Italy and had resided there a while, I composed, in conformity with the insignificant talent God has lent me and, be it said without vanity, in a short time, a little Latin work for one, two, and three
vocal parts, with two subordinate violins or similar instruments, in the
musical style I then met with there; and how I caused the same to be set
up and printed in Venice under the title *Symphoniae sacrae;* none of this
shall be concealed from you here.

Since, at that time, from copies of the work, part of which had been
exported to Germany and had there fallen into the hands of musicians,
there came to my ears a report that the work was there thought to be of
real value, further, that it was being diligently performed in various distinguished places with German words in place of Latin adapted throughout; I regarded this as a special incentive to me to attempt another little
work of the same sort in our German mother tongue; and, after a bold
beginning, I accordingly finished the same at length, with God's help,
together with other works of mine (such as are here included).

Since then, however, and up until the present, I have been no little
dissuaded from giving these out in a public edition, not only by the
wretched times which still continue unabated in our beloved fatherland,
unfavorable no less to music than to the other free arts, but also, and indeed above all, by the modern Italian manner used therein, still hidden
from the majority, both as regards the composition and the proper performance of it, by means of which (in the opinion of the keen-witted Signor
Claudio Monteverdi in the foreword to the Eighth Book of his madrigals)
music is thought to have at length attained its final perfection.[7]

Indeed (to admit the truth here reluctantly), experience has thus far
repeatedly shown that this same modern music, whether Italian or after
the Italian manner, together with the measure proper for it and for the

7 See pp. 53–55 above.

notes of lesser value therein introduced, will neither rightly adapt itself to most of us Germans on this side, as many of us as are not bred to it, nor yet becomingly depart from us; in that (doubtless even in those places where one has thought to have good music) things thus composed are often so abused, defamed, and as it were actually broken that to an intelligent ear they can occasion nothing less than disgust and annoyance, to the author and to the praiseworthy German nation a wholly unjustified disparagement, as though the latter were in fact unskilled in noble music (as indeed there is no lack of such accusations on the part of certain foreigners).

But inasmuch as this little work, completed some years ago, was at that time humbly presented as manuscript to the serene all-powerful Prince and Lord, Lord Christian V, Prince in Denmark, Norway, and of the Goths and Wends, etc., as is, with other matters, to be seen from the foregoing most humble dedication; and inasmuch as I have since learned how many pieces of my composition, carelessly and incorrectly copied, scattered far and wide (as is then usual), have come into the hands of distinguished musicians; I have been obliged, therefore, to take the same once more in hand myself, and, after carrying out a thorough revision, I communicate them herewith through publication to those who may seek pleasure in them.

Now, since I should needlessly address myself to competent musicians, trained in good schools, if I were to call to their attention the pains I have expended herein (and, after the glory of God, it is to please these alone that the present few copies are now come to light); and since the manner herein introduced will be by no means displeasing to them;

Then to the others, especially to those who neither know nor practice the proper beat for the afore-mentioned modern music and its notes of lesser value and also the steady broadened way of bowing the violin which we Germans have (but who may wish nonetheless to perform something of this), this my friendly request: that before they undertake to employ one or other of these pieces in public they will not be ashamed on this account to seek instruction in advance from those familiar with this manner and will spare themselves no pains in private practice lest perchance on the contrary there accrue to them and to the author himself, through no fault of his, instead of the expected thanks, an unexpected ridicule.

Further, inasmuch as in the concerto "Es steh Gott auf," etc., I have been guided, in some few details, by Signor Claudio Monteverdi's madrigal "Armato il cor," etc., and also by one of his chaconnes with two tenor voices, I leave the question of how far I have gone in this to those familiar with the afore-mentioned compositions.[8] But let no one on this account suspect my remaining work unduly, for I am not accustomed to dress my works in borrowed plumage.

Finally, I make this further offer: that, if God continue to prolong my life, I shall, with His help, publish without delay still others of my admittedly unworthy *opera*, and, first among these, works of such a sort that even those who neither are nor intend becoming musicians *ex professo* may use them, it is hoped, and with the better effect.

Vale.

TERTIA PARS—OPUS XII

[*Dresden, 1650*]

To the most serene high-born Prince and Lord

Lord Johann Georg
Duke of Saxony, Jülich, Cleve, and Berg; Arch Marshal and Elector
of the Holy Roman Empire; Landgrave in Thuringia;
Margrave of Meissen, also of Upper and Lower
Lausitz; Burgrave of Magdeburg; Count
of the March and Ravensberg;
Lord of Ravenstein.

Most gracious Elector and Lord: Just as Your Electoral Serenity can, I trust, graciously call to mind and recollect for how long a time, now thirty-five years, I have in most humble submission and due fidelity been your constant servant, and just as you will not be less likely to recall how I have at all times loyally and industriously offered up the little talent lent me by God and have waited upon you with it, both in Your Electoral Serenity's Court Chapel and also in connection with other events that have occurred within this time and with various past solemnities;

So similarly there remains constantly with me in vivid memory how, during the past tedious thirty-year succession of wars, Your Electoral Serenity has never entirely withdrawn your favor and helping hand, either from the other free arts, or yet from the noble art of music, but has continued to assist them to the utmost, and especially how (during

---

8 For the concerto by Schütz see his *Sämmtliche Werke,* VII, 87–97; Monteverdi's "Armato il cor" and "Zefiro torna" may be consulted in the Appendix of the same volume or in Vol. 9 of Malipiero's edition of Monteverdi's works. The bass of Monteverdi's "Zefiro torna" was also used by Benedetto Ferrari in 1637 and by Tarquinio Merula in the same year (cf. Hugo Riemann, *Handbuch der Musikgeschichte,* II, 2. Teil [2d ed., Leipzig, 1922], 55–61, 121–124, 489–492).

the continued unrest in our universally beloved fatherland, the German nation) you have shown my unworthy person evidences of favor of all sorts: that in the year 1628 and again in 1629, for the continuance of my profession, you not only graciously allowed me to visit Italy (in order that I might there inform myself about the new and now usual manner of music introduced since my first return thence) and greatly furthered this enterprise, but also graciously permitted me, this my journey completed, at the further request of His Majesty of Denmark, Christian IV, now at rest in God,[9] to spend some time at his Royal Chapel, to head the *Directorium* (at that time offered me unsolicited), and in this way to preserve my small knowledge of music through constant practice and bring to it further experience.

Nor ought in this connection to be passed over in silence the most gracious means granted me some time ago by Your Electoral Serenity whereby the publication or giving out of my musical work can in future be even further forwarded and its printing facilitated.

For this high and mighty benefit I shall for the rest of my life remain justly bound to express to Your Electoral Serenity my most humble thanks and shall in addition do my utmost, through further most humble attendance (as long as my now diminished powers permit), to deserve again Your Electoral Serenity's many-sided favor and to continue in the possession of this same consolation in future.

And to this end is also directed the most humble dedication of this, my twelfth little work, which, with Your Electoral Serenity's lofty name at its head, I send forth into the world herewith; not only as a public witness of my proper and constant gratitude, but also to make known to everyone, above all to those whom my compositions may please, through what circumstance, favor, and furtherance the same are now brought to light and (should God grant me life) may continue to appear in future, and that the thanks and the honor (should anything of value be found in them) is due to Your Electoral Serenity alone.

Hence then to yourself my most humble and most diligent request that you may graciously deign to receive and accept from me in electoral favor the well-intended and faithfully devoted dedication and presentation of this my unsolicited work, not completed without effort, and that you may continue to favor me, your old and faithful servant, with that mercy and grace which until now you have used toward me.

Whereupon, together with many thousands, I wish with all my heart

---

9 Christian IV had died in 1648, the year following the publication of the second part of the *Symphoniae sacrae*.

that, to the advantage of your great electoral house and as a consolation to your loyal subjects, almighty God may preserve Your Electoral Serenity in good and constant health for many years to come and that, after the heavy burden of war, so long endured, He may grant you to enjoy to the full the restoration of order [10] in your honorable land, brought about through His mercy (for which everlasting thanks) and to rejoice in this and apply and employ the same fruitfully in the furtherance of the glory of God and the preservation of the good free arts.

Dated, Dresden, on the Feast of St. Michael Archangel in the year 1650.

> Your Electoral Serenity's
> Most humble and dutiful
> Heinrich Schütz

Dear gracious reader:

For all that there is no doubt that competent and experienced musicians will know in advance and of themselves how properly to order and employ this my present musical work, as well as the others that have been published; since, however, this leaf will otherwise have to remain vacant or empty, I have deemed it good to cause some few memorials to be here listed, hoping that no one will object to hearing in some measure my opinion, as the author's, about it.

1. Thus the complementary parts added to this work *ad beneplacitum* are to be found in four separate books, and from the index to the thorough bass part is to be seen to what concertos they belong and how many of them belong to each, whereby in general this further point seems noteworthy, that although in the index just mentioned most complementary music is only listed as being in four parts and although only four printed parts are supplied, the same may (if copied out again) be doubled and as it were divided into two choirs, for example vocal and instrumental, and ordered with the others. The rest is left to the judgment of the competent conductor.

2. Above the bass for the organ I have had the signatures entered with all possible care. The Italians are for the most part accustomed today to use no figures in this connection, objecting that experienced organists do not need them and without them know how to play along according to the counterpoint, while the inexperienced will not find the musical concord or agreement even when one places a figure immediately above

---

10 A reference to the end of the Thirty Years' War (1648).

it. Which then in itself is doubtless true enough, for to play along properly above the thorough bass and to content a musical ear thereby is not such a simple matter, for all that many a one may think so. That, however, in my previously published compositions I make use of these same signatures follows the precept: *Abundans cautela non nocet*.[11]

3. The organ must be registered with discretion (according to whether the complementary parts are added or left out).

4. Finally, I wish in this place hereby once again to call attention to all that has previously been pointed out to the reader in the published second part of my *Symphoniae sacrae* regarding modern music or the present manner of composition and touching the proper and suitable beat for it.

Commending us all faithfully to Divine Providence in mercy.

The Author.

---

11 Abundant caution does no harm.

12. Georg Muffat

Born about 1645, this South German composer was organist at the Strassburg Cathedral till 1674. From there he visited Paris where he studied Lully's style. About 1678 he became organist to the Bishop of Salzburg, visited Vienna and Rome, and in 1690 was made organist, and in 1695 choirmaster to the Bishop of Passau. Muffat published several important collections of suites for string orchestra with basso continuo; their forewords contain discussions of the French and Italian styles and instructions concerning the playing of stringed instruments and the execution of ornaments. Another well-known work of Muffat's is his *Apparatus musico-organisticus* (1690), of importance for the history of organ playing and organ music.

Georg Muffat was the father of an equally distinguished composer for the organ and harpsichord, Gottlieb (Theophil) Muffat.

Florilegia [1]

FLORILEGIUM PRIMUM
[Augsburg, 1695]

Foreword

THE AUTHOR'S FOREWORD TO THE GRACIOUS AMATEUR

HERE YOU have my pieces, composed in Salzburg before I came to Passau and conforming in the main to the French ballet style, now submitted to you, gracious amateur, for your entertainment and approval. Heard with pleasure by several princes and also praised by others of the higher nobility, they are published at the repeated entreaty of good friends and with the approbation of distinguished musicians, both Italian and Ger-

---

1 Texts: *Denkmäler der Tonkunst in Oester-* reich, I2 (Vienna, 1894), 10–11; II2 (Vienna, 1895), 19–20, 28; XI2 (Vienna, 1904), 8–10.

Muffat prints each of these forewords in four languages—Latin, German, Italian, and French.

man. To these importunities I have given in the more gladly, observing that in Germany the French style is gradually coming to the fore and becoming the fashion. This same style, which formerly flourished in Paris under the most celebrated Jean Baptiste Lully, I have diligently sought to master, and, returning from France to Alsace, from whence I was driven by the last war, I was perhaps the first to bring this manner, not displeasing to many professional musicians, into Austria and Bohemia and afterwards to Salzburg and Passau. Inasmuch as the ballet compositions of the aforesaid Lully and other things after his manner entirely reject, for the sake of flowing and natural movement, all other artifices —immoderate runs as well as frequent and ill-sounding leaps—they had at first the misfortune, in these countries, to displease many of our violinists, at that time more intent on the variety of unusual conceits and artificialities than on grace; for this reason, when occasionally produced by those ignorant of the French manner or envious of foreign art, they came off badly, robbed of their proper tempo and other ornaments. When, however, they were exhibited with greater perfection, first in Austria by certain foreign violinists, soon afterwards in Bavaria by His Electoral Serenity's excellent musicians, they were more maturely considered, and many, in order to conform to the genius of the princes and lords applauding such music, began to form a better opinion of it, to accustom themselves to its style and grace, and even to study it. No doubt they discovered the truth of what an extremely discerning prince once said to me, touching this style: namely, that what they had learned previously was more difficult than what, to charm the ear, they needed to have learned. Now that the ill-considered contempt for the aforesaid ballet style has gradually fallen off, it has seemed to me that I might the more confidently come forward with my admittedly insignificant pieces, which, though they appear simple, are the more in need of the artistry and favor of our violinists. To give reasons for the names prefixed to each fascicle seems needless, especially since these have been named, only to distinguish one from another, either for some cause, effect, or other circumstance peculiar to myself or for some state of the affections which I have experienced.[2]

It still remains for me to remind and request such musicians as are as yet unfamiliar with the aforesaid style that, when notes are enclosed in such brackets as these ⌐⌐ ⌐⌐ , they are to play the first time those notes which precede the sign of repetition ∫ :||: , the second time omit-

---

2 The Latin titles of the seven suites making up the *Florilegium primum* might be translated: Piety, The Joys of the Hopeful, Gratitude, Impatience, Solicitude, Flatteries, Constancy.

ting these altogether, straightway skipping over instead to those notes which follow immediately after the sign of repetition just mentioned :||:. This sign, $\int$, whether at the very beginning or after the sign of repetition :||:, marks the note from which, omitting the preceding altogether, one must begin; it is also to be observed when it occurs near the middle of the second part or somewhat further from the end. Although I find not displeasing the practice of some who, having in this case first repeated the whole second part once more in its entirety, begin again at the aforesaid sign $\int$ and repeat this much alone a third time, this is a matter to be settled by the musicians before the performance. The beat or measure governed by the signs 2 and ¢, divided into two parts, must be given once again as fast as that following the sign C, divided into four. Moreover, the time of those pieces comprehended by the names *Ouverture*, *Prélude*, and *Symphonie* is to be beaten rather slowly when it is marked 2, a little more briskly for the *Ballet*, in any case more slowly than one beats at the sign ¢, which last, in the *Gavotte*, is not so precipitate as in the *Bourrée*. Further, although at the sign 2 the measure is very slowly divided into two parts, the notes have nearly the same value as they have with the Italians at the sign C and the additional direction "Presto," when the measure is divided into four; the difference between the two is simply that in the latter case one must not, as in the former and better, give to successive quavers a dotted rhythm, but must, on the contrary, play them evenly. The *Symphonie* of the fourth fascicle provides an example of this. As to the other signs, ³⁄₂ requires a restrained movement, ¾ a gayer one, yet uniformly somewhat slow in *Sarabandes* and *Airs*, lively in the *Rondeau*, very brisk in *Menuets*, *Courantes*, and many other dances, as also in the Fugues appended to the *Ouvertures*. The remaining pieces, such as are called *Gigues* and *Canaries*, need to be played the fastest of all, no matter what the time signature.

Gracious amateur, may it please you to accept this my *Florilegium primum*, protecting it from the envious and grudging, and excusing such errors of mine and of the press as may have crept in. Await what is promised at the end of the work. Farewell and favor him who would deserve your favor.

.   .   .   .   .   .

Friendly amateur, I had planned, for the better advancement and greater glory of our Germany in its higher flights into the musical arts, to append to these ballets certain observations perhaps not displeasing to

you, touching the performance of the same, having promised—in my *Apparatus Musico-Organisticus,* delivered five years ago, at the time of his royal coronation, into the all-serenest hands of our invincible Emperor Leopold—to attach something noteworthy and useful of this nature to all my forthcoming musical works. But since the limited time allowed me to complete this work did not permit my properly arranging the aforesaid observations, I have put these off to append them to my *Florilegium secundum,* in precisely the same style as this, which, if the present work finds acceptance, shall follow it without delay. In this same *Florilegium secundum* you may expect my new pieces, composed in Passau no less for the fitting reception of distinguished visitors than for the better ballet exercise of the youthful higher nobility; in the meantime another work of instrumental music, in an unusual but lofty style, has begun to sweat under the Passau printing press.[3]

FLORILEGIUM SECUNDUM
[*Passau, 1698*]

Foreword

When I remarked, friendly reader, that the first garland of my ballet pieces, printed and published at Augsburg in 1695, early last year, as a precursor of various musical works of mine to follow in the future, had not only been kindly received by many, especially by those amateurs who prized its natural and flowing style and for whose entertainment it was after all chiefly designed, but had further given rise to a great demand for my other promised ballets; I thought it proper to submit for your worthy intellectual entertainment and kindly approval this my second garland, enriched by many pieces, more amusing—thanks to the variety of its inventions, and, it is to be hoped, more valuable—thanks to the utility of its added observations. It contains no small part of the ballets recently composed in Passau and performed with great applause at this illustrious court, both for dancing and at many instrumental concerts. The which, though also serving in various other connections—for example, as chamber music, table music, or night music—still owes its origin more to Your Reverend Highness' zealous concern for the education of the youthful higher nobility resident at your court than to my desire to tickle the ear.

---

3 The *Auserlesene Instrumental-Music* of 1701 (see pp. 89–92 below).

For, when Your Reverend Highness proposed to determine what progress those high and well-born gentlemen, your nephews, and those noble gentlemen, your pages, had made in their studies and noble exercises, hence also in dancing, Herr Christian Leopold Krünner, groom of the chamber and most deserving court dancing-master to Your Reverend Highness aforesaid, besought me to compose entirely new airs for certain ingenious inventions which he had conceived in order that, enhanced by theatrical costumes and apparatus, the dancing might be the more impressive. And when I had complied with this request of his to the best of my meager ability, Your Reverend Highness regarded this our work with such gracious eyes that you ordered us to prepare, for a further exercise in dancing, more arrangements of the same kind and also to perform these even before princes and other distinguished visitors, yourself taking gracious pleasure in such things as often as they were produced.

All this I have wished to point out to you in advance, friendly reader, so that, if anything in these pieces should strike your ears as strange or vulgar, you will ascribe it, not at all to a sterility or rudeness of style, but to the exigencies of the natural representations belonging to the dance, of which you may form an idea from the engraving diligently printed at the head of the thorough bass and violin parts.[4]

Then, although I should unwillingly be reckoned among those who adopt every idea that occurs to them, regarding it as the more praiseworthy, the more extravagant it is; among those to whom these lines of Horace apply so well:

> Nimium patienter utrumque
> Ne dicam stulte mirati; [5]

it sometimes happens, nonetheless, that for the better suggestion of certain words, manners, or gestures, one must defer a little. For this reason, since to avoid all excess great caution is required, I have sought diligently to soften, by means of the sweetness of agreeable consonances, whatever seemed unusual in the upper voice, namely the violin, and also to lend distinction, by means of the artful setting of the inner voices and the bass, to whatever seemed overly vulgar.

Aside from this, you have in this second garland my first observation, promised to you in the foregoing, showing how such ballets ought properly to be played according to the ideas of the late Monsieur Jean

---

4 The engraving is not reproduced in the critical edition.

5 *The Art of Poetry*, 271–272. Too tolerant, not to say foolish, was their admiration of both. [Fairclough]

Baptiste de Lully; observations written at the request of those who, as yet insufficiently instructed in this proper manner, have a desire to know in what it chiefly consists or in how it may be distinguished from the manner and opinion of others. All of which I wish to state as briefly as possible, readily admitting, at the same time, that others (of whom already there are many in these parts), violinists by actual profession and in addition well versed in the aforesaid manner, might have ordered this business much better than I. And I protest that, in what I am about to say, there is no intention to detract in the least from the well-earned reputation of many other celebrated violinists (whose flourishing abundance in Germany I myself acknowledge most respectfully); nor are these to be regarded as of little competence, even though not used to this new manner, for they have other qualities which concern the art more directly and more highly, and would beyond a doubt not only equal but easily excel the foreigners, were they to add to the musical assurance, the manual dexterity, and the store of artifice already at their command, the animated and agreeable charm of the Lullists.

Finally, I have added at the end of this work a catalogue of these partitas, with their keys and the years of their performance, and of my other things, already published or still to follow; to this I would direct your attention, so that, if perchance you meet in the works of others things more or less similar to my ideas, you may discover from my chronology that the theft is not to be charged to my account, and so that, being apprised of what I plan to work on for your entertainment and further advantage in music, you may receive this my painstaking the more kindly. Farewell.

FIRST OBSERVATION

ON THE PERFORMANCE OF BALLETS IN THE LULLIAN-FRENCH MANNER

·   ·   ·   ·   ·

The art of playing ballets on the violin in the manner of the most celebrated Jean Baptiste Lully (here understood in all its purity, admired and praised by the world's most excellent masters) is so ingenious a study that one can scarcely imagine anything more agreeable or more beautiful.

To reveal to you, gracious reader, its chief secrets, know that it has at one time two aims: namely, to appeal to the ear in the most agreeable way and to indicate properly the measure of the dance, so that one may recognize at once to what variety each piece belongs and may feel in one's affections and one's feet, as it were without noticing it at all, an inclination to dance. For this there are, in my opinion, five considerations necessary. First, one must, for purity of intonation, stop the strings accurately. Second, the bow must be drawn in a uniform way by all the players. Third, one must bear constantly in mind the time signature, or tempo and measure, proper to each piece. Fourth, one must pay strict attention to the usual signs of repetition introduced and also to the qualities of the style and of the art of dancing. Fifth, one must use with discernment certain ornaments making the pieces much more beautiful and agreeable, lighting them up, as it were, with sparkling precious stones. Of which the following distich:

> Contactus, plectrum, tempus, mos, atque venustas
> Efficient alacrem, dulcisonamque chelyn.[6]

. . . . .

May it then please you, gracious amateur, to receive kindly this my first observation, until now kept secret, but now most diligently brought together in this brief order for your approval and communicated to you, and to protect the same generously, in accordance with your inborn inclination toward music, from all envious persons and from interpreters opposed to my ideas. Should you find in this work something defective, ascribe it to my want of ability, crediting its merits to Almighty God, as the dispenser of all grace, and praying Him that He may vouchsafe to the Christian world, and especially to our beloved Germany, more peaceful times, pleasing to the Muses; and that He may graciously grant to me—wandering about Parnassus, variously troubled, despite all envy —continued life and health under the all-serenest shadow of the Austrian eagle and the most gracious protection of the miter of Lamberg-Passau and also such a disposition of affairs and affections as is required for the better explanation of this subject and for the completion of further work designed for your pleasure.

---

[6] Fingering, bowing, and tempo, usage, ornamentation;
These to the viol will bring liveliness, sweetness of tone.

Auserlesene Instrumental-Music

[*Passau, 1701*]

Foreword

AFTER HAVING printed and published my two garlands, or *Florilegia*, of agreeable ballet pieces, the first at Augsburg in the year 1695, the second at Passau in the year 1698, I present to you, sympathetic reader, this first collection of my instrumental concertos, blending the serious and the gay, entitled "of a more select harmony" because they contain (in the ballet airs) not only the liveliness and grace drawn intact from the Lullian well, but also certain profound and unusual affects of the Italian manner, various capricious and artful conceits, and alternations of many sorts, interspersed with special diligence between the great choir and the trio of soloists. These concertos, suited neither to the church (because of the ballet airs and airs of other sorts which they include) nor for dancing (because of other interwoven conceits, now slow and serious, now gay and nimble, and composed only for the express refreshment of the ear), may be performed most appropriately in connection with entertainments given by great princes and lords, for receptions of distinguished guests, and at state banquets, serenades, and assemblies of musical amateurs and virtuosi.

The idea of this ingenious mixture first occurred to me some time ago in Rome, where I learned the Italian manner on the clavier from the world-famous Signor Bernardo [7] and where I heard, with great pleasure and astonishment, several concertos of this sort, composed by the gifted Signor Arcangelo Corelli, and beautifully performed with the utmost accuracy by a great number of instrumental players.

Having observed the considerable variety in these, I composed several of the present concertos, which were tried over at the house of the aforesaid Signor Arcangelo Corelli (to whom I am deeply indebted for many useful observations touching this style, most graciously communicated to me); then, with his approbation—just as was long ago the case with the Lullian ballet style on my return from France—I brought to Germany, as the first, some specimens of this harmony, until then unknown in these parts, and, increasing their number to twelve, performed them successfully on highly distinguished occasions at various times and

---

7 Pasquini.

places (as is then enigmatically implied in the titles prefixed to each concerto). The hearing granted in Vienna, at the imperial royal coronation in Augsburg, also in Munich, Salzburg, and Passau—*most graciously* by Their Imperial and Royal Majesties, *graciously*, however, by several electoral and other princes—to these my admittedly insignificant compositions; the great kindness generously shown on their account to my unworthy self; the approbation of a master most celebrated for his delicate discrimination; and the acclamation of my listeners, which has spread even to distant lands; all these things will easily console me for the fault-finding and envious persons who have risen up against this work and whose malicious undertakings have at all times foretold a happy issue for me. As to you, understanding reader, may it please you to make sympathetic trial of this first collection and to observe the observations which follow, in order that you may attain my herein intended goal and the full emphasis of the composition.

OF THE NUMBER AND CHARACTER OF THE PLAYERS AND INSTRUMENTS

1. Should you be short of string players, or wish to try over these concertos with only a few, you may form a perfect little trio, at all times necessary, from the following voices: Violino primo concertino, Violino secundo concertino, and Basso continuo e Violoncino concertino. Your bass, however, will go better on the small French bass than on the double bass used hereabouts, and to this may be added, for the greater ornamentation of the harmony, a harpsichord or theorbo, played from the very same part. Further, it is to be noted that, besides observing the directions *piano* and *forte*, all should play with a full tone at the direction T or *tutti*, softly and tenderly at the direction S or *solo*.

2. With four string players you may make music by adding to the three principal voices just mentioned the Viola prima, with five by adding to these the Viola secunda.

3. Should still more players be available, add to all the parts aforesaid the three remaining ones, namely, the Violino primo, Violino secundo, and Violone or Basso continuo of the concerto grosso (or great choir), assigning to each of these, as reason and the number of available musicians may dictate, either one, two, or three players. In this case, to make the harmony of the bass the more majestic, a large double bass will prove most serviceable.

4. But insofar as you may have a still greater number of musicians at your disposal, you may assign additional players, not only to the first and second violin parts of the great choir (concerto grosso), but also to the two inner viola parts and to the bass, further ornamenting this last

with the accompaniment of harpsichords, theorbos, harps, and similar instruments; as to the little choir or trio, for it is always to this that the word "concertino" refers, let it be played singly, but at the same time superlatively well, by your three best string players with the accompaniment of an organist or theorbo player, never assigning more to a part, unless in some unusually vast place where the players of the great choir are exceptionally numerous, then assigning two at the most.

5. Should there be among your musicians some who can play and modulate the French oboe or shawm agreeably, you may with the best effect use two of these instead of the two violins, and a good bassoon player instead of the French bass, to form the concertino or little trio in some of these concertos; provided you choose only concertos in those keys, or transposed to those keys, in which the instruments just mentioned are of some use, provided also that, if some few things therein should lie too high or too low, you replace these instruments with violins or transpose to a more convenient octave. In this fashion I have often performed successfully the first, third, fourth, eighth, ninth, and tenth concertos in their original keys and the seventh in a transposition from E-flat to E major.

OF THE MANNER TO BE OBSERVED IN PERFORMING THESE CONCERTOS

6. The note in the concerto grosso standing at the very beginning or entering after a rest or *suspirium* is to be sounded without hesitation, with a full tone, and boldly by each and every player, unless the word *piano* directs otherwise, for this note, were one to slight it or sound it only timidly, would weaken and obscure the whole harmony.

7. At the direction *piano* or *p* all are ordinarily to play at once so softly and tenderly that one barely hears them, at the direction *forte* or *f* with so full a tone, from the first note so marked, that the listeners are left, as it were, astounded at such vehemence.

8. In directing the measure or beat, one should for the most part follow the Italians, who are accustomed to proceed much more slowly than we do at the directions *Adagio, Grave, Largo,* etc., so slowly sometimes that one can scarcely wait for them, but, at the directions *Allegro, Vivace, Presto, Più presto,* and *Prestissimo* much more rapidly and in a more lively manner. For by exactly observing this opposition or rivalry of the slow and the fast, the loud and the soft, the fullness of the great choir and the delicacy of the little trio, the ear is ravished by a singular astonishment, as is the eye by the opposition of light and shade. Though this has often been reported by others, it can never be said or enjoined sufficiently.

9. To each voice, hence also to the inner and lower voices, should be assigned, not only the mediocre and weaker players, but also a few of the able ones, who should regard it as no disgrace to lead these voices for you as worthily as they would lead the others, contrary to the deep-rooted prejudice of certain haughty persons, who faint away on the spot if one does not assign them to the violin or some other prominent part.

10. In the opening sonatas and fugues and in the affecting Graves that are interpolated, the Italian manner is to be chiefly observed, and, in the suspensions, the note tied over, the note sounding the dissonance in another voice, and the note resolving the dissonance aforesaid (those experienced in this art will readily understand this) are to be played at all times with the same full tone, lifting the bow (in Italian, *staccato*), detaching them rather than weakening them by prolonging them timidly.

11. Inasmuch as the force and charm of these compositions largely depends on the connection between successive movements, special care is to be taken that, after a sonata, air, or interpolated Grave, no noticeable wait or silence, above all no annoying tuning of the violins, should interrupt the continuous order; on the contrary, provided only the last notes of the several periods be held out to their full value and the repetitions observed as otherwise usual, but so that the more serious airs are repeated twice only, the livelier ones three times on occasion, but the Graves never, it is earnestly requested that the listeners be maintained in continuous attention from beginning to end, until, at a given moment, all end the concerto together, forcibly and, as it were, unexpectedly.

12. Finally, since nothing is so exquisite or lofty that, if heard too often, it does not depreciate, and since it is to be presumed that there will be no lack of bunglers enamored of this style, who, if they merely misplace without judgment *forte* and *piano*, *solo* and *tutti*, and other such matters, piling up threadbare stupidities in disorder, will imagine that they have attained the zenith of art; it is my advice that these concertos should be performed neither too often nor one after another, two —still less, more than two—in succession, but rather in moderation— sometimes only one previously tried over in private—after a partita more usual in style (of which many may be found in my *Florilegia*), observing a suitable variety of key—at the end of an important function, and then with all possible ardor, ornament, and magnificence. Having considered all this duly, may it please you, understanding reader, to regard this work kindly and to await my *Florilegium tertium*, or third garland of ballet pieces,[8] and other works. Farewell.

---

8 This promised continuation never appeared.

13. F. E. Niedt

Friedrich Erhardt Niedt describes himself in 1700 as a notary public living in Jena. Later on he became a resident of Copenhagen, where he died sometime before 1717. The first part of his principal writing, the *Musikalische Handleitung*, was published in Hamburg in 1700; a second part followed in 1706, and in 1717, after the author's death, the third part was brought out by Johann Mattheson.

Niedt was one of the first German writers to teach the art of accompaniment from a thorough bass. That his little treatise was well thought of in its day is evident not only from Mattheson's editorial work on the third part and from his reprint of the second, but also from the extracts copied from it by J. S. Bach and incorporated in his "Precepts and Principles," a collection of rules compiled in 1738 for the use of his pupils. One section from this compilation of Bach's is translated by David and Mendel in *The Bach Reader* (New York, W. W. Norton & Co., Inc., 1945); there is a complete translation in the third volume of the English Spitta (Appendix XII).

Before introducing his reader to the study of the thorough bass itself, Niedt entertains him with a foreword in the shape of a short satiric novel in which he reproves his German contemporaries for clinging obstinately to an antiquated system of musical notation and pokes fun at the arrogant incompetence of the old-fashioned provincial music-teacher. This is included here as a brief but characteristic specimen of a literary variety which enjoyed a widespread if short-lived popularity in Germany toward the end of the seventeenth century, as witness Johann Kuhnau's *Musikalischer Quacksalber* (1700) or the various similar productions published between 1676 and 1691 by Wolfgang Caspar Printz.

Musikalische Handleitung [1]

[1700]

Foreword

1. PHOEBUS IN HIS fiery chariot had by this time climbed so high along the heavenly ramparts that the white shroud of winter, shaming itself before him, had had once more to grant our quarter of the globe an open countenance. Already Flora had dressed the trees in gay attire; Pomona, too, had again bedecked the trees' bald crown with a becoming wig; and Ceres, hard at work, was helping the fields, already sown and teeming, to a joyous bearing of their fruits. At this season, all things are so alive and astir that I too was unwilling to sit longer imprisoned by my four walls; very early one morning I went out into the open country, thinking to contemplate with my five senses the wonderwork of nature. No sooner had I gone a little distance from the town than my nostrils were filled with the agreeable perfume of the loveliest flowers and plants; these at the same time gave no less pleasure to my eyes; I was tempted to touch and to pick a few of them and to taste them, some delightfully sweet, others agreeably sour; to my ears, however, the most pleasant thing of all was that the winged field musicians were making, with many variations, so gay a music. As though enchanted by these sensual pleasures I went on, knowing not where, until I arrived unexpectedly at a deep glen, through the midst of which a limpid stream swept by, putting a stop to my walk which, as it was, had already been rather a long one. Only then did I notice that I was somewhat tired. Accordingly I lay down for a moment, stretched out on the ground, and should actually have been overtaken by a gentle sleep had this not been prevented by a buzzing sound which presented itself, *per intervalla*, to my ears. At this I raised myself a little, looking toward the place from which this buzzing voice seemed to be coming. It was at my right—a cheerful wood with trees of every sort all thrown together. Seeing this, I surmised that a bittern might perhaps have settled there to act as *basso* to the other delightful songsters. But when the sound seemed to be coming nearer and nearer and to be growing louder and louder, I sprang up nimbly, thinking to run away, for I feared that there might by chance be in the neighborhood a satyr with a hunting horn, and I thought it inadvisable to await his arrival.

2. But, lo and behold, at that moment there came trotting right up to me two men on horseback, one of whom addressed me as follows: "Good friend, if you too are of our company, then follow us to the place agreed upon." My answer was that I knew nothing of any company, hence nothing of the place

---

1 Text: The second edition (Hamburg, 1706). I have omitted part of § 14 and all of § 15.

of which he spoke, but that I was thoroughly upset by an adventure that had befallen me. Questioned about this, I recounted it to them, whereupon they fell to laughing heartily at my expense. On my betraying some annoyance at this, the second horseman spoke, bowing politely to make good the presumed affront. "My friend," he said, "do not take our laughter amiss; we could not help it. I will soon relieve your fears by waking you from your dream. Know then that we are hastening to an appointed *collegium musicum* which the celebrated musician Florimon designs to hold today and at which he has invited us, as members, to appear. Now we may readily imagine that he will have caused his apprentices to bring all sorts of instruments to the place, above all a fine big positive organ on which he is to play the thorough bass himself. This he will at once have tested to see whether the removal and delivering of it from his home have put it out of tune. No doubt but what some uncouth sound or other found its way to your ears and that you fancied this to have come, first, from a bittern, but finally, from the actual horn of a forest deity. The flute that is peeking out of your pocket makes me think that you must be of our profession, or at least an amateur and friend to noble music. So do not begrudge the effort of following us thither. I assure you that you will count it fortunate that the scare you had will have been the cause of your enjoying the merry company with us and that Master Florimon will not be displeased to see us bringing you along *pro hospite*, especially when we tell him what a terrible fright he unwittingly gave you."

3. The great politeness of this person induced me to reply to him in kind, and I thanked him politely for his friendly offer. At the same time I gave him to understand that, while I was a devotee of music, I had not as yet so perfected myself in it (though my student days were long since over) that I could take part in everything extempore; that nothing more agreeable could befall me than to be permitted to see gathered in one place so great a number of musicians, doubtless all of them well drilled, and to listen to their harmonious exercises; and that this would spur me on to pursue the noble art the more industriously so that, if I studiously applied myself, I might one day reach such a point that I could take my place in the company of masters. "Then follow us confidently," replied my guide; "the way is short, but should you be pleased to mount my horse, I will the while accompany you on foot." This too great honor I declined, thanking him again, and with the two of them holding their horses to a leisurely pace on my account, I soon reached the middle of the wood. Here there stood a rather deserted palace and in this a great paved hall where Master Florimon, with the permission of the local authorities, had caused his instruments to be brought in great number so that the invited musicians and amateurs might use them according to their pleasure and preference.

4. After my two guides had given up their horses to be led out to pasture by a servant assigned to this task, they went up with me into the hall, where Master Florimon, standing at the door, gaily bade us welcome. The first of my companions, whose name was Tacitus, sought to apologize for my presence

and explained in a few words how and for what reasons he and his comrade had brought me along with them. "Gentlemen," Master Florimon replied, "no apologies are necessary—this man too shall be a welcome guest." With this he showed us to a long table, about which twelve musicians were already seated, awaiting Tacitus and his companion. We greeted them cordially, as they in turn did us, rising from their seats and asking us to be pleased to sit down in their company, something to which we offered no great objection. Master Florimon alone remained standing by the table at his positive organ, which had been set up facing the open window, so that its sound, when it was touched, might ring through the woods, sending back a doubled echo.

5. To make a long story short, the music was now to begin. Master Florimon, as director of the *chorus musicus*, distributed the parts, deciding who should play the first violin, who the second, and so forth; he himself remained at the thorough bass; I chose the role of a listener. First there was played an agreeable sonata, set by the director himself; this was followed by other things of his, composed with special art. Each participant was now busied in letting his skill be seen and heard, yet things did not go so smoothly but that from time to time one heard a little pig, even a full-grown sow; still, the whole came to an end without undue confusion, for it is written: *In fine videbitur cujus toni*. Master Florimon swallowed his displeasure as best he could, not wishing to shame those openly who had soiled his fine work with their swine. Instead, he caused his apprentices to pour out for each person a fair-sized glass of good wine; this all emptied together, *more Palatino*, for instrumentalists also know how to turn to their advantage the proverb: *Cantores amant humores*. After this they fell to making music again, but the parts were now differently distributed, so that he who had previously played a violin was given a *viola da braccio*, and vice versa. Master Florimon himself undertook to handle the *viola da gamba* and requested Tacitus to play the thorough bass; beside him, Mopsus took up his stand to reinforce him with a *violone*, and although I was also offered a part to play, the company was in the end content with the excuse of my incompetence— thus, once again, I could to my greater satisfaction be an observer. Everything went as before, except that after every piece there was a rest of one hundred full measures, during which time each player, if he cared to, sent for a glass of wine. I must admit that the composition was so beautiful and that the greater part of the company played, this time too, with such remarkable art and so valiantly, that Orpheus with his lyre, nay, Apollo with all his Muses, would have had to concede the prize to this assembly, if only Mopsus and Negligentius, and Corydon too, had not at times screwed up their art to rather too high a point.

6. The whole company had at length grown tired of making music, for nothing is so good and so pleasant to hear that the ear does not finally call a halt; one may have too much, even of a good thing: *Omne nimium vertitur in vitium*. Enough is as good as a feast. In my own case, however, the word was

Venter caret auribus; the belly has no ears, and it cannot make a meal of fleeting sounds. For by this time the sun was ready to set, and I had not had the least thing to eat since watching it rise. Who, then, was more cheerful than I when Master Florimon had a good cold supper brought in and served up? I fell to with a will at the piece of roast mutton that had been placed before me, at the same time forcing myself, as best I could, not to wolf everything down at once, lest I be taken for a shameless glutton. With the food there was also a good drink of wine, further an excellent malt liquor, and to this last we finally gave our preference.

7. With this, as the beer began to find its mark, there arose among the gentlemen musicians all sorts of discourse touching their art, just as sailors, when they meet, are wont to talk of their winds, peasants of their cattle, hunters of their dogs, and every man of what he can do and can understand. Yet, the rule being that he who has learned the least and has the fewest brains in his head will give himself out, when he drinks, as the cleverest master of all, we had here to have just this experience. Mopsus, who had previously been the worst music corrupter, wished now in his conceit to pass for the best organist and composer, in a word, for the most excellent *musicus.* He bragged a good deal of how he had served full eight years under a world-famous master and of how, with great and tireless industry, he had at length reached such a point that he could not only put everything into the German tablature by himself, but also, after a brief inspection, play it off. In this connection he had a fling at those who hold music to be an easy matter and boldly declared that a man may far more quickly become a *Magister,* nay, even a *Doctor* of all three faculties, than an accomplished *musicus.* His neighbors, to be sure—an organist named Fidelio from the town of Lauterbach—sought to contradict him, saying that he had heard that there was one famous master who set no store whatever by the laborious German tablature and could yet teach music, as though from the ground up, to an intelligent person so that in little time he need not be ashamed to play for anyone. At this Mopsus nearly jumped out of his skin. "Pray hold your tongue," said he to Fidelio; "you don't know what you're talking about; I too have heard all about the fellow who feeds you music with a spoon; what they say about him is foul and fabricated—nothing but big talk." With rather more modesty his good friend Corydon added: "After all, my dear Fidelio, you may safely believe what Master Mopsus says; to be sure, I too have heard great things of this master, but it is my opinion that, if they are true, they must be accomplished by forbidden, supernatural arts." Negligentius spoke up also and held that one ought just to keep the old way; that would be the best plan and our elders were after all no fools. The good Negligentius had been for fifty-six years organist at Springenfeld. At these words, the entire rest of the company would soon have come to blows, had not Master Florimon interposed his authority and kept at hand a few of his staff, who presented themselves at the entrance to the hall with some old hunting pikes, so that they might make peace,

should there perchance be fighting. Of these fellows Mopsus was so thoroughly afraid that on their appearance he began at once to pull in his horns.

8. When things had become more quiet, Florimon addressed himself to Tacitus, Capellmeister at Klingewoll, in this fashion: "Dear sir, I commend the modesty with which you have listened patiently to so many absurdities, you who in my opinion have a greater understanding of the art than any of us." "Master Florimon," Tacitus replied, "I have heard these precepts from my youth: 'No one speaks amiss by keeping silent,' and similarly, 'Never answer until you are asked.' What then? Says not the all-wisest of kings: 'Answer not a fool according to his folly, lest thou also be like unto him'?" [2] "Aha!" cried Corydon. "Now you mean me and my fellows; may you, etc!" "Come on, boys!" Florimon shouted. "This way with your hunting pikes!" They lost no time over it. Florimon, however, held them off, a little to one side of the table, with his arm. At this the trembling Corydon said: "Reverend Master Florimon, I will gladly keep still. It was only in jest that I spoke as I did. I pray you, do let Master Tacitus go on for a while with his talk. I myself know well enough that he speaks but little, yet, when at length the words begin to flow, what he says is worth hearing."

9. "I am ready," continued Tacitus, "to respect the prejudices of everyone, and I wish to quarrel with no one on this account; at the same time, it is annoying"—the gentlemen-at-arms, standing near the table with their boar-hunting halberds, made him somewhat bold, for Florimon was his friend—"to hear many pronouncing judgment on a matter they do not understand and to have Hans Lassdünkel bragging at all times and in all places. It would be much better if he were quiet as a mouse; thus he would often not even betray his lack of understanding and, did one not afterwards find him out a bungler, would remain a good *musicus*. As I know from my own case, at a time when I still had the least understanding of music, I was to my way of thinking the most excellent of masters; since having had my eyes opened by my last teacher, I have even been ashamed of myself." "Pardon me, sir, for interrupting you," said Florimon at this. "I am well aware that you have had two teachers who sought in various and contrary ways to teach you the musical *Fundamenta;* some say you owe your science largely to the first; others say, to the last; please be so kind as to tell us yourself what your frank opinion about this is." "Were I to do so," Tacitus objected, "I should have to tell the whole story of my life." "Just this," said Florimon, "will be the thing most pleasing to us to hear, and, sir, you will greatly oblige the whole company—especially, perhaps, Masters Mopsus and Corydon—if you will humor me in this." Tacitus replied: "To oblige Milord Florimon, it shall be willingly done. Yet I shall make this condition in advance: should I be forced to relate my own stupidities, let no one laugh up his sleeve at me who has perhaps been in his day—and may for that matter still be at this moment—a greater fool than I."

---

2 Proverbs 26:4.

10. As to my early childhood, then, I see no great necessity for speaking of it, and, to tell the truth, I have actually forgotten the greater part of it; this much, however, I do recall—that I had a father and mother of honorable descent who, with great care and diligence, kept me from my sixth year on at school and—besides reading, writing, and arithmetic—at music, that is, at singing and fiddling, for to this I had a great inclination. Then, when I was nearly twelve, my father (who could do no more and no better for me than to see to it that I learned something honest in my youth) brought me to a master who enjoyed throughout the countryside the reputation of being the best organist. He was called Orbilius—and the name suited him, for, as you will presently hear in detail, he was a horrible tormentor of his pupils; further, he had been made organist in the right place, namely, in Poltersheim—a place well known to some of you, though, should you not recall it at the moment, your womenfolk, when you get home, can doubtless show you where it lies. With this Orbilius I had first of all to make the acquaintance of the letters of the German tablature and of the crow's feet, written above and beside them, that purport to indicate the time, further, of the keys of the clavier. Before I had properly (and still not completely) grasped this, two years had already gone by. Meanwhile I reflected: "Alas, had you but known the organist's art was so difficult, you might well have given up your inclination to it. Look here! You already understand the notes by which one otherwise sings and fiddles; were your master to use these in teaching you at the clavier, it would no doubt be a good thing!" To be sure, this was not such a stupid idea on my part, but if I was an apprentice, it followed that my master must be still cleverer than I. My first piece, which was to teach me to place my fingers properly according to the *applicatur*, had the imposing title "Bergamasco"—the melody is otherwise a familiar country song, "Ripen Garsten wille wi meyen," etc., sung by the boys in the streets—and I cannot imagine what the special secret is that this piece hides and that makes it such a favorite with so many organists that they have their pupils learn it first of all. After this my master also taught me to play a couple of *sarabandes*, a *courante simple*, and a *ballo*, all with imposing titles, further, the chorale "Erbarm dich mein, O Herre Gott," etc. Then came dreadful long *praeludia*, *toccate*, *ciaconne*, *fughe*, and more such zoological marvels; these I was to learn by heart, since (as my teacher sternly told me) "unless you first master these admirable pieces perfectly, you good-for-nothing, you will never in all the world learn one *basso continuo*, for it is from these splendidly worked-out written models that you, you lout,

you loafer, must learn the manner of the *basso continuo*." I still did not know that by this he meant thorough bass, which I had heard all about before in connection with singing; for this reason I wondered what sort of creature a *basso continuo* might be. In those days I had only a blind man to lead me; now, having had my eyes opened by my later teacher, I see that it is in thorough bass, and not in *toccate* and things of that sort, that science lies; that, provided he first have some understanding of the notes, a pupil who begins at once with thorough bass will grasp it as quickly—indeed, even more quickly—than one who has already played for several years from German tablature; what is more, that, once he has had some practice in it and knows how to vary it, he will be able to play off a *toccata* or a *fuga* or the like, of himself and, as they say, out of his own head, while he who has already put three whole books of *ciaconne* and more such things into tablature, and has learned to play them, will be unable to play half a line of thorough bass. But, to return to my story, I worked hard, and many a time, over those splendid pieces of writing, my master roughly boxed my ears, slapped my face, rapped me on the nose, pinched my ears, and pulled my hair; at other times I was treated to live coals, the strap, and more such delicacies. Willy-nilly, he was determined to beat music into my head. But, for all his good intentions, this would not do; the more he abused me, the more stupid I became; indeed, be it said in all modesty that, though I had to work for at least half a year over a single *toccata* or *praeludium* and *fuga*, when I came to play it—just when things were going splendidly and at their best— I stuck fast all of a sudden and could recall neither beginning nor end. At this, from my master's kindly fists there rained down on my ears some three score blows; meanwhile he consoled me with words like these: "May you be this, that, and the other, you bloodhound! Even the sparrows on the roof will learn before you do!" In this wise I had spent seven years with my master before I could play five *praeludia* and the chorale, or German psalm, in two parts.

11. "In truth," said Florimon, "I must confess that Master Tacitus did not advance any too quickly during his years of apprenticeship. It is my desire to know more about how he finally became the splendidly experienced musician that he is today, but, before I make him a formal request for this, he will. be pleased to drink a glass of wine. After the impassioned story he has just told us, I know that it will do him no harm; each member of the company shall pledge him with his glass." No one could refuse this. Tacitus then went on with his story.

At length (he said) my master took up the thorough bass with me; from the first I was in terror, thinking "Now you will really begin to catch it!" I had noticed that whenever he and the cantor tried anything over together they often came to blows over the thorough bass; I could only conclude that my own head would still more often be the target. In instructing me, my master's procedure was as follows. He showed me neither rules nor figures—even to him the numerals standing above the bass were no better than towns in Bohemia; he simply played the bass through for me once or twice, saying: "You must play it thus and so—that's the way I learned it." But if I was not getting on, you would have been entertained to see the admirable means my master found to teach me the art after his own fashion. The *sexta* was situated behind my right ear, the *quarta* behind my left, the *septima* on my cheeks, the *nona* in my hair, the false *quinta* on my nose, the *secunda* on my back, the *tertia minor* across my knuckles, the *tertia major* and *quinta* on my shins; the *decima* and *undecima* were special sorts of boxes on the ear. Thus, from the whereabouts of the blow or kick, I was supposed to know what to play; the best part of it was that continual kicking in the shins made my feet right active on the pedals, the use of which I was also beginning to learn at this time. Besides this, my master showed me how to put thorough bass into tablature, provided I could get hold of the complete composition; at times, however, there was stuff in this that neither of us could play as it stood. Once he hit upon an extraordinary measure; since with no foundation none of his teaching could drive the thorough bass through my head, he actually decided to kick it into me. Seizing my hair, he pulled me down from the organ bench on which I was sitting before the keyboard, threw me to the ground, lifted me way up by the hair so that, when I fell back, my head struck sharply against the floor, and then trampled all over me, stamping on me for some time. At length, when the *basso continuo* had quite robbed him of his senses, he dragged me from the room toward a flight of stairs leading to the street, saying as he did so: "Here is an end to your apprenticeship and here you have your indentures (for I shall throw these in for good measure)!" So saying, he would have pushed me downstairs, so that with so much learning my head would probably have been crushed, once and for all, had I not misunderstood this too and grabbed him by the legs so that he tumbled with me down the stairs, head over heels into the street. No harm was done, although a reddish sap began to flow from our mouths and noses. At first I feared that my lesson might be flowing away with it, but I soon realized that it was only ordinary blood, the loss of which disturbed me the less when I saw that my teacher was in similar trouble and that people who (as usually happens) had come running up in droves were making fun of the crazy Orbilius, were tearing me from him (for they knew him as a Tartar), and were concerned lest he should actually beat me to death.

12. Bloody as I was, I let my teacher march back up the stairs with his wife and her maid, the two of whom had helped him to his feet after the bad fall that he had taken, for I thought: "I have no desire for further dealings of this sort with you—it is best that we should simply part company." At this I went in to the nearest house, where my neighbor gave me a cordial reception and advised me that, inasmuch as my parents, before their death, had settled in full with Orbilius for his teaching and, in addition to this, had left me a little money so that I might try my luck in the world, I ought, now that I had attained my majority, to betake myself elsewhere—with my understanding of my art, I would no doubt find a situation sooner or later. I followed this well-meant advice and sent to my teacher's house for my clothes and other belongings. Orbilius sought at first to prevent their being taken away, but when I began to threaten, telling him that I would bring a swarm of lawyers about his ears and that I had already engaged one for this purpose, he thought better of it, especially since he had many enemies in the council and elsewhere. In giving up my things, he sent word that, wherever I might go, I was to speak no ill of what had happened to me during my years of apprenticeship and that in particular I was to keep to myself the indentures he had given me at the end. "Good!" I thought. "Go on being yourself! I have now been with you for all of nine years and I know you like a book—I shall not advise any honest man to apprentice a child to you." The very next day I found work on a traveling van and set out into the world, I cared not whither, for now that all my friends were dead, I was as much at home in one place as in another.

13. After wandering for some time hither and yon I arrived at length in the province of Marcolphia where, one Sunday, I went into a village church. Here, on an old organ of five stops, a simple-hearted organist was prancing about in great style; sometimes he used his whole fist with all five fingers at once and, to make sure of a sufficient uproar, at every cadence he helped himself out with his nose. This was in his opinion a most artistic *secretum*, and he told me later on that, if he had known that I too was of his profession, he would have been unwilling to show it openly in my presence. After the sermon I begged that I might have the

honor of playing just once on his instrument. To this he at first turned a cold shoulder, but he soon changed his mind, for I had decked myself out in quite handsome clothes and there are many for whom clothes make the man. "Well, sir," he said to me, "perhaps it can be done if only you are sure of your business so that you won't stumble—but wait —I know what to do—I shall stand right here behind you so that if needs be I can help you out at the keyboard and assure your getting through without disgrace." I was somewhat annoyed with him for not taking me at once for a master; nevertheless I sat down and played one of my most artful *praeludia manualia* and, for a close, a *sonata* (such things I regularly carried with me in my pocket, ready for any emergency). Hearing these, the village organist thrust out his nose and pricked up his ears and the people in the church were on the point of dancing. At this I was so set up that I secretly thought even my old master Orbilius insignificant in comparison with myself, imagining that wherever a place as organist might be open, it must inevitably go to me while my competitors stood to one side. And to be sure, what I imagined actually came to pass, for on that very day a visiting nobleman was also in the church. After the service he sent for me and, when I had paid him my respects, he addressed me as follows. "My good friend, in church today your public performance on the organ gave me such great pleasure that with all my heart I should like to see you in a good position. I can even help in no small way to bring this about; inasmuch as in the town of Dantzfurt, which lies near my residence, the organist has just died, and inasmuch as I have some influence with the ancient and honorable council of that town, so that without my consent they will call no one to the post, I myself will help you to get it, but with the proviso that you marry my lady's chambermaid, who has faithfully served Her Ladyship—and myself too, although with perfect honesty—so that I may thus help two people to a livelihood at once." I accepted this proposal, thanked him most respectfully, and immediately set out with him for his estate, where we arrived that very evening.

·   ·   ·   ·   ·

14. To make a long story short, the marriage contract was drawn up the next day. Cornaria, my intended, gave me as a token a handsome gold ring and promised to supply me in future with abundant linens; I for my part engaged to deliver to her at the first possible moment, as a pledge of my love, a present that I would have made for her by a celebrated artist. In the meantime, letters were sent off to the ancient

and honorable town council of Dantzfurt, and the courier returned with a reply in writing, addressed to my lord patron. His recommendation would be given special weight and the ability of his celebrated master was not questioned (who was more puffed up by this than I?); nevertheless, since it was presumed that the citizens would not be willing to relinquish their traditional right and would insist upon the presentation of the candidate by the council, I was to be good enough to present myself for hearing and trial on the eighth day *a dato*, which would be St. Margaret's, at the beginning of the dog days. My Cornaria and I lived in a fool's paradise; with the permission of her noble mistress, she visited me in my room some six or seven times a day; there nothing was heard but amorous discourse, and at this Cornaria proved much more adept than I.

.   .   .   .   .

16. Now the time came when I was to give my trial performance in Dantzfurt before assuming my new office. Fortunately for me, the town cantor was an old man who had forgotten what little he had ever known about music. Here "birds of a feather flocked together," as the saying goes, and I did not need to plague myself about the thorough bass, which I feared like the Devil himself. Thus, seeing that I could make my own choice and play what I pleased, the trial came off well, and people were at once congratulating me right and left on my appointment, of which, in the opinion of the ancient and honorable council, no one was worthier than I. Since the customary annual inventory was to take place that same evening, I was immediately invited; there, over the banquet table, after the pastors, the burgomasters, and the lord of the manor had praised my recent and duly delivered masterpiece, I began myself to brag of my art. I expressed my contempt for all the other masters I had heard of, pulled the most celebrated people to pieces, and knew how to find fault with everyone, now on this score, now on that, for example, for not holding such and such a finger properly, for not having any elegant movement and presence in their bodies when they played, for not being able to make any proper trills with their feet on the pedals, and many other such stupidities. One parson extolled a certain organist of his acquaintance from whom he had taken a few months' lessons on the clavier. By this time, after all, I was clever enough not to contradict him openly; still, this praise of someone else cut me to the quick and I began at once to fear that my authority would be somewhat the worse for it. My only desire was that everyone should

praise me alone, and to this end I gave all possible encouragement and opportunity. Well, I stayed from now on in the town, near the church, in the house in which the former organist had lived and in which, with my permission, his widow and children continued to live. I sent my dearest Cornaria an account of all that had happened, telling her in particular that I had come to the sort of place where there were people who understood music thoroughly and who looked on me as the most celebrated organist in the world. To tell the truth, I was actually a sorry bungler and knew nothing more presentable to play than what was written in my book.

17. But hear how the tables were turned. My dearest Cornaria sent me the melancholy tidings that that noble gentleman, my patron and champion, had suddenly died, from which I could readily conclude that I need no longer expect with my dear one any such generous portion as my lord had promised me. Into the bargain, the old cantor died the next week, and, when it was time to hear the new candidate, I was told to bring him the things that he should sing at his trial. I excused myself, saying that I did not as yet have my things with me, but the new cantor quickly disposed of this, replying: "Indeed! Then let him spend a few hours in composing something new!" At once it became the pleasure of all the overseers that I should do this and that it should likewise be a new trial of my art. The only one displeased with the arrangement was myself. For, having previously sought to pass myself off as the complete musician, to admit that I could not compose would have compromised my dignity. The trial was to take place the following day. I sat down and, scratching my head, debated with myself the course that I would take—whether to stay or to run away. At length I hit upon the remedy (so I imagined, at least)—I brought out all my fugues and hunted through them for one to which to fit the text *Laudate Dominum omnes gentes*. This I then arranged in such a way that, when on the organ I played the subject in the pedals, the cantor would sing the bass along with me, just as I played it. The following morning the trial was to be held in the church, in the presence, not only of the assembled gentry and overseers, but also of a great throng of citizens who of their own accord had gathered there. The new cantor had with him two instrumentalists who offered to play along on violins or zinks. I told them, however, that it was a trial of vocal music that was contemplated, not one of instrumental music, and that for this reason I had omitted the instruments in the new piece that I had composed. With this excuse they were obliged to content themselves. Told to begin, I first improvised a

praeambulum on the full organ; then, when it was time for the cantor to begin his *Laudate Dominum*, I left most of the stops out so that the organ might peal the more merrily. The cantor beat time with one hand and sang out boldly with a fine deep voice, while the instrumentalists, who were standing by, laughed up their sleeves until I thought they would burst. Seeing what was going on, I presumed that they were laughing at the cantor for rumbling so much. But when the cantor came to a rest, turned to them, and joined in the laughter—indeed, could not stop laughing, even after he began to sing again—I soon saw which way the wind was blowing, that the laughter must be aimed at me, and at this I was so overcome that I was ready to give up the ghost on the spot. When the piece was at an end, the cantor drew from his pocket various things for voices and instruments and asked me to play a thorough bass to them in order that the company in the church might have a further treat. There I stood in my true colors.

"Gentlemen, don't laugh at me so much"—here Tacitus betrayed a slight annoyance—"some one of you who is laughing now with the rest may one day have the same experience." So saying, he continued his narrative.

18. After this (he said) I had to come out with the truth, and so, seeking to cover up my ignorance as best I could, I answered the cantor as follows: "If only you had given me the things yesterday so that I could first have put them into tablature or, failing this, have looked them over once or twice, I should have been glad to accommodate you; having neglected to do this, you will not misinterpret it if I do not at once accept this closely figured bass to play." In the meantime a boy came running up to the organ, calling to the new cantor that the overseers wished to speak to him. As I learned later, they were well satisfied with his voice, but wished to go on listening to him; he might now choose some of his own things and tell the organist that, in accompanying them, he should save his art for another time and play softly so that they might hear better what was being sung (they assumed that it required special skill to get all the organ-pipes to play at one time). To this the cantor replied, with a somewhat contemptuous smile: "By all means, gentlemen; I should be glad to do so if only the bungler (by this he meant me) knew how to play." This struck them as very peculiar, and, thinking that the cantor would not thus speak behind his back of so excellent a master unless it was from envy, they immediately sent for me also and asked whether I was not able to play right off the things the cantor had with him. Here I offered again my previous excuses; I was ready to die

of shame, still more so when the cantor spoke up once more. "Gentlemen," he said, "we will perforce make shift, for one of the two instrumentalists who came here with me can play the thorough bass; let the other play one violin and I will engage both to sing and play the other." This was most agreeable to the entire company, so there was nothing for me to do but to remain in the lower church with the rest while the three of them, to my great dismay, played one thing after another—so sweetly that the citizens who were present began to grumble openly against the council for having been so quickly taken in by the Arch-Imposter (so they called me) whom they had accepted as organist. "They ought to chase the loafer back to where he came from!" Hearing this, I hurriedly made my decision and addressed myself to the assembled company, saying that, since there was evidently not room enough for both the cantor and myself, I would prefer asking to be released to being continually at odds with him. Thus I got out of the affair with little honor and danced merrily away from Dantzfurt again. The cantor, on the other hand, was at once engaged, together with his two instrumentalists (for until now the place had had no town musicians of its own). The arrangement was that one of the two should play the organ in church as organist, receiving for this the regular salary; in addition to this he was to be in attendance at weddings and other formal revelries with the other, to whom a given annual pension was assured in writing; the two were to divide the profits as they pleased.

19. Thus I had had all my trouble and vexation for nothing. My chief consolation in it was that I had not yet married Cornaria and could thus withdraw on the pretext that our courtship had been inspired by the promise that I should become organist in Dantzfurt and that, now that nothing had come of this, the council having, after my patron's death, set the cantor on me in order to rid themselves of me, my former promise was no longer binding. With this the good Cornaria was obliged to content herself and I, for my part, am as well satisfied, for in due course she married an elderly widower whose forehead, since this his second marriage, has put forth such shoots that, from his wife Cornaria, he has received the name Cornutus.

20. What next? What was I to do now? Passing myself off for a master of music had certainly turned out badly for me. I decided, accordingly, to apprentice myself all over again to Master Prudentius, the same organist of whom the parson previously mentioned had said in further praise that he was an extraordinarily able composer. And although he lived in the town of Schönhall, more than sixty miles away,

I preferred making this long journey to remaining the rest of my days an ignoramus and a ruined man. When I arrived, I found Master Prudentius at home, busily at work on his music; he received me most cordially, bade me sit down and, after a few moments' pause, desired me to let him know where I had come from. He took me for a likely fellow, and indeed I might well have passed for one if clothes could make a good-for-nothing into an honest man, for I had provided myself with a fine new suit and, although it was my entire capital, still had a little money left over. I told Prudentius candidly how matters stood with me, how very badly I had been disappointed in my expectations, and how I had come to him so that he might teach me something honest; if he were willing to oblige me in this and to give me sound instruction in music, I would not only pay him adequately for his trouble—I would also gratefully sing his praises the rest of my life. Master Prudentius then went on to ask who had been my teacher, how long I had studied, and what method my master had employed in teaching me. After I had answered all these questions modestly and had once more begged him to receive and accept me as his obedient apprentice, he gave me this heartening answer: "My friend, perceiving how very earnestly you desire to become a thorough musician, I cannot find it in my heart to send you away empty-handed, even though I have already a full day's work every day. And so, if you have money enough to maintain yourself here for a year, I will within that time so instruct you in the real fundamentals and in the organist's art that, from being a false organist (*Argenist*) you will become a true one (*Organist*). For my trouble I ask not one farthing, for if you will only promise me to be industrious and to employ your art to the glory of God I will instruct you for nothing, every morning from seven to eight. Aside from this, you may come to my house whenever you please and practice by yourself in a room where there are several claviers." Was ever man happier than I? The same day I arranged with a baker for my year's board, and the next morning and every other morning after that I went at the appointed time to Master Prudentius, who began at once by instructing me in thorough bass, saying: "In this lies the whole basis of practical music and of composition and with this I begin with all my pupils. Thus they have the advantage that, instead of having to plague themselves with the troublesome tablature, only to remain forever paper organists, even though they have studied for many years, they become in a short time good thorough musicians." Under my new teacher, I employed my time as industriously as I knew how; he, for his part, spared no pains to instruct me faithfully and, when the year was over, he addressed me as follows: "Now, my dear Tacitus, basing my teaching on the fundamentals, I have so instructed you in music that you may, from now on, bear the name, not of a false organist, but of a true one and of a thorough musician and composer. Go your way, employ your art to the glory of God, and should you meet with anyone who is desirous of learning music, impart it to him for nothing, just as you received it from me and just as I, at your entreaty, faithfully dictated it to you." Thus, with many tears and sincere protestations of gratitude, I took leave of Master Prudentius and found my way back to my fatherland, where—as you gentlemen are well aware—I have now been active for some years in my present capacity.

"To oblige Master Florimon I have had to make this story rather diffuse; If in so doing I have made myself irksome to any other member of this company, I shall be glad to ask his pardon."

21. Thus Tacitus ended his narrative, making good his long silence by his long speech. Master Florimon thanked him for it becomingly and, after the drinks had gone round again once or twice, addressed the company as follows: "I must admit that Master Prudentius began with Tacitus in the right way. I am acquainted with the man myself, and I know that he introduces his pupils to the thorough bass at once and that within one year, if only they already know their notes and can count twenty, they so perfect themselves in it that it becomes a joy. I also know that, as a part of his instruction, he shows them how to make fugues and other such things extempore and that from time to time, once they are fairly presentable in such music as requires the thorough bass, he gives them music that is fully written out—as though for an amusement and in order that they may be able to reproduce the embellishments in it. This is much easier for them to learn than the German tablature, and I have no patience with what some say against it—that one ought to keep the old way. All honor to our German ancestors, who in their day brought things to an extremely high point with the tablature! Sixty years ago, or perhaps a few years earlier, one could scarcely find a single German organist who played the thorough bass or read from notes. But now that a better, more correct, and easier way has been discovered, why should we not abandon the old one? The Italians never have had a German tablature, but have used notes since longer than one can remember; just this is the real reason why they were able to maintain so long their superiority in music over us Germans."

22. Master Negligentius interrupted Florimon at this point. "What you say is nonetheless offensive to many an honest German organist—let the Italians just dare to make a claim like that again!" To which Florimon modestly replied: "Very true! I too am well aware that there are today many German organists who are not much inferior to the foreigners—nay, are in certain respects superior to them. On this we agree. The reason is that they become

accustomed to play the thorough bass so very much earlier than formerly. Were they to follow the teaching of Prudentius, whom one can never praise enough, and to make this the very beginning, they would discover its excellent effect, even in their pupils. What is more, we should no longer hear the impudent assertion that anyone who has not studied for nine or ten years, but has acquired his art in a shorter time, must have been to school with a wizard. Uninformed pronouncements of this kind remind me of the peasant who, when asked to decide the quarrel between the nightingale and the cuckoo as to which was the better singer, delivered himself of the following bovinity: 'Both are excellent singers, but the cuckoo sings a better *choral* music, while the nightingale's voice is better suited to the *figural*.' Even so, he was not as inept a critic as the clown who, when chosen as their judge, gave to Pan, the shepherd-god with the reed pipes, the preference over Phoebus, who played artfully on instruments of all sorts, for which reason this uncouth fellow, whose name was Midas, was deservedly endowed by Phoebus with the ears of an ass."

23. What further topics Florimon and the others went on to discuss, how they made merry far into the night, and what other delightful compositions they sang and played, all this I shall pass over in silence, recording simply that not long after this I enrolled myself as a pupil of Master Tacitus, who faithfully instructed me, just as Prudentius had faithfully instructed him.

24. And now, just as my teacher faithfully instructed me, so—in this, the first part of my *Musical Tutor; or, Thorough-Bass Instructor*, as also in the second part to follow—I shall faithfully impart the whole to those of you who love music and seek learning, and, to begin with, how properly to play a thorough bass, hoping that I shall thus be rendering a conspicuous service to many, as I am bound by Christian charity to do, and ignoring what certain prejudiced critics may say of it.

Operatic Rivalry in France:
Pro and Contra Lully

14. François Raguenet

With the Abbé François Raguenet (born at Rouen in 1660) began the impassioned and obstinate controversies about the opera that were to hold under their sway the artistic and literary circles in France throughout the eighteenth century. No matter whether the controversy was fought out between the followers and detractors of Lully, as was the case with Raguenet and Le Cerf de La Viéville; whether it was transferred to the field of comic opera, as in the "Querelle des Bouffons" (see Chapter XIV); or whether it assumed the aspect of a fight for or against the major operatic reform embodied in the works of C. W. von Gluck (see Chapter XV)—the underlying issue was fundamentally the same—should the musical expression in the opera be entirely autonomous, or should it be determined by the exigencies of the dramatic action?

Raguenet had visited Rome in 1698 and had there become an ardent admirer of Italian music. Returned to France, he published in 1702 his *Parallèle des Italiens et des Français en ce qui regarde la musique et les opéras,* in which he took Lully and his imitators severely to task while extolling the merits of Italian musicians. The date and circumstances of Raguenet's death are not known, but there are reports that he took his own life about 1722.

Parallèle des Italiens et des Français [1]

[*1702*]

THERE ARE SO many things wherein the French music has the advantage over the Italian, and as many more wherein the Italian is superior to the French, that, without a particular examination into the one and the other, I think it impossible to draw a just parallel between 'em or entertain a

1 Text: The original edition of the anonymous English translation of 1709, attributed by Sir John Hawkins to J. E. Galliard. Only a very few of the translator's notes are reprinted here; all of these are included, however, in the edition prepared by the present editor for the *Musical Quarterly*, XXXII (1946), 411–436.

right judgment of either. The operas are the compositions that admit of the greatest variety and extent, and they are common both to the Italians and French. 'Tis in these the masters of both nations endeavor more particularly to exert themselves and make their genius shine, and 'tis on these, therefore, I intend to build my present comparison. But in this there are many things that require a particular distinction, such as the language, the composition, the qualifications of the actors, those of the performers, the different sorts of voices, the recitative, the airs, the symphonies, the chorus, the dance, the machines, the decorations, and whatever else is essential to an opera or serves to make the entertainment complete and perfect. And these things ought to be particularly inquired into before we can pretend to determine in favor either of the Italian or French.

Our operas are writ much better than the Italian; they are regular, coherent designs; and, though repeated without the music, they are as entertaining as any of our other pieces that are purely dramatic. Nothing can be more natural and lively than their dialogues; the gods are made to speak with a dignity suitable to their character, kings with all the majesty their rank requires, and the nymphs and shepherds with a softness and innocent mirth peculiar to the plains. Love, jealousy, anger, and the rest of the passions are touched with the greatest art and nicety, and there are few of our tragedies or comedies that appear more beautiful than Quinault's operas.

On the other hand, the Italian operas are poor, incoherent rhapsodies without any connection or design; all their pieces, properly speaking, are patched up with thin, insipid scraps; their scenes consist of some trivial dialogues or soliloquy, at the end of which they foist in one of their best airs, which concludes the scene. These airs are seldom of a piece with the rest of the opera, being usually written by other poets, either occasionally or in the body of some other work. When the undertaker of an opera has fixed himself in a town and got his company together, he makes choice of the subject he likes best, such as Camilla, Themistocles, Xerxes, &c. But this piece, as I just now observed, is no better than a patchwork, larded with the best airs his performers are acquainted with, which airs are like saddles, fit for all horses alike; they are declarations of love made on one side and embraced or rejected on the other, transports of happy lovers or complaints of the unfortunate, protestations of fidelity or stings of jealousy, raptures of pleasure or pangs of sorrow, rage, and despair. And one of these airs you are sure to find at the end of every scene. Now certainly such a medley as this can never be set in competition with our operas, which are wrought up with great exactness and marvelous conduct.

Besides, our operas have a farther advantage over the Italian in respect of the voice, and that is the bass, which is so frequent among us and so rarely to be met with in Italy. For every man that has an ear will witness with me that nothing can be more charming than a good bass; the simple sound of these basses, which sometimes seems to sink into a profound abyss, has something wonderfully charming in it. The air receives a stronger concussion from these deep voices than it doth from those that are higher and is consequently filled with a more agreeable and extensive harmony. When the persons of gods or kings, a Jupiter, Neptune, Priam, or Agamemnon, are brought on the stage, our actors, with their deep voices, give 'em an air of majesty, quite different from that of the feigned basses among the Italians, which have neither depth nor strength. Besides, the interfering of the basses with the upper parts forms an agreeable contrast and makes us perceive the beauties of the one from the opposition they meet with from the other, a pleasure to which the Italians are perfect strangers, the voices of their singers, who are for the most part castrati, being perfectly like those of their women.

Besides the advantages we claim from the beauty of our designs and the variety of voices, we receive still more from our chorus, dances, and other entertainments, in which we infinitely excel the Italians. They, instead of these decorations, which furnish our operas with an agreeable variety and give 'em a peculiar air of grandeur and magnificence, have usually nothing but some burlesque scenes of a buffoon, some old woman that's to be in love with a young footman, or a conjurer that shall turn a cat into a bird, a fiddler into an owl, and play a few other tricks of legerdemain that are only fit to divert the mob. And, for their dancers, they are the poorest creatures in the world; they are all of a lump, without arms, legs, a shape, or air.

As to the instruments, our masters touch the violin much finer and with a greater nicety than they do in Italy. Every stroke of their bow sounds harsh, if broken, and disagreeable, if continued. Moreover, besides all the instruments that are common to us as well as the Italians, we have the hautboys, which, by their sounds, equally mellow and piercing, have infinitely the advantage of the violins in all brisk, lively airs, and the flutes, which so many of our great artists [a] have taught to groan after so moving a manner in our moanful airs, and sigh so amorously in those that are tender.

In short, we have the advantage of 'em in dress. Our habits infinitely excel all we see abroad, both in costliness and fancy. The Italians them-

---

[a] Philbert, Philidor, Descouteaux, and the Hotteterres.

selves will own that no dancers in Europe are equal to ours; the Combatants and Cyclops in *Perseus*, the Tremblers and Smiths in *Isis*, the Unlucky Dreams in *Atys*, and our other entries are originals in their kind, as well in respect of the airs composed by Lully, as of the steps which Beauchamp has adapted to those airs. The theatre produced nothing like it till those two great men appeared; 'tis an entertainment of which they are the sole inventors, and they have carried it to so high a degree of perfection that, as no person either in Italy or elsewhere has hitherto rivaled 'em, so, I fear, the world will never produce their equal. No theater can represent a fight more lively than we see it sometimes expressed in our dances, and, in a word, everything is performed with an unexceptionable nicety; the conduct and economy, through the whole, is so admirable that no man of common understanding will deny but that the French operas form a more lively representation than the Italian and that a mere spectator must be much better pleased in France than Italy. This is the sum of what can be offered to our advantage in behalf of our music and operas; let us now examine wherein the Italians have the advantage over us in these two points.

Their language is much more naturally adapted to music than ours; their vowels are all sonorous, whereas above half of ours are mute or at best bear a very small part in pronunciation, so that, in the first place, no cadence or beautiful passage can be formed upon the syllables that consist of those vowels, and, in the next, the words are expressed by halves, so that we are left to guess at what the French are singing, whereas the Italian is perfectly understood. Besides, though all the Italian vowels are full and open, yet the composers choose out of them such as they judge most proper for their finest divisions. They generally make choice of the vowel *a*, which, being clearer and more distinct than any of the rest, expresses the beauty of the cadence and division to a better advantage. Whereas we make use of all the vowels indifferently, those that are mute as well as those that are sonorous; nay, very often we pitch upon a diphthong, as in the words *chaîne* and *gloire*, which syllables, consisting of two vowels joined together, create a confused sound and want that clearness and beauty that we find in the simple vowels. But this is not the most material part to be considered in music; let us now examine into its essence and form, that is, the structure of the airs, either distinctly considered or in relation to the different parts of which the whole composition consists.

The Italians are more bold and hardy in their airs than the French; they carry their point farther, both in their tender songs and those that are more sprightly as well as in their other compositions; nay, they often unite styles which the French think incompatible. The French, in those compositions that consist of many parts, seldom regard more than that which is principal, whereas the Italians usually study to make all the parts equally shining and beautiful. In short, the invention of the one is inexhaustible, but the genius of the other is narrow and constrained; this the reader will fully understand when we descend to particulars.

It is not to be wondered that the Italians think our music dull and stupefying, that according to their taste it appears flat and insipid, if we consider the nature of the French airs compared to those of the Italian. The French, in their airs, aim at the soft, the easy, the flowing and coherent; the whole air is of the same tone, or, if sometimes they venture to vary it, they do it with so many preparations, they so qualify it, that still the air seems to be as natural and consistent as if they had attempted no change at all; there is nothing bold and adventurous in it; it's all equal and of a piece. But the Italians pass boldly and in an instant from b-sharp to b-flat and from b-flat to b-sharp; [2] they venture the boldest cadences and the most irregular dissonance; and their airs are so out of the way that they resemble the compositions of no other nation in the world.

The French would think themselves undone if they offended in the least against the rules; they flatter, tickle, and court the ear and are still doubtful of success, though everything be done with an exact regularity. The more hardy Italian changes the tone and the mode without any awe or hesitation; he makes double or treble cadences of seven or eight bars together upon tones we should think incapable of the least division. He'll make a swelling [b] of so prodigious a length that they who are unacquainted with it can't choose but be offended at first to see him so adventurous, but before he has done they'll think they can't sufficiently admire him. He'll have passages of such an extent as will perfectly confound his auditors at first, and upon such irregular tones as shall instill a terror as well as surprise into the audience, who will immediately conclude that the whole concert is degenerating into a dreadful dissonance; and betraying 'em by that means into a concern for the music, which seems to be upon the brink of ruin, he immediately reconciles 'em by such regular cadences that everyone is surprised to see harmony rising again, in a manner, out of discord itself and owing its greatest beauties to those irregularities which seemed to threaten it with destruction. The Italians venture at everything that is harsh and out of the way, but then they do it like people that have a right to venture and are sure of success. Under a notion of being the greatest

---

b By the Italians called *messa di voce*.   2 That is, from major to minor and from minor to major.

and most absolute masters of music in the world, like despotic sovereigns they dispense with its rules in hardy but fortunate sallies; they exert themselves above the art, but, like masters of that art whose laws they follow or transgress at pleasure, they insult the niceness of the ear which others court; they master and conquer it with charms which owe their irresistible force to the boldness of the adventurous composer.

Sometimes we meet with a swelling to which the first notes of the thorough bass jar so harshly as the ear is highly offended with it, but the bass, continuing to play on, returns at last to the swelling with such beautiful intervals that we quickly discover the composer's design, in the choice of those discords, was to give the hearer a more true and perfect relish of the ravishing notes that on a sudden restore the whole harmony.

Let a Frenchman be set to sing one of these dissonances, and he'll want courage enough to support it with that resolution wherewith it must be sustained to make it succeed; his ear, being accustomed to the most soft and natural intervals, is startled at such an irregularity; he trembles and is in a sweat whilst he attempts to sing it. Whereas the Italians, who are inured from their youth to these dissonances, sing the most irregular notes with the same assurance they would the most beautiful and perform everything with a confidence that secures 'em of success.

Music is become exceedingly common in Italy; the Italians sing from their cradles, they sing at all times and places, a natural uniform song is too vulgar for their ears. Such airs are to them like things tasteless and decayed. If you would hit their palate, you must regale it with variety and be continually passing from one key to another, though you venture at the most uncommon and unnatural passages. Without this you'll be unable to keep 'em awake or excite their attention.

But to be more particular, as the Italians are naturally much more brisk than the French, so are they more sensible of the passions and consequently express 'em more lively in all their productions. If a storm or rage is to be described in a symphony, their notes give us so natural an idea of it that our souls can hardly receive a stronger impression from the reality than they do from the description; everything is so brisk and piercing, so impetuous and affecting, that the imagination, the senses, the soul, and the body itself are all betrayed into a general transport; 'tis impossible not to be borne down with the rapidity of these movements. A symphony of furies shakes the soul; it undermines and overthrows it in spite of all its care; the artist himself, whilst he is performing it, is seized with an unavoidable agony; he tortures his violin; he racks his body; he is no longer master of himself, but is agitated like one possessed with an irresistible motion.

If, on the other side, the symphony is to express a calm and tranquillity, which requires a quite different style, they however execute it with an equal success. Here the notes descend so low that the soul is swallowed with 'em in the profound abyss. Every string of the bow is of an infinite length, lingering on a dying sound which decays gradually till at last it absolutely expires. Their symphonies of sleep insensibly steal the soul from the body and so suspend its faculties and operations that, being bound up, as it were, in the harmony that entirely possesses and enchants it, it's as dead to everything else as if all its powers were captivated by a real sleep.

In short, as for the conformity of the air with the sense of the words, I never heard any symphony comparable to that which was performed at Rome in the Oratory of St. Jerome of Charity on St. Martin's Day in the year 1697 upon these two words—*Mille saette* ("A thousand thunderbolts"). The air consisted of disjointed notes, like those in a jig, which gave the soul a lively impression of an arrow and that wrought so effectually upon the imagination that every violin appeared to be a bow, and their bows were like so many flying arrows, darting their pointed heads upon every part of the symphony. Nothing can be more masterly or more happily expressed. So that, be their airs either of a sprightly or gentle style, let 'em be impetuous or languishing, in all these the Italians are equally preferable to the French. But there is one thing beyond all this which neither the French nor any other nation besides themselves in the world ever attempted; for they will sometimes unite in a most surprising manner the tender with the sprightly, as may be instanced in that celebrated air, "Mai non si vidde ancor più bella fedeltà," &c.,[3] which is the softest and most tender of any in the world, and yet its symphony is as lively and piercing as ever was composed. These different characters are they able to unite so artfully that, far from destroying a contrary by its contrary, they make the one serve to embellish the other.

But if we now proceed from the simple airs to a consideration of those pieces that consist of several parts, we there shall find the mighty advantages the Italians have over the French. I never met with a master in France but what agreed that the Italians knew much better how to turn and vary a trio than the French. Among us, the first upper part is generally beautiful enough, but then the second usually descends too low to deserve

---

3 From the opera *Camilla*, by M. A. Bononcini.

our attention. In Italy the upper parts are generally three or four notes higher than in France, so that their seconds are high enough to have as much beauty as the very first with us.[4] Besides, all their three parts are so equally good that it is often difficult to find which is the subject. Lully has composed some after this manner, but they are few in number, whereas we hardly meet with any in Italy that are otherwise.

But of compositions consisting of more parts than three, the advantages of the Italian masters will still appear greater.[5] In France, it's sufficient if the subject be beautiful; we very rarely find that the parts which accompany it are so much as coherent. We have some thorough basses, indeed, which are good grounds and which, for that reason, are highly extolled by us. But where this happens, the upper parts grow very poor; they give way to the bass, which then becomes the subject. As for the accompaniments of the violin, they are, for the most part, nothing but single strokes of the bow, heard by intervals, without any uniform coherent music, serving only to express, from time to time, a few accords. Whereas in Italy, the first and second upper part, the thorough bass, and all the other parts that concur to the composition of the fullest pieces, are equally finished. The parts for the violins are usually as beautiful as the air itself. So that after we have been entertained with something very charming in the air, we are insensibly captivated by the parts that accompany it, which are equally engaging and make us quit the subject to listen to them. Everything is so exactly beautiful that it's difficult to find out the principal part. Sometimes the thorough bass lays so fast hold of our ear that in listening to it we forget the subject; at other times the subject is so insinuating that we no longer regard the bass, when all on a sudden the violins become so ravishing that we mind neither the bass nor the subject. 'Tis too much for one soul to taste the several beauties of so many parts. She must multiply herself before she can relish and digest three or four delights at once which are all beautiful alike; 'tis transport, enchantment, and ecstasy of pleasure; her faculties are upon so great a stretch, she's forced to ease herself by exclamations; she waits impatiently for the end of the air that she may have a breathing room; she sometimes finds it

---

4 Freneuse replies to this objection of Raguenet's in his Second Dialogue (Jacques Bonnet, *Histoire de la musique* [Amsterdam, 1725], II, 69): "The first upper parts of the Italians squeak because they are too high; their second upper parts have the fault of being too close to the first and too far from the bass, which is the third part."

5 Compare Freneuse (*ibid.*, II, 74–75): "'Is it in the choruses that the advantage of the Italians is supposed to lie? . . . Everyone knows that choruses are out of use in Italy, indeed beyond the means of the ordinary Italian opera house.

. . . How many singers do you suppose an Italian company has?' 'Say twenty or twenty-five, Monsieur, as in our own.' 'Nothing of the sort, Madame; usually six or seven—seven or eight. Those marvelous opera companies in Venice, Naples, and Rome consist of seven or eight voices. . . . When the composer of an opera aspires to the glory of having included a chorus in his work, as a rarity, it is these seven or eight persons as a group who form it, all singing together—the king, the clown, the queen, and the old woman.' "

impossible to wait so long, and then the music is interrupted by an universal applause. These are the daily effects of the Italian composition which everyone who has been in Italy can abundantly testify; we meet with the like in no other nation whatsoever. They are beauties improved to such a degree of excellence as not to be reached by the imagination till mastered by the understanding, and when they are understood our imaginations can form nothing beyond 'em.

To conclude, the Italians are inexhaustible in their productions of such pieces as are composed of several parts, in which on the other side the French are extremely limited. In France, the composer thinks he has done his business if he can diversify the subject; as for the accompaniments you find nothing like it in them; they are all upon the same chords, the same cadence, where you see all at once, without any variety or surprise. The French composers steal from one another or copy from their own works so that all their compositions are much alike. Whereas the Italian invention is infinite, both for the quantity and diversity of their airs; the number of 'em may modestly be said to be without number; and yet it will be very difficult to find two among 'em that are alike. We are daily admiring Lully's fertile genius in the composition of so many beautiful different airs. France never produced a master that had a talent like him; this I'm sure no one will contradict, and this is all I desire to make it appear how much the Italians are superior to the French, both for the invention and composition; for, in short, this great man, whose works we set in competition with those of the greatest masters in Italy, was himself an Italian. He has excelled all our musicians in the opinion of the French themselves.[6] To establish, therefore, an equality between the two nations, we ought to produce some Frenchman who has in the same manner excelled the greatest masters in Italy, and that by the confession of the Italians themselves; but this is an instance we have not yet been able to produce. Besides, Lully is the only man ever appeared in France with a genius so superior for music; whereas Italy abounds in masters, the worst of which may be compared to him; they are to be found at Rome, Naples, Florence, Venice, Bologna, Milan, and Turin, in which places there has been a long succession of them. They have had their Luigi, their Carissimi, their Melani, and their Legrenzi; to these succeeded their Buononcini, their Corelli, and their Bassani, who are still living and charm all Europe with their excellent productions. The first seemed to have robbed the art of all her beauties; and yet those that followed have at least rivaled 'em in an infinite number of works of a stamp perfectly new; they grow up there every day

---

6 "In the opinion of the French themselves" should be "In the French style itself."

and seem to claim the laurel from their predecessors; they are flourishing in all parts of Italy, whereas in France a master like one of them is looked on as a Phoenix; the whole realm has been able to produce but one in an age, and 'tis to be feared no age hereafter will ever be able to supply the loss of Lully. 'Tis therefore undeniably evident that the Italian genius for music is incomparably preferable to that of the French.

We have had no masterly compositions in France since Lully's death, so that all true lovers of music must despair of any new entertainments among us; but if they take the pains to go into Italy, I'll answer for 'em; let their heads be never so full of the French compositions, they'll renounce 'em all that they may have room enough for the Italian airs, which bear not the least resemblance to those in France, though this is an assertion no one can rightly comprehend that has not been in Italy; for the French have no notion of anything fine in music that doth not resemble some of their favorite airs.

These are the advantages the Italians have over the French in point of music, generally considered. Let us now examine wherein they excel 'em in relation to the operas. And that some order may be observed in the examination of so many things as concur to the forming of an opera, I think it proper to begin first with the music, in which some judgment of the recitative and symphony is first to be made before we descend to the singers themselves, who are to be considered in a twofold sense, as musicians and actors; the instruments and those that touch them, the decorations, and machines will likewise require a place in this examination.

There is no weak part in any of the Italian operas, where no sense is preferable to the rest for its peculiar beauties; all the songs are of an equal force and are sure to be crowned with applause, whereas in our operas there are I know not how many languishing scenes and insipid airs with which nobody can be pleased or diverted.

It must be confessed that our recitative is much better than that of the Italians, which is too close and simple; it's the same throughout and can't properly be called singing. Their recitative is little better than downright speaking, without any inflection or modulation of the voice, and yet there is this to be admired in it—the parts that accompany this psalmody are incomparable, for they have such an extraordinary genius for composition that they know how to adapt charming concords, even to a voice that does little more than speak, a thing to be met with in no other part of the world whatsoever.

What has been said of their music in general, with regard to ours, will be of equal force if we consider their symphony in particular. The symphony in our operas is frequently poor and tiresome, whereas in Italy it's equally full and harmonious.

I observed in the beginning of this parallel how much we had the advantage over the Italians in our basses, so common with us and so rare to be found in Italy; but how small is this in comparison to the benefit their operas receive from their castrati, who abound without number among them, whereas there is not one to be found in all France. Our women's voices are indeed as soft and agreeable as are those of their castrati, but then they are far from being either so strong or lively. No man or woman in the world can boast of a voice like theirs; they are clear, they are moving, and affect the soul itself.

Sometimes you hear a symphony so charming that you think nothing in music can exceed it till on a sudden you perceive it was designed only to accompany a more charming air sung by one of these castrati, who, with a voice the most clear and at the same time equally soft, pierces the symphony and tops the instruments with an agreeableness which they that hear it may conceive but will never be able to describe.

These pipes of theirs resemble that of the nightingale; their long-winded throats draw you in a manner out of your depth and make you lose your breath. They'll execute passages of I know not how many bars together, they'll have echoes on the same passages and swellings of a prodigious length, and then, with a chuckle in the throat, exactly like that of a nightingale, they'll conclude with cadences of an equal length, and all this in the same breath.

Add to this that these soft—these charming voices acquire new charms by being in the mouth of a lover; what can be more affecting than the expressions of their sufferings in such tender passionate notes; in this the Italian lovers have a very great advantage over ours, whose hoarse masculine voices ill agree with the fine soft things they are to say to their mistresses. Besides, the Italian voices being equally strong as they are soft, we hear all they sing very distinctly, whereas half of it is lost upon our theatre unless we sit close to the stage or have the spirit of divination. Our upper parts are usually performed by girls that have neither lungs nor wind, whereas the same parts in Italy are always performed by men whose firm piercing voices are to be heard clearly in the largest theatres without losing a syllable, sit where you will.

But the greatest advantage the Italians receive from these castrati is that their voices hold good for thirty or forty years together, whereas our women begin to lose the beauty of theirs at ten or twelve years' end. So that an actress is hardly formed for the stage before she loses her voice and another must be taken to supply her place, who, being a stranger to the theatre, will at least be out in the action if she comes off tolerably well in the singing and won't be fit to perform any considerable parts under five or six years' practice. We think it a mighty matter in France if we can brag of five or six good voices among thirty or forty actors and actresses that are employed in the opera. In Italy they are almost all of equal merit; they seldom make use of indifferent voices where there is so great a variety of good ones.[7]

As for the actors, they must be considered either as musicians that have a part to sing or players that are to act on the theatre; in both these capacities the French are infinitely outdone by the Italians.

In all our operas we have either some insignificant actor that sings out of tune or time, or some ignorant actress that sings false and is excused, either because she is not as yet thoroughly acquainted with the stage or else she has no voice, and then she is borne with because she has some other way of pleasing the town and withal makes a handsome figure. This never happens in Italy, where there is not a voice but what may very well be liked; they have neither man or woman but what perform their parts so perfectly well that they are sure to charm an audience by their agreeable manner of singing though their voices are not extraordinary, for music is nowhere so well understood as in Italy. At which we are not to wonder when we consider that the Italians learn music as we do to read; they have schools among 'em where their children are taught to sing as soon as ours learn their A B C; they are sent thither whilst they are very young and continue there for nine or ten years, so that by that time our children are able to read true and without any hesitation, theirs have been taught to sing with the same judgment and facility. To sing at sight with them is no more than to read so with us. The Italians study music once for all and attain it to the greatest perfection; the French learn it by halves, and so making themselves never masters of it, they are bound always to be scholars. When any new piece is to be presented in France, our singers are forced to con it over and over before they can make themselves perfect. How many times must we practice an opera before it's fit to be performed; this man begins too soon, that too slow; one sings out of tune, another out of time; in the meanwhile the composer labors with hand and voice and screws his body into a thousand

---

[7] Compare Freneuse (*ibid.*, II, 123): "Six or seven voices suffice for an Italian opera; it is thus not extraordinary that they should all be of more or less equal merit. Nevertheless they seldom are so, although one does in truth hear some who are admirable. In France, where we require forty or fifty, it is not necessary that the members of the chorus and those who have only a little air in passing should sing as beautifully as the others."

contortions and finds all little enough to his purpose. Whereas the Italians are so perfect and, if I may use the expression, so infallible, that with them a whole opera is performed with the greatest exactness without so much as beating time or knowing who has the direction of the music. To this exactness they join all the embellishments an air is capable of; they run an hundred sort of divisions in it; they in a manner play with it and teach their throats to echo in a ravishing manner, whereas we hardly know what an echo in music means.

In their tender airs they soften the voice insensibly and at last let it die outright. These are beauties of the greatest nicety, a nicety not only unknown to, but impracticable by the French, whose upper parts are so weak that when they come to soften 'em, they are quite smothered and you hear no more of 'em. However, these echoes, these abatements of the voice, add such a grace to the Italian airs that very often the composer finds 'em more charming in the mouth of the singer than they were at first in his own imagination. And in this the Italian operas have a double advantage over the French, since that which makes 'em better singers makes 'em also better actors. For playing, as it were, with the music and singing exactly true, without obliging themselves to attend either the person that beats the time or anything else, they have full leisure to adjust themselves to the action, and having nothing else to do but to express the passions and compose their carriage, they must certainly act much better than the French, who being not such thorough masters of the music, are wholly busied in the performance. We have not one man in all our operas fit to act a lover, except Du_ény, but, besides that he sings very false and has little or no skill in music, his voice is not comparable to that of the castrati. If a principal actress, such as La Rochoix, should step aside, all France can't afford another to supply her place.[8] Whereas in Italy, when one actor or actress is out of the way, they have ten as good ready to succeed 'em, for all the Italians are born comedians and are as good actors as they are musicians. Their old women are incomparable figures, and their buffoons excel the best of the sort we ever saw on our stage.

The Italians have this farther advantage over us, which is that their castrati can act what part they please, either a man or a woman as the cast of the piece requires, for they are so used to perform women's parts that no actress in the world can do it better than they. Their voice is as soft as a woman's and withal it's much stronger; they are of a larger size than women, generally speaking, and appear consequently more majestic. Nay,

---

8 I saw that woman at Paris; she was a good figure enough and had a tolerable voice, but then she was a wretched actress and sung insufferably out of tune. [Translator's note]

they usually look handsomer on the stage than women themselves. Ferinni, for example, who performed the part of Sybaris in the opera of *Themistocles* at Rome in the year 1685 is taller and more beautiful than women commonly are.[9] He had I know not what air of grandeur and modesty in his countenance; dressed, as he was, like a Persian princess, with his plume and turban, he looked like a real queen or empress, and probably no woman in the world ever made a more beautiful figure than he did in that habit. Italy abounds with these people; you'll find a great choice of actors and actresses in every town you come at. I saw a man at Rome who understood music as well as the best of our performers and at the same time he was as good an actor as our Harlequin or Raisin, yet by profession he was neither singer nor comedian. He was a solicitor and quitted his employment in the carnival time to perform a part in the opera; when that was done, he returned again to his business.[10] It's therefore much easier, as we have made it appear, to perform an opera in Italy than in France.

The Italians have, besides all this, the same advantage over us in respect of the instruments and the performers as they have in regard of the singers and their voices. Their violins are mounted with strings much larger than ours; their bows are longer, and they can make their instruments sound as loud again as we do ours. The first time I heard our band in the Opéra after my return out of Italy, my ears had been so used to the loudness of the Italian violins that I thought ours had all been bridled. Their archlutes are as large again as our theorbos and their sound consequently louder by half; their bass-viols are as large again as the French, and all ours put together don't sound so loud in our operas as two or three of those basses do in Italy. This is certainly an instrument much wanted in France; 'tis the basis on which the Italians in a manner build the whole consort; 'tis a sure foundation, equally firm as it is deep and low; it has a full mellow sound, filling the air with an agreeable harmony in a sphere of activity extending itself to the utmost bounds of the most capacious places. The sound of their symphonies is wafted by the air to the roof in their churches and even to the skies in open places. And for those that play on these instruments, we have very few can come near 'em here in France. I have seen children in Italy not above fourteen or fifteen years old play the bass or treble admirably well in symphonies they never saw before and in such symphonies as would puzzle the best of our masters,

---

9 Upon inquiry I'm informed that Ferinni never perform'd on any theatre in Rome but that of Tordinona and that the opera of *Themistocles* was never represented on that theatre, so that I believe the author has either mistaken or forgot the name of the opera.—[Translator's note] Possibly the opera in question is Zannettini's *Temistocle in bando*, performed in Venice, 1683.

10 The lawyer here mention'd is called Paciani, a man well known at Rome; his performances on the theatre are purely for his pleasure. [Translator's note]

and this they do often over the shoulders of two or three others that stand between them and the score. 'Tis wonderful to see these striplings with a side look take off the most difficult pieces at first sight. They beat no time to the bands in Italy, and yet you never find 'em out in the measure or the tune. You must rummage all Paris to fit out a good band; 'tis impossible to find two such as that in the Opéra. At Rome, which is not a tenth part so populous as Paris, there are hands enough to compose seven or eight bands, consisting of harpsichords, violins, and theorbos, equally good and perfect. But that which makes the Italian bands infinitely preferable to those in France is that the greatest masters are not above performing in 'em. I have seen Corelli, Pasquini, and Gaetani play all together in the same opera at Rome, and they are allowed to be the greatest masters in the world on the violin, the harpsichord, and theorbo or archlute, and as such they are generally paid 300 or 400 pistoles apiece for a month, or six weeks at the most. This is the commonest pay in Italy, and this encouragement is one reason why they have more masters there than we have with us. We despise 'em in France as people of a mean profession; in Italy they are esteemed as men of note and distinction. There they raise very considerable fortunes, whereas with us they get but a bare livelihood. From hence it is that ten times more people apply themselves to music in Italy than France. Nothing is more common in Italy than performers, singers, and music. The singers in the Navona Square at Rome and those on the Rialto at Venice, which hold the same rank there as our ballad singers on Pont Neuf do with us, will often join three or four in a company; and one taking the violin, another the bass, and a third a theorbo or guitar, with these instruments they'll accompany their voices so justly that we seldom meet with much better music in our French consorts.

To conclude all, the Italian decorations and machines are much better than ours; their boxes are more magnificent; the opening of the stage higher and more capacious; our painting, compared to theirs, is no better than daubing; you'll find among their decorations, statues of marble and alabaster that may vie with the most celebrated antiques in Rome; palaces, colonnades, galleries, and sketches of architecture superior in grandeur and magnificence to all the buildings in the world; pieces of perspective that deceive the judgment as well as the eye, even of those that are curious in the art; prospects of a prodigious extent in spaces not thirty foot deep; nay, they often represent on the stage the lofty edifices of the ancient Romans, of which only the remains are now to be seen, such as the Colosseum which I saw in the Roman College in the year 1698 in the same perfection in which it stood in the reign of Vespasian, its founder, so that these decorations are not only entertaining, but instructive.

As for their machines, I can't think it in the power of human wit to carry the invention farther. In the year 1697 I saw an opera at Turin wherein Orpheus was to charm the wild beasts by the power of his voice.[11] Of these there were all sorts introduced on the stage; nothing could be more natural or better designed; an ape, among the rest, played an hundred pranks, the most diverting in the world, leaping on the backs of the other animals, scratching their heads, and entertaining the spectators with the rest of his monkey tricks. I saw once at Venice an elephant discovered on the stage, when in an instant that great machine disappeared and an army was seen in its place, the soldiers having, by the disposition of their shields, given so true a representation of it as if it had been a real living elephant.

The ghost of a woman, surrounded with guards, was introduced on the Theatre of Capranica at Rome in the year 1698; this phantom, extending her arms and unfolding her clothes, was with one motion transformed into a perfect palace, with its front, its wings, its body and courtyard all formed by magical architecture; the guards striking their halberds on the stage were immediately turned into so many water-works, cascades, and trees that formed a charming garden before the palace. Nothing can be more quick than were those changes, nothing more ingenious or surprising. And in truth the greatest wits in Italy frequently amuse themselves with inventions of this nature. People of the first quality entertain the public with such spectacles as these without any prospect of gain to themselves. Signor Cavaliere Acciajoli, brother to the cardinal of that name, had the direction of those on the Theatre Capranica in the year 1698.

This is the sum of what can be offered in behalf of the French or Italian music by way of parallel. I have but one thing more to add in favor of the operas in Italy which will confirm all that has been already said to their advantage; which is that, though they have neither choruses nor other diversions in use with us, their entertainments last five or six hours together and yet the audience is never tired, whereas after one of our representations, which does not hold above half so long at most, there are very few spectators but what grow sufficiently weary and think they have had more than enough.[12]

---

11 This was the *Orfeo* of Antonio Sartorio; Loewenberg gives the date of the first performance in Turin as March 20, 1697.

12 The Italian operas don't usually last five or six hours, as this author imagines, the longest being not above four. 'Tis true that sometimes at Vienna the late Emperor Leopold would have operas of the length the author mentions, provided they were good, being a great admirer of the Italian music; besides he composed himself and played on the harpsichord to perfection.—[Translator's note] Compare Freneuse (*ibid.*, II, 50): " 'That was a mighty short opera,' said the Countess when [Campra's] *Tancrède* was over. 'And that is already handsome praise,' the Chevalier said; 'you will not say as much for the Italian operas that last five or six hours and that will seem to you to have lasted eight or nine.' "

15. Le Cerf de La Viéville, Seigneur de Freneuse

Jean Laurent le Cerf de La Viéville, Lord of Freneuse, was born in 1647 and died in 1710. He was an ardent admirer of Lully and deeply affected by Raguenet's attack on him in his *Parallèle des Italiens et des Français*. Freneuse answered Raguenet in his *Comparaison de la musique italienne et de la musique française*, the first part of which first appeared in 1704. In the following year (1705) a second edition of this first part was brought out together with a second part containing the *Traité du bon goût en musique* which is reproduced below. Raguenet having published an answer to the writings of Freneuse in 1705, the latter reciprocated by adding a third part to his *Comparaison* in 1706. All three parts were then reprinted and added, in 1725, to the second edition of Pierre Bourdelot's and Jacques Bonnet's *Historie de la musique*.

From the Comparaison de la musique italienne et de la musique française

[*1705*]

"Traité du bon goût en musique" [1]

"You ARE methodical in your divisions, monsieur," replied Mademoiselle M. " 'To bring to the opera attention, a certain knowledge, a familiarity with these entertainments, and good taste.' Indeed, without attention there is no way of judging of things. One judges of them the better for

---

1 Text: Jacques Bonnet, *Histoire de la musique* (Amsterdam, 1725), III, 258–262, 275–278, 280–283, 285–287, 292–294, 297–299, 301–309, 313–316, 318–322. The "Treatise on Good Taste" forms part of the sixth dialogue of the *Comparaison*. The speakers are the Marquis des E——, the Chevalier de —— (the author himself), the Comtesse du B——, and Mlle. M—— ——; the scene is the home of the Countess. Unless otherwise noted, the examples cited are from the operas of Lully.

being accustomed to see others of their kind and even for having several times seen the things which are under discussion. At the sixth performance of a play I discuss it better than at the first. And then, good taste. We can be attentive, monsieur, when we please, and no opera can be wholly new to us. May we have from you, if you please, that third thing so essential and so rare. Teach us what good taste is, the secret of acquiring it and keeping it, and the indications that one has acquired it and has kept it. Would not that be enough, madame?"

"Yes," said the Countess. "I shall be glad if anyone will teach me how to distinguish perfectly the beauties of music and their different value and how to become attached to them. Speak, monsieur le Marquis, and by so doing relieve us of the fatigue of our excursion into learning."

"I intend," said the Marquis, "to rely upon that lad there to take the pains to give you the explanation you have asked for. As I have never read any author who has treated of good taste, even of good taste in general, in a precise manner, and as I have never seen any who treated of good taste in music in any manner, I fear that my own ideas would not be sharply defined."

"And would mine be any more so?" asked the Chevalier. "If I am to say what I have imagined on the subject, I must have Madame's command. Without an absolute order to serve as my excuse for opening, for undertaking the discussion of so new and so difficult a matter, I should not have the boldness to do so."

The beautiful Countess smiled.

"See that smile," said the Marquis. "There is your order, a very pleasant one."

"It is small pay," replied the Chevalier, "if I must content myself with a smile for the danger I am about to incur. But as you have observed, the ladies are cruelly reserved in this age. I shall expound to you then, since Madame so commands me, what eight or ten years of attentive assiduity at the Opéra, long reflections at the close of performances, and my study of the nature of amusement have led me to conclude concerning good taste. You will find that it could be applied to several other fine arts: to painting, to eloquence, to poetry. I freely agree that all these arts have a bond of union which makes what can be said of each of them almost common to all, and I take for a good omen that what is said of any one is, in part, true of the others.

"But nevertheless, music will be found to have some particular and distinctive attribute of its own. Besides, monsieur le Comte was right, madame, in suspecting me of wishing to justify the principles of the an cients.[2] I am for the men of that age and the women of this. It is on the side of the principles of ancient music that I have all the while been seeking to enlist you; I praised them to you on purpose at the time of our second conversation; [3] I shall continue to follow them; and I am very well pleased that we have refuted M. Perrault's book,[4] in order to have the right to follow these principles with entire freedom.

"There are two great ways of knowing good and bad things: by our inward feeling and by the rules. We know the good and the bad only by these means. What we see and what we hear pleases us or displeases us. If one listens only to the inward feeling, one will say, 'It seems to me that that is good, or that it is not.' On the other hand, the masters, the skilled, following the observations they have made, have established precepts in every craft. These comprised whatever had seemed to them to be the best and the surest. The established precepts are the rules, and if one consults them regarding what one sees and what one hears, one will say that this is good or is not good, according to such and such a rule, or for such and such a reason. These masters were men; were they incapable of being deceived? The authority of the rules is considerable, but after all it is not a law. Inward feeling is still less sure, because each should distrust his own, should distrust that it is what it should be. Who will dare flatter himself that he has a fortunate nature, endowed with sure and clear ideas of the good, the beautiful, the true? We have all brought into the world the foundation of these ideas, more or less clear and certain, but since our birth we have received, and this it is sad and painful to correct, a thousand false impressions, a thousand dangerous prejudices, which have weakened and stifled within us the voice of uncorrupted nature.

2 Rightly understood, the controversy between Raguenet and Freneuse is not so much concerned with the rival claims of French and Italian music as with those of a "classic" and a "modern" style. As such, it is simply a part of the larger quarrel between the ancients and the moderns, begun in France by Boileau, Fontenelle, and the brothers Charles and Claude Perrault, and continued in England by Temple, Wotton, and Swift. Raguenet's book is pro modern in that its title is an obvious paraphrase of Charles Perrault's *Parallèles des anciens et des modernes en ce qui regarde les arts et les sciences* (1688–97) and in that it appeared with an "Approbation" by Fontenelle. The reply of Freneuse is pro classic in that it repeatedly quotes with approval from Boileau, the chief partisan of the ancients, and in that it includes an attack on Claude Perrault. Cf. his first dialogue (Bonnet, *op. cit.*, II, 17–18): "M. de Fontenelle is entitled to his opinions. In comparison with the Italians, the French musicians are our ancients. Aside from this, M. de Fontenelle is interested only in exalting the French above other nations in poetry, physics, and the other sciences within his province: thus if he abandons

the glory of France in music, this carries no weight." Cf. also his reply to Raguenet's *Defense du Parallèle* (Paris, 1705) in his third book (Bonnet, *op. cit.*, IV, 188): "When I say that, in comparison with the Italians, the French musicians are our ancients, this simply means that, compared with Italians, whose great vogue did not begin in France until ten years ago or thereabouts, our composers, to whom we have been attached for thirty, forty, sixty years, have had to share the disgrace of the ancients, if we are to believe M. de Fontenelle, who likes to prefer the latest arrivals. And our composers are also ancients in view of their character, their simplicity, and their naturalness, qualities which M. de Fontenelle is not accustomed to rating very highly. For all his attempts at dialectic, M. l'Abbé cannot prove my little jest to be far-fetched or obscure."

3 The fifth dialogue, a conversation on musical history, opera, and the life of Lully.

4 The present dialogue began with a discussion of Claude Perrault's "De la musique des anciens," first published in his *Essais de physique*, II (1680).

"I think that in this uncertainty and confusion the remedy is to lend to the inward feeling the support of the rules, that our policy should be to correct and strengthen the one by the other, and that it is this union of the rules and the feeling which forms good taste. To listen attentively to the inward feeling, to disentangle it, and then to purify it by the application of the rules; there is the art of judging with certainty, and therefore I am persuaded that good taste is the most natural feeling, corrected or confirmed by the best rules."

.   .   .   .   .   .

"Oh, monsieur, what are these rules? I cannot consult them unless you . . ."

"There are little ones and great ones, madame, and we have touched upon both sorts in our conversation. The little rules are those of composition, on which twenty treatises have been written, of which I do not cite a single one, because I am waiting for somebody to write a twenty-first one that will be good.[a] Just as faults of versification are condemnable and perceptible in the best poets (witness the saying of M. le Duc de Montausier that Corneille should be crowned as a poet and whipped as a versifier), the same is true of faults of composition in the best musicians. An air in which these are found loses something of its value. Our masters have sufficiently instructed us in the little rules, and a little reflection will make us remember to pay attention to them when they are violated . . ."

"An example, Chevalier, an example. Precepts without examples only disquiet and distress me . . ."

"But these examples can hardly be cited from memory, and besides, examples of faults and minutiae are not easy to find in Lully, the only composer I wish to cite here, and it is dangerous to propose to find them. No matter, madame, you will make a beautiful excuse for the audacity and the novelty of my criticisms. For example, then, it is a little rule of composition, founded in part on the necessity of expressing, of depicting, to use low notes or high notes with words which represent a low or a lofty object. Colasse has been praised for having observed this rule in very remarkable fashion in the passage of *Thétis et Pélée*,

Les cieux, l'enfer, la terre et l'onde [5]

On the contrary, at the end of the first act of *Acis et Galatée*, where Polyphemus says,

[a] Since that time, Etienne Roger has published that of Masson. [Masson's *Nouveau traité*, first published in Paris in 1694, was reprinted by Roger of Amsterdam about 1710.—Ed.]

[5] The skies and hell, the earth, the ocean.

Je suis au comble de mes voeux [6]

the note to which the word *comble* (summit) is sung is very low, the lowest note of all that line. *Comble* called for a high note, and strictly speaking, that negligence is assuredly a fault which detracts from the value of the admirable melody of that recitative. Little rules, which, for all that, enter into consideration.

"You know the great rules, mademoiselle," continued the Chevalier, turning toward Mademoiselle, who was amusing herself by looking at her scarf, "indeed we have gone over them to the point of weariness."

"Yes," she replied, "but go ahead as if I didn't know them." [b]

"Very well, mademoiselle. A piece of music should be natural, expressive, harmonious. In the first place, natural, or rather, simple, for simplicity is the first part, the first sign of the natural, which is almost equally an ingredient in these three qualities. In the second place, expressive. In the third place, harmonious, melodious, pleasing—take your choice. These are the three great, the three important rules which one must apply to the airs that the inward feeling has approved, and it is they which in the last resort decide."

" 'Fore heaven, monsieur le Chevalier," said Mademoiselle, "how greatly I should be obliged to you if you would just once define for me in precise words those terms which you use as a stand-by. 'Natural, simple.' What, in precise words, do you call simple and natural? . . ."

"Ah, well, I hate all obscurity just as you do, and I am delighted that you should prevent me from leaving those terms in any way obscure. I call natural, in the literal sense, the music which is composed of notes that present themselves naturally, which is not composed of notes that are farfetched or out of the ordinary. I call simple the music which is not loaded with ornaments, with harmonies. I call expressive an air of which the notes are perfectly suited to the words, and a symphony which expresses perfectly what it aims to express. I call harmonious, melodious, pleasing, the music which fills, contents, and tickles the ear.

.   .   .   .   .   .

"A last rule, which must be added to the little rules and the three great rules, and which clarifies and fortifies both groups, is always to abhor excess. Let us make it a habit and a merit to have contempt, distaste, and aversion without quarter for all that contains anything superfluous. Let us hate even an expression which is of the right character but which goes beyond the appropriate degree of force. And to return to where we were,

---

b *Le bourgeois gentilhomme,* Act I.   6 I reach the summit of my hopes.

when your inward feeling has caused you to enjoy an air, which moreover conforms to the minor rules, make sure, by examining it in the light of the three great rules and the rule of just proportion, that your heart and your senses have not been deceived. After which, mademoiselle, be at rest; be assured that the air is truly one to be esteemed.

"You are going to ask me for an example, an air which the great rules condemn. Gladly, madame, and from Lully, since it is a question of satisfying you. Listen to that air of *Phaëton*,[c]

> *Que l'incertitude*
> *Est un rigoureux tourment!*

It will flatter your ear, and I do not think that there are faults in it. An attentive ear will confirm the opinion that it is simple, agreeable, natural. Examine whether it is expressive; you will perceive that it is not. Lybia is lamenting the rigor of a sorrowful uncertainty. How does she lament it? In a gay tone and movement. How excuse the incongruity arising from this gaiety and from a sort of pleasantry caused by the repetition of the verses? Perhaps Quinault incited Lully to this vicious pleasantry. But why did Lully accept these words and follow them, increasing the defect? It would seem to me that, taking the words as they stand, the falsity of expression which prevails in the air makes it bad, and I should like neither to sing it nor to hear it, in spite of my veneration for its author."

"I have seen," said the Marquis, "a man of wit, who is a scholar and a musician, who likewise criticized the duet of the prologue of *Persée*,

> *La grandeur brillante*
> *Qui fait tant de bruit*, etc.,

finding in it a misplaced gaiety. If it were an ambitious man expressing in this tone the unhappiness of ambition, I too believe that the gaiety would be a grave fault. But it is a philosopher who is describing the evils from which he has sheltered himself, evils at which he laughs. Is he not right in depicting them gaily and laughingly? The words,

> *Notre sort est tranquille;*
> *C'est un bien qui nous doit rendre heureux*,

justify the movement and the amiable gaiety of the whole duet.

"Indeed, I have no doubt that constant adherence to these principles and exact care in applying them in detail to all the music that one hears will really lead one to good taste. One who took the pains to judge always

---

c Act II, Scene iii.

in this manner would in less than a year be able to judge without thinking about it."

"Trust us to do so," said the Countess. "But although we must not let ourselves be blinded by the reputation of composers, cannot their favorable or unfavorable reputation serve to give a certain assurance to the judgments we have already formed? Am I not justified in saying, 'My heart, my ear, all the rules agree in persuading me that "Bois épais" [7] is a charming air. And it is by Lully, a new pledge of the correctness of my taste. This other air does not flatter my ear, nor does it touch me; it has neither sweetness nor expression. And it is by Charpentier.[8] Yes, I am judging it rightly; it is bad.' Would that be bad reasoning, Chevalier?"

"Not at all, madame, anything but bad. It is clear that the reputation of the composers, which would be a dangerous guide before we judge, is excellent for confirming our opinions after we have judged. But the memory of Charpentier is greatly obliged for citing him so appositely. Apparently you are of the opinion of the Abbé de Saint Real,[d] that it is less forbidden to maltreat dead authors than living ones."

"But," said the Countess, "could there not be some other method of judging music, not so long and not so trying, some way of judging it at a glance and in a phrase? Try to find for me, Marquis, the secret of consoling my indolence, or rather my vivacity, which indeed accepts the principles which we have just run over, but which is hampered by them and tired of them."

"Yes, madame," the old noble promptly replied, "I will find for you the secret of judging in a phrase. I will make you judge by a silent and summary application of your principles. It will not be so sure, but it will ordinarily be just, and moreover, easy and convenient. You do not wish to take the pains to judge by reasoning. Judge by comparison, which is the method of courtiers, as La Bruyère, I believe, somewhere says. You will need to carry in your head two airs representing the two qualities, one good and one bad; that is, good and bad by almost unanimous consent, and two symphonies, one good and one bad, and you must have all their beauties and all their faults at the tip of your fingers. You must have the knowledge of the least of the beauties and faults of these two airs and these two symphonies ever at command and thoroughly familiar, and compare with these models the airs and symphonies you hear.

---

d *De la critique,* chap. ii.

7 From his *Amadis,* II, iv.

8 Born in Paris, Charpentier studied in Rome with Carissimi; he returned to France a partisan of Italian music and became Lully's principal adversary.

"These latter you will esteem in proportion to their resemblance to the others, and the idea of this resemblance alone, accordingly as it strikes you more or less forcibly, will cause you to say, with greater or less force, 'I like that air; that symphony does not please me.' I am convinced that the ablest connoisseur should not neglect to combine with the judgments based on reasoning these judgments by comparison, from which will be derived an additional clearness, well adapted to confirm our feelings. For a man of wit, a man of the world, who knows how to make the most of this taste derived from comparison, it will perhaps be sufficient. It is a facility which is flattering to indolence and a fortunate resource for ignorance. I shall praise every symphony which approaches the one that accompanies the air of *Acis et Galatée*, 'Qu'une injuste fierté,' of the passacaglia of *Armide*, etc. I shall admire every sad air which imitates 'Bois épais,' every lively air which resembles that of *Amadis*, which all France, from the princess to the serving maid in the tavern, has so often sung,

Amour, que veux-tu de moi?

And so on. The precept is not complicated, and its application will not be fatiguing."

.   .   .   .   .

"Now," said the Countess, "let us judge of the degrees of value of airs. So far we have not spoken of the degrees of beauty. But indeed, Chevalier, I understand that you are on the point of telling me that no one knows how to determine these degrees, that the more perfectly an air complies with the rules the better it is, and the further it departs from them the worse, and that it depends on the skill of the connoisseur to measure these degrees of perfection or of imperfection."

"Beyond doubt that will be my answer, madame," said the Chevalier. "Meanwhile there are precepts with regard to this matter. First, infringements of the little rules are as nothing in comparison with violations of the great ones. Listen to a lesson of Holy Week which begins with a sixth, but go out when one begins with a roulade. In the second place, the pleasures of the heart being, by the principles we have established, superior to those of the ear, an air which offends against the laws that are directed toward touching the heart offends more than one which disregards merely those which aim to satisfy the ear. Let us forgive two similar cadences which are too near to each other, or a poor thorough bass, and let us never forgive a melody which is cold and forced. There you have two ideas which will help us to make up our minds about the degrees of good and bad of a piece.

"In the third place, the most beautiful thing is that which is equally admired by the people and by the learned or by all the connoisseurs. Then, after this, I should admire more that which is generally admired by all the people. Finally, that which is admired by all the learned. Mademoiselle likes precise definitions. The learned are the masters of music, the musicians by profession, stubborn about the rules. The people is the multitude, the great mass, which has not risen to special knowledge and has only its natural feeling as its guide and as the warrant for its judgments. The connoisseurs are those who are neither altogether of the people nor altogether learned, half the one and half the other, a shade less learned than of the people, that is to say, crediting the rules a shade less than natural feeling; and this definition is my own.

. . . . .

"As to the half-learned, they are in music what they are in any art, in anything whatever, the most contemptible and the most insupportable of all men. Let us attach more importance to the opinion of a good bourgeois of the Rue St. Denis than to that of the apprentice-composers, these chevaliers of accompaniment, whose efforts and whose vanity have turned topsy-turvy the little taste they might have had;

> Of the folk who, attended by one scurvy lute,
> Say, 'my bass,' and make marvelous doctors.*

"Therefore, mesdames, I persist in maintaining the rank which I have assigned to the suffrages of those who judge of our operas: the people and the learned or the connoisseurs; the people alone; the connoisseurs alone; the learned alone. That order is good. I see in *Thésée* the first scene of the second act:

> *Doux repos, innocente paix,* etc.;

the third scene of the third act:

> *Princesse, scavez-vous ce que peut ma colère,* etc.;

the fifth scene of the fourth act:

> *Eglé ne m'aime plus, et n'a rien à me dire,* etc.;

admired equally by our people and by our learned. I believe without any difficulty that these scenes are the most beautiful, and I have verified that

---

* Imitated from Molière's *Les Fâcheux,* scene of the hunter, II, vii.

they will pass for such with the connoisseurs. I see the first and fourth scenes of the fourth act,

> *Cruelle, ne voulez-vous pas*, etc.,

and

> *Faut-il voir contre moi tous les enfers armés*, etc.,

loved by the people, who are moved to tenderness by them. I do not hesitate to prefer them greatly to

> *Prions, prions la déesse*, etc.,

of Act I, Scene vi, and to the entire part of the Grand Priestess, a part so imbued with learning, which makes the learned esteem it in spite of its coldness. In this way there are in Lully two hundred expressive pieces which touch the multitude, and I should not hesitate to prefer them to the admirable trio, 'Le fil de la vie,' [t] one of the most perfect learned pieces and one of the most acceptable to the learned that Lully has left. I am ready to maintain against all comers that the public's favorite scenes in *Proserpine*,[g]

> *J'ai peine à concevoir d'où vient le trouble extrème*, etc.,

and

> *Venez-vous contre moi défendre un téméraire*, etc.,

are worth far more than the learned scenes of *Les Ombres heureuses*,

> *Loin d'ici, loin de nous*, etc.

The despair of Roland is of far greater merit than the profound beauties of the part of Logistille, etc.[9]

·   ·   ·   ·   ·   ·

"When I heard, for example, the air of *Amadis*,

> *Amour, que veux-tu de moi*, etc.,

sung by all the kitchen maids of France, I was right in thinking that this air was already certain to have the approbation of everybody in France of a degree between that of princess and that of kitchen maid; that this air had passed through all those degrees to reach the lowest, and had captured the esteem and the suffrage of all people of quality, of all the learned, of that immense number of persons of distinction on whose lips it had been, and remarking that it had succeeded in touching the kitchen maid as it had succeeded in touching the princess, that it pleased equally

---

t *Isis*, Act IV.   9 Characters in Lully's *Roland*.
g Acts II and IV.

the learned and the ignorant, the intelligences of the highest order and of the lowest, I concluded that it must be very beautiful, very natural, very full of true expression, to have moved so many different hearts and flat-tered so many different ears. But an air of the Pont-Neuf, which has begun among the populace and which spreads among the populace, has only the approval of the populace, and the humbler folk of France, very unlike those of Athens and not attending the theater as those of Athens did, have not a natural feeling pure enough to entitle their suffrage to count when it stands alone. You will not count it, madame, except when it comes after your own. But you will please permit the more or less lively approbation of the populace to be a sixth measure, which I was forgetting, of the degree of beauty of musical works. These are our principles; all follows logi-cally."

"Yes," said the Marquis, "they bring you, willy-nilly, to that con-clusion. And that characterization of the people, the connoisseurs, and the learned makes me realize that we must listen to the reasoning of the learned, defer to the feeling of the connoisseurs, and study how the people are moved. I conceive that above all this, the study of how the people are moved by theatrical representations can infinitely clarify and facilitate our judgments and help us to make them true. At the first three representations of an opera, let us concern ourselves only with ourselves; it will keep us sufficiently occupied, unless long habituation leaves our minds exceptionally free. But at the fourth and later performances let us apply ourselves to studying in what manner and how greatly the people are touched. The value and the degree of value of pieces will certainly be revealed by the impression which they make on the heart of the people and by the vivacity of that impression. When Armida works herself up to stab Rinaldo in the last scene of the second act, I have twenty times seen everybody seized by terror, holding his breath, motionless, all the soul in the ears and eyes, until the air of the violin which ends the scene gave leave to breathe, then at that point breathing again with a murmur of delight and admiration. I had no need to reason. That unanimous re-sponse of the people told me with certainty that the scene was of over-powering beauty.[10] A number of times in Paris, when the duet of *Persée*, so learnedly written and so difficult,

Les vents impétueux, etc.,

was well given, I have seen the entire public, similarly attentive, remain for the half of a quarter-hour without breathing, with their eyes fixed

---

10 For this scene see Schering, *Geschichte der Musik in Beispielen* (Leipzig, 1931), No. 234. Rameau analyzes Armida's monologue in his *Nouveau système* (1726) and in his *Observations* (1754) replies to Rousseau's criticism of it in his *Lettre sur la musique française* (1753).

upon Phineus and Merope, and when the duet was finished, nod to each other to indicate the pleasure it had given them. Certainly a beautiful passage: expressive learning, beautiful roulades.

"I am so much of the Chevalier's opinion, namely, that the public is an oracle for the fine arts, that I could even like to study and put faith in the responses of a particular section of the public to certain things which come especially within their province, which concern them, and about which they have a particular feeling. I remember that at the beginning of a performance of *Hésione*,[11] in that scene, the fifth of the second act, in which Venus begs Anchises for his love, which he has refused (I don't know why, since Venus was hardly made to have refusals flung in her face, and since on the faith of the legend he was by no means cruel to her), and when he leaves her, saying,

> *À vos regards tout doit rendre les armes;*
> *Si je n'adore pas leur pouvoir éclatant,*
> *Je sens du moins qu'un coeur qui veut être constant*
> *Doit craindre de voir tant de charmes,*[12]

I remember, I say, that at these last verses, I saw all the ladies look at each other and smile. The ignoble advances of Venus had distressed their vanity; now a universal joy returned to their faces. I had no need of discussion to know that the language and the expression of the passage were most graceful. The natural response of those ladies, more skilled than we in matters of gallantry, their air, the contentment in their eyes, were my warrant, and I could rely upon them. Should one of the learned have asserted that the music did not match the words, I should have assured him that if the music had not been as graceful as the words, the passage would have made a less general and less lively impression on the ladies.

"Let us then add this to our other rules: to study at the Opéra the response of the public and of particular groups from the public, in so far as certain things are more within their range and their competence. Here is another secret for throwing a clear and immediate light on the subject of our thoughts, a secret likewise derived from our principles, to which we cannot adhere too closely. A thousand fashionables who daily judge music at haphazard and in a way to move pity do so only from having no

---

11 Opera by André Campra.

12 Your dazzling glances overcome all arms;
    If I withhold the worship to them due,
    At least I feel that one whose heart would
        fain be true
    Should fear to gaze upon such potent
    charms.

principles to adhere to. Our principles are such that we may well adhere to them without reserve."

"While we are on the subject of these principles," replied Madame du B., "pray, give me also, messieurs, those which will enable me to judge of voices, singers, and players of instruments, so that I shall be able to pass on the merit of any of these with the same clearness and the same certainty as on the music which they execute. When we learn to sing or to play an instrument, our masters burden us with a quantity of little observations which become a confused jumble, because we are not taught to refer them to certain general principles."

"That is what the masters forget, madame," replied the Marquis, smiling. "But you are right; it would be clearer and more convenient later if they said, in so many words, that the perfection of a voice, of singing, and of the playing of an instrument depends only on this. I am going to explain the method which I have devised and adopted to judge of the players of instruments, the voices, and the singers that I hear; you may use it if it pleases you.

"A perfect voice should be sonorous, of wide range, sweet, exact (*nette*), lively, flexible. These six qualities, which nature combines only once in a century, are ordinarily present in half measure. A voice of wide range and of a beautiful tone (*son*), a touching tone, is a great, a beautiful voice, and the sweeter it is, in addition, a thing rarer in great voices than in others, the more beautiful I believe it to be. A lively and flexible voice is a pretty voice, a pleasing voice, and the more exact it is, in addition, the less, in my opinion, will it be subject to hoarseness and coughing, the frequent drawbacks of pretty voices, and the more I shall esteem it. Bacilly [h] esteems these little voices as much as the great ones; they interested him. My friend and I, who like noble, bold, penetrating tones, are of a different taste. We are for the great voices, and we shall allow the little voices to embellish their tunes ever so neatly with no regrets on our part.

"I reduce the merit of a singer to three things: accuracy, expression, neatness (*propreté*). I reduce the merit of a player upon an instrument to three other things: exactness (*netteté*), delicacy, getting the most out of his instrument. The first thing required of a singer is correct pitch. If he sings without accompaniment, he cannot sing off pitch except by insensibly raising or lowering the tone, so that at the end of the air he is higher or lower than he was at the beginning. The first of these faults is

h *Art de chanter*, Part I, ch. vii.

that of voices too loud or too shrill, the coarse basses and the voices of women; the second that of weak chests. If one is singing with accompaniment, one sings falsely by not taking or by leaving the pitch prescribed by the harmony which the accompaniment must create.

"Expression on the part of a singer consists in entering, in a spirited and appropriate manner, into the feeling of the verses he sings, to inform them with passion is the term, as one who understands them and is the first to feel them. On the whole, the recitative and the smaller airs should be sung lightly, the great airs more consciously (*en s'écoutant davantage*), bringing out the full force of each note. It is noticeable that the fault of beginners is to sing too fast, that of the good provincial singers to go a little too slowly. Neatness (*propreté*) is that great mass of little observations, unknown to the Italians but so well known to our own masters, and which by their combined effect afford great pleasure, I assure you. To open the mouth, to produce (*porter*) the tones in the right way, to prepare, ornament (*préparer, battre*), and finish a cadence gracefully, etc. I listen attentively to a singer; the number of minutiae which must be observed does not embarrass me because I arrange them each under one of these three heads, and in case he satisfies me under these three heads, I do not ask him for a fourth. Of the three qualities to which I reduce the merit of a player, exactness is the principal one, especially for the players of instruments which are played directly by the fingers, without a bow. Count that of five hundred players of the lute, the harpsichord, etc., there will not be one who succeeds in playing as exactly (*nettement*) as one has the right to ask. And without exactness, what is a piece for the lute or the harpsichord? A noise, a jangling of harmonies in which one understands nothing. I would sooner listen to a hurdy-gurdy. After this precious exactness comes delicacy. It is in instruments what neatness (*propreté*) is in singing. It is at capturing delicacy that all those little observations aim that your masters burden you with.

"Last, to get the most out of the instrument. It is certainly necessary that an instrument should sound (*parle*), and it is true that to make it sound well is an art and a most important talent, but let us not lose sight of the capital maxim of monsieur le Chevalier, the golden mean. In truth, mademoiselle, your Italians carry too far a certain desire to elicit sound from their instruments. My intelligence, my heart, my ears tell me, all at once, that they produce a sound excessively shrill and violent. I am always afraid that the first stroke of the bow will make the violin fly into splinters, they use so much pressure. Besides, you comprehend that the sovereign perfection of an instrumentalist and of a singer would be to ally the three qualities, and if they could, to combine them in equal proportions. But I think I have observed that they never have all three in equal measure; the best instrumentalist, the best singer exceeds in some one point and is mediocre as regards the other two; at best, he excels in two and is passable in the third. I must remember further to say to you that keeping the measure with inviolable precision is in singing a part of accuracy, and in the playing of instruments the principal cause of exactness."

"I tender you my thanks, monsieur," said the Countess. "What you have said will comfort me and enlighten me. Let us continue our exploration of good taste. To acquire it, then, we shall accustom ourselves to judge of everything by listening to our natural feeling, and by confirming this with the aid of the little and the great rules; we shall pay attention, after judging, to the reputation of the composers; we shall consider our judgments final only after hearing pieces for the third or fourth time; we shall combine judgment by comparison with that by reasoning. At the Opéra we shall study with care the responses of the spectators; and we shall let our own judgment and that of the public be confirmed by the decrees of time. Is that all? Has good taste been completely acquired?"

"One more little practice to observe, madame," said the Chevalier. "As, with all that, we shall not at once become good judges, but shall now and then be mistaken, we shall form the habit of observing and eliminating our misconceptions. We shall at times examine our judgments as strictly as we examine the works of others, and when we find that we have committed an error, we shall follow it step by step; we shall retrace our way to the origin of our misconception, and after finding it we shall make precise note of this cause. The better we shall have noted it, the less subject we shall be to falling into it again. This practice is of great utility in every way and leads very quickly and very directly to good taste.

. . . . . .

"But if it is agreeable to you, we shall agree that the greatest possible evidence of good taste is to give praise where praise is due. We are under no obligation to find fault when we hear a piece of music that shocks us. We can leave the hall or we can remain silent. But I think that praise is a tribute which one owes to whoever has deserved it.

> And grudging mortals only when compelled
> Will offer incense to the rarest virtues.[1]

"It is an injustice to those mortals who make a profession of being wits, and a right-minded man praises and even delights in praising when he

---

1 Antoine de La Fosse. *Polixène*, a tragedy, Act I, Scene ii.

feels that someone has succeeded in pleasing him. Lully took pleasure in applauding the music of others which satisfied him. He said a number of times that the symphony to which has been written that irreverent potpourri of words,

Je gage de boire autant qu'un Suisse, etc.,[18]

seemed to him to be one of the most graceful he knew for any kind of instrument, especially for wind instruments. (Indeed, take note of this, you will have difficulty in finding another which rolls along (*roule*) or rather leaps so agreeably.) And he praised Lambert [14] and old Boësset [15] every day. M. Ménage [j] answered the Cardinal de Retz, who had asked him for a little instruction in how to become a judge of poems, 'Monseigneur, always say the thing is worthless; you can hardly go wrong.' Still, Monseigneur le Cardinal de Retz would sometimes have gone wrong, for after all there are some good poems. There are also some good musical works.

"The exquisite mark of good taste, then, is to praise those and only those. And that is not enough; the degree of praise must correspond to the degree of value of the work. To praise more or less than this is bad taste, and I am persuaded that here is the reef on which the greatest number of people are wrecked. He who can praise with reason and in due proportion will be a perfect connoisseur; do not doubt it, but recognize him by this perilous test. Do you not often laugh, madame, at the terms which certain persons use to express approval and the grand words they fill their mouths with? Do not expect a moderate eulogy from them. Just as what displeases them is always detestable, frightful, abominable, so what pleases them is never less than admirable, incomparable, inimitable, and the poor Abbé R[aguenet] thereby became lamentably addicted to —— we noticed it sufficiently at the time. But none the less, Ménage gave sensible advice, and we can see that one is more commonly and more shamefully wrong in praising too much than in praising too little. What torrents of ridiculous praise! How many Madelons in this world, who 'would sooner have written an "oh, oh" than an epic poem!' [k] How many learned ladies who are in love with a '*quoi qu'on die!*' [l] And the unfortunate thing about these exaggerated praises is that they dishonor those who receive them. Those stiff people,[m] from whom politeness never extorts

j Ménage, Vol. II, p. 280.
k *Les Précieuses ridicules*, Scene x.
l *Les Femmes savantes*, Act III, Scene ii.
m La Bruyère.

18 I wager I can drink as much as a Swiss, etc.
14 Michel Lambert, composer of several books of airs, was Lully's father-in-law and collaborated with him on the music of the *Ballet des arts* (1663).
15 Antoine Boësset, composer of *airs de cour*, is for Freneuse one of the principal representatives of classicism in French vocal music.

a word more than they think is their duty, are or seem to be more polite in this respect than the others. One is fortunate to have the courage to reply, as Segrais once did to Mademoiselle: '*Mordi!* would your Highness be any the fatter for having made me say something silly?' "

"Monsieur le Chevalier," said Mademoiselle M., coldly, "be on your guard, you too, against that ugly habit of overpraising."

. . . . . .

"Come, mademoiselle," said the old noble, "let's convert each other. And let's convert each other good-naturedly and quickly, for we haven't the time to disagree. You see that that lad there is a conscientious man and that his good faith is rather dry than dubious. He is not singing master for the Français, and it does not appear that he has ever had a share in the profits of the Opéra. Indeed, I advise you to believe him."

"I am sorry to be still unable to surrender," replied Mademoiselle M. "But even if your reasoning were unanswerable, I have a resource which would stand me in lieu of everything. It is the example of so many persons of eminent rank who are enchanted by Italian music. I rely upon their taste, which constitutes an authority superior to all your arguments."

"In the matter of taste, mademoiselle," retorted the Chevalier, "great nobles are only men like ourselves, whose name proves little. Each has his voice and the voices are equal, or at least it is not their quality which will determine their weight. But in case you put your trust in authorities, we have one on our side to whom you can defer. The King—

> I should name another name to you, madame
> Knew I of any higher."[n]—

the King, I say, is on our side. But I am no courtier. I do not wish to stress that name, however great it may be, or to maintain that it decides. Let us put aside from the person of the King all the splendor which his rank and his reign bestow upon it, and let us regard him only as a private person in his kingdom. It is only rendering him the justice which one would not refuse to a minister out of favor to say that of all the men of Europe he is one of those born with the greatest sense and the most direct and just intelligence. He loves music and is a competent judge of it. The great number of ballets in which he has danced and of operas composed expressly for him or of his choice, the honor he has done to Lully and to so many other musicians in permitting them to approach him, attest that he loves music. That he is a good judge of it, this same love of the art, his

---

n *Britannicus,* Act II, Scene iii.

familiarity with it, and the personal qualities that no one could refuse to concede that he possesses, are the proof. It is certain that the fashion of hailing with rapture the beauty of the operatic pieces now brought to us from Italy in bales has not yet reached him. Even in Lully's lifetime the King enjoyed a beautiful Italian piece when one was presented to him. He had a motet of Lorenzani [16] sung before him five times. He was fond of the air of M. de La Barre, attributed to Luigi, etc.° He had, as he still has, among his singers some *castrati*, in order to have them sing airs from time to time, a thing in which I agree that they are excellent. But for all that he was attached to the opera of Lully, to the music and musicians of France, and since the death of Lully he has not changed his taste; he has stoutly adhered to it, though there have been attempts to make him change it."

"If the recent story which a thousand persons have been telling is true," said the Marquis, "it is specific and shows very well that the magnificence and the lively pace of the Italian symphonies have failed to please him. Don't you know the story, ladies? A courtier of some importance who had extolled these symphonies to the King, brought him little Batiste, a French violinist of surprising natural aptitude who had studied for three or four years under Corelli. The interests of Italy were in good hands. You can imagine that little Batiste had studied his lesson besides. He played rapid passages which would have made Mademoiselle faint with delight or terror before Madame gave the word. The King listened with all the attention that Italy could desire, and when Italy waited to be admired, said, 'Send for one of my violinists!' One came; his name is not given; apparently it was one of mediocre merit, who happened to be at hand.

" 'An air from *Cadmus*,' said the King.

"The violinist played the first one that occurred to him, a simple, unified air; and *Cadmus* is not, of all our operas, that from which one would have chosen to select an air if the incident had been premeditated.

" 'I can only say to you, sir,' said the King to the courtier, 'that is my taste; that is my taste.' "

"I had already heard the story," interposed Madame du B. "They say that nothing is truer, and they say too that after Monseigneur, whose extreme fairness is recognized by all France, had heard Batistin [17] and Marchand of the King's Band play the violoncello, he greatly preferred

o *Le Mercure galant*, August, 1678, p. 246. ["Dolorosi pensieri," by J. C. La Barre, mistakenly attributed to Luigi Rossi.—Ed.]

16 Paolo Lorenzani, Italian composer resident in Paris from 1678 to 1694, was influential as a representative of Italian music in France.

17 Jean Baptiste Stuck, Italian-born violoncellist and composer of German extraction, a resident of Paris during the greater part of his life.

the Frenchman to the Italian, in spite of the efforts and the insinuations of those who had presented the latter to him."

"The grand total, messieurs the partisans of Italy," said the Marquis, "is this. Do you yield to reason? Reason pronounces for us. Do you respect the authority of illustrious connoisseurs?

We reign over a heart alone worth all the rest.[p]

And in consequence, reconcile yourselves to believing that not only are the Italian operas greatly inferior to ours on the stage, which was the first question, but that the Italian operas on paper, and divided into vocal part and symphonies, are always absolutely bad in the first respect and rarely good in the second, this being the fundamental subject of the last disputes of our pretty musician. She has said that she would give us the cards for a little game of omber. May she be pleased to do so. Mademoiselle, who does not play, will have to go halves with monsieur le Chevalier."

. . . . . .

[p] Prologue to *Armide.*

IV

Critical Views of Italian Opera: Addison and Marcello

16. Joseph Addison

One of the greatest English essayists and men of letters, Addison (1672–1719) was the leading contributor to the periodicals *The Tatler*, *The Spectator* and *The Guardian*, published by his friend Richard Steele from 1709 to 1713. Particularly important are Addison's contributions to *The Spectator*. The paper stood for reason and moderation in an age of bitter party strife. In his essays, Addison shows himself an able painter of life and manners. His witty, distinguished writings exerted an important influence on criticism, not only in England but also in France and Germany.

From The Spectator [1]

Tuesday, March 6, 1711.
Spectatum admissi risum teneatis?—Hor.[2]

AN OPERA may be allowed to be extravagantly lavish in its decorations, as its only design is to gratify the senses, and keep up an indolent attention in the audience. Common sense, however, requires, that there should be nothing in the scenes and machines which may appear childish and absurd. How would the wits of King Charles's time have laughed to have seen Nicolini [3] exposed to a tempest in robes of ermine, and sailing in an open boat upon a sea of pasteboard! What a field of raillery would they have been let into, had they been entertained with painted dragons spitting wildfire, enchanted chariots drawn by Flanders mares, and real cascades

1 Text: As edited by G. Gregory Smith for Everyman's Library (London, 1907), I, 20–23, 49–52.
2 Could you, my friends, if favored with a private view, refrain from laughing?—*Ars poetica*, 5. [Fairclough]

3 Nicolini, who sang in London at the Theatre in the Haymarket during the seasons of 1708 to 1712 and 1715 to 1717, created the principal castrato roles in Handel's operas *Rinaldo* and *Amadigi*.

in artificial landscapes! [4] A little skill in criticism would inform us, that shadows and realities ought not to be mixed together in the same piece; and that the scenes which are designed as the representations of nature, should be filled with resemblances, and not with the things themselves. If one would represent a wide champaign country filled with herds and flocks, it would be ridiculous to draw the country only upon the scenes, and to crowd several parts of the stage with sheep and oxen. This is joining together inconsistencies, and making the decoration partly real and partly imaginary. I would recommend what I have here said to the directors, as well as to the admirers, of our modern opera.

As I was walking in the streets about a fortnight ago, I saw an ordinary fellow carrying a cage full of little birds upon his shoulder; and, as I was wondering with myself what use he would put them to, he was met very luckily by an acquaintance, who had the same curiosity. Upon his asking him what he had upon his shoulder, he told him, that he had been buying sparrows for the opera. Sparrows for the opera! says his friend, licking his lips; what, are they to be roasted? No, no, says the other; they are to enter towards the end of the first act, and to fly about the stage.

This strange dialogue awakened my curiosity so far, that I immediately bought the opera, by which means I perceived the sparrows were to act the part of singing birds in a delightful grove; though, upon a nearer inquiry, I found the sparrows put the same trick upon the audience, that Sir Martin Mar-all [5] practised upon his mistress; for, though they flew in sight, the music proceeded from a consort of flagelets and bird-calls [6] which were planted behind the scenes. At the same time I made this discovery, I found, by the discourse of the actors, that there were great designs on foot for the improvement of the opera; that it had been proposed to break down a part of the wall, and to surprise the audience with a party of an hundred horse; and that there was actually a project of bringing the New River into the house, to be employed in jetteaus and water-works. This project, as I have since heard, is postponed till the summer season; when it is thought the coolness that proceeds from fountains and cascades will be more acceptable and refreshing to people of quality. In the meantime, to find out a more agreeable entertainment for the winter season, the opera of *Rinaldo* is filled with thunder and lightning, illuminations

---

4 These references are without exception to the stage machinery of Handel's *Rinaldo*.

5 Character in Dryden's comedy of the same name. In Act V, Sir Martin acts out the singing of a serenade to the lute, while the actual singing and playing is done in an adjoining room by his man. The scheme miscarries.

6 Almirena's cavatina "Augelletti che cantate" (*Rinaldo*, I, vi) has an accompaniment for flauto piccolo (or "flageolett" as Handel calls it in his autograph score), two flutes, and strings.

and fire-works; which the audience may look upon without catching cold, and indeed without much danger of being burnt; for there are several engines filled with water, and ready to play at a minute's warning, in case any such accident should happen. However, as I have a very great friendship for the owner of this theatre, I hope that he has been wise enough to insure his house before he would let this opera be acted in it.

It is no wonder that those scenes should be very surprising, which were contrived by two poets of different nations,[7] and raised by two magicians of different sexes. Armida (as we are told in the argument) was an Amazonian enchantress, and poor Signor Cassani (as we learn from the persons represented) a Christian conjuror (Mago Christiano). I must confess I am very much puzzled to find how an Amazon should be versed in the black art; or how a good Christian (for such is the part of the magician) should deal with the devil.

To consider the poets after the conjurors, I shall give you a taste of the Italian from the first lines of his preface: Eccoti, benigno lettore, un parto di poche sere, che se ben nato di notte, non è però aborto di tenebre, mà si farà conoscere figliolo d'Apollo con qualche raggio di Parnasso. "Behold, gentle reader, the birth of a few evenings, which, though it be the offspring of the night, is not the abortive of darkness, but will make itself known to be the son of Apollo, with a certain ray of Parnassus." He afterwards proceeds to call Mynheer Hendel the Orpheus of our age, and to acquaint us, in the same sublimity of style, that he composed this opera in a fortnight. Such are the wits to whose tastes we so ambitiously conform ourselves. The truth of it is, the finest writers among the modern Italians express themselves in such a florid form of words, and such tedious circumlocutions, as are used by none but pedants in our own country; and at the same time fill their writings with such poor imaginations and conceits, as our youths are ashamed of before they have been two years at the university. Some may be apt to think that it is the difference of genius which produces this difference in the works of the two nations; but to show there is nothing in this, if we look into the writings of the old Italians, such as Cicero and Virgil, we shall find that the English writers, in their way of thinking and expressing themselves, resemble those authors much more than the modern Italians pretend to do. And as for the poet himself,[8] from whom the dreams of this opera are taken, I must entirely agree with Monsieur Boileau, that one verse in Virgil is worth all the clinquant or tinsel of Tasso.[9]

---

7 Aaron Hill and Giacomo Rossi.
8 Torquato Tasso, from whose *Gerusalemme liberata* the story of *Rinaldo* is drawn.

9 *Satire*, IX, 176.

But to return to the sparrows; there have been so many flights of them let loose in this opera, that it is feared the house will never get rid of them; and that in other plays they make their entrance in very wrong and improper scenes, so as to be seen flying in a lady's bed-chamber, or perching upon a king's throne; besides the inconveniences which the heads of the audience may sometimes suffer from them. I am credibly informed, that there was once a design of casting into an opera the story of Whittington and his cat, and that in order to do it, there had been got together a great quantity of mice; but Mr. Rich, the proprietor of the playhouse, very prudently considered, that it would be impossible for the cat to kill them all, and that consequently the princes of the stage might be as much infested with mice, as the prince of the island was before the cat's arrival upon it; for which reason he would not permit it to be acted in his house. And indeed I cannot blame him: for, as he said very well upon that occasion, I do not hear that any of the performers in our opera pretend to equal the famous pied piper, who made all the mice of a great town in Germany follow his music, and by that means cleared the place of those little noxious animals.

Before I dismiss this paper, I must inform my reader, that I hear there is a treaty on foot with London and Wise (who will be appointed gardeners of the playhouse) to furnish the opera of Rinaldo and Armida with an orange-grove; and that the next time it is acted, the singing birds will be personated by tom-tits: the undertakers being resolved to spare neither pains nor money for the gratification of the audience.

Thursday, March 15, 1711.
Dic mihi, si fias tu leo, qualis eris?—Mart.[10]

There is nothing that of late years has afforded matter of greater amusement to the town than Signor Nicolini's combat with a lion [11] in the Haymarket, which has been very often exhibited to the general satisfaction of most of the nobility and gentry in the kingdom of Great Britain. Upon the first rumor of this intended combat, it was confidently affirmed, and is still believed by many in both galleries, that there would be a tame lion sent from the Tower every opera night, in order to be killed by Hydaspes; this report, though altogether groundless, so universally prevailed in the upper regions of the playhouse, that some of the most refined

---

10 Tell me, if you became a lion, what sort of lion will you be?—*Epigrammata*, XII, xcii. [Ker]

11 In the opera *L'Idaspe fedele* by Francesco Mancini, first performed in London, April 3, 1710.

politicians in those parts of the audience gave it out in whisper, that the lion was a cousin-german of the tiger who made his appearance in King William's days, and that the stage would be supplied with lions at the public expense, during the whole session. Many likewise were the conjectures of the treatment which this lion was to meet with from the hands of Signor Nicolini: some supposed that he was to subdue him in recitativo, as Orpheus used to serve the wild beasts in his time, and afterwards to knock him on the head; some fancied that the lion would not pretend to lay his paws upon the hero, by reason of the received opinion, that a lion will not hurt a virgin; several, who pretended to have seen the opera in Italy, had informed their friends, that the lion was to act a part in High-Dutch, and roar twice or thrice to a thorough bass, before he fell at the feet of Hydaspes. To clear up a matter that was so variously reported, I have made it my business to examine whether this pretended lion is really the savage he appears to be, or only a counterfeit.

But before I communicate my discoveries, I must acquaint the reader, that upon my walking behind the scenes last winter, as I was thinking on something else, I accidentally justled against a monstrous animal that extremely startled me, and upon my nearer survey of it, appeared to be a lion rampant. The lion, seeing me very much surprised, told me, in a gentle voice, that I might come by him if I pleased: "For," says he, "I do not intend to hurt anybody." I thanked him very kindly, and passed by him. And in a little time after saw him leap upon the stage, and act his part with very great applause. It has been observed by several, that the lion has changed his manner of acting twice or thrice since his first appearance; which will not seem strange, when I acquaint my reader that the lion has been changed upon the audience three several times. The first lion was a candle-snuffer, who being a fellow of a testy, choleric temper, overdid his part, and would not suffer himself to be killed so easily as he ought to have done; besides, it was observed of him, that he grew more surly every time he came out of the lion, and having dropped some words in ordinary conversation, as if he had not fought his best, and that he suffered himself to be thrown upon his back in the scuffle, and that he would wrestle with Mr. Nicolini for what he pleased, out of his lion's skin, it was thought proper to discard him; and it is verily believed, to this day, that had he been brought upon the stage another time, he would certainly have done mischief. Besides, it was objected against the first lion, that he reared himself so high upon his hinder paws, and walked in so erect a posture, that he looked more like an old man than a lion.

The second lion was a tailor by trade, who belonged to the playhouse, and had the character of a mild and peaceable man in his profession. If the former was too furious, this was too sheepish for his part; insomuch that after a short, modest walk upon the stage, he would fall at the first touch of Hydaspes, without grappling with him, and giving him an opportunity of showing his variety of Italian trips. It is said, indeed, that he once gave him a rip in his flesh-colored doublet; but this was only to make work for himself, in his private character of a tailor. I must not omit that it was this second lion who treated me with so much humanity behind the scenes.

The acting lion at present is, as I am informed, a country gentleman, who does it for his diversion, but desires his name may be concealed. He says, very handsomely, in his own excuse, that he does not act for gain; that he indulges an innocent pleasure in it; and that it is better to pass away an evening in this manner than in gaming and drinking: but at the same time says, with a very agreeable raillery upon himself, that if his name should be known, the ill-natured world might call him, "the ass in the lion's skin." This gentleman's temper is made out of such a happy mixture of the mild and choleric, that he outdoes both his predecessors, and has drawn together greater audiences than have been known in the memory of man.

I must not conclude my narrative, without taking notice of a groundless report that has been raised to a gentleman's disadvantage, of whom I must declare myself an admirer; namely, that Signor Nicolini and the lion have been seen sitting peaceably by one another, and smoking a pipe together behind the scenes; by which their common enemies would insinuate, that it is but a sham combat which they represent upon the stage: but upon inquiry I find, that if any such correspondence has passed between them, it was not till the combat was over, when the lion was to be looked upon as dead, according to the received rules of the drama. Besides, this is what is practised every day in Westminster Hall, where nothing is more usual than to see a couple of lawyers, who have been tearing each other to pieces in the court, embracing one another as soon as they are out of it.

I would not be thought, in any part of this relation, to reflect upon Signor Nicolini, who in acting this part only complies with the wretched taste of his audience; he knows very well, that the lion has many more admirers than himself; as they say of the famous equestrian statue on the Pont Neuf at Paris, that more people go to see the horse than the king who sits upon it. On the contrary, it gives me a just indignation to see a person whose action gives new majesty to kings, resolution to heroes, and softness to lovers, thus sinking from the greatness of his behavior, and degraded into the character of the London Prentice. I have often wished, that our tragedians would copy after this great master in action. Could they make the same use of their arms and legs, and inform their faces with as significant looks and passions, how glorious would an English tragedy appear with that action which is capable of giving a dignity to the forced thoughts, cold conceits, and unnatural expressions of an Italian opera! In the meantime, I have related this combat of the lion, to show what are at present the reigning entertainments of the politer part of Great Britain.

Audiences have often been reproached by writers for the coarseness of their taste; but our present grievance does not seem to be the want of a good taste, but of common sense.

17. Benedetto Marcello

Born at Venice in 1686 to patrician parents, Marcello was distinguished both as a composer and as a writer. His most significant and best-known musical work is the *Estro poetico-armonico*, a collection, in eight volumes, of settings of fifty Psalms for one to four voices with *basso continuo* and a few instruments. Marcello was also a composer of instrumental music.

Among his literary works, the satire *Il teatro alla moda* (c. 1720) is the most famous. It marks, within the Italian scene, the spontaneous reaction of those concerned with the musical theater as a temple of dramatic art against all those—singers, composers, men of the stage—who wanted to use it for the gratification of their personal vanities. Although more than two centuries old, the witty work has lost none of its interest.

From Il teatro alla moda [1]

[*1720*]

THE

THEATER

A LA MODE

OR

Safe and easy METHOD of properly composing and producing
Italian OPERAS according to modern practice
in which

1 Text: Tessier's edition (Venice, 1887), pp. 51–79. For a reproduction of the original title page and an explanation of its satiric vignette and imprint, see R. G. Pauly, "Benedetto Marcello's Satire on Early 18th-Century Opera," *Musical Quarterly*, XXXIV (1948), 222–233, with refer- ences to important studies by Malipiero and Rolandi. A complete translation of the *Teatro alla moda*, by Mr. Pauly, is published in the *Musical Quarterly*, XXXIV (1948), 371–403, and XXXV (1949), 85–105.

cidental details of the opera will be prisons, stilettos, poisons,
, hunting the wild ox, earthquakes, sacrifices, settlements of
mad scenes, etc., because by such unexpected things the public
dinarily thrilled; and if it should ever be possible to introduce
which some of the characters should sit down and others should
p in a grove or garden while a plot was being laid against their
should wake up (something never seen in an Italian theater),
ld reach the very acme of the marvelous.

odern poet need not devote much labor to the style of his drama,
that it must be heard and understood by the multitude, but
sire to make it more intelligible he will leave out the customary
nd will use long periods, which are not customary, being lavish
thets when he finds it necessary to fill out some line of a recitative
netta.

ill provide himself, further, with a large number of old operas,
hich he will take his subject and setting, changing only the verse
w names of characters. He will do the same thing in adapting
from French into Italian, from prose into verse, or from tragic
, adding or taking out characters according to the needs of the
rio.

has no other resource, he will become a great schemer in order to
e operas, joining forces with another poet, furnishing the subject
iting a share of the verses, under an agreement to divide the pro-
f the dedication and the profits of publication.

he will absolutely never allow the singer to make his exit without
tomary *canzonetta*, especially when, by a vicissitude of the drama,
ter must go out to die, commit suicide, drink poison, etc.

will never read the entire opera to the impresario, though he will
snatches of some of the scenes to him and repeatedly recite bits from
ene of the poison or the sacrifice or the chairs or the bears or the
ments of contracts; adding that if such a scene as that deceives his
ations, there is no use in writing operas any more.

the good modern poet be careful to understand nothing at all of
, for such knowledge was characteristic of the ancient poets, accord-
Strabo, Pliny, Plutarch, etc., who did not separate the poet from
usician or the musician from the poet, as was true of Amphion,
mmon, Demodocus, Terpander, etc., etc., etc.

e ariettas should have no relation whatever to the recitative, but the
should do his best to introduce into them for the most part the terms
erfly," "mosquito," "nightingale," "quail," "bark," "canoe," "jes-

Are given useful and necessary recommendations to Poets, Composers
of Music, Singers of either sex, Impresarios,
Musicians, Designers and Painters of Scenes, Buffo parts,
Costumers, Pages, Supernumeraries, Prompters, Copyists,
Protectors and MOTHERS of Lady Singers, and other
Persons connected with the Theater

DEDICATED

BY THE AUTHOR OF THE BOOK

TO ITS COMPOSER

[Vignette]

Printed in the SUBURBS of BELISANIA for ALDIVIVA
LICANTE, at the Sign of the BEAR in the BOAT
For sale in CORAL STREET at the
GATE of ORLANDO'S PALACE
And will be reprinted each year with new additions

TO THE POETS

In the first place the modern poet will not need to read or ever to have
read the ancient Latin and Greek authors, because not even the ancient
Greeks or Romans ever read the moderns.

Likewise he will not need to profess any understanding of Italian meter
or verse, except for some superficial notion that a line is composed of seven
or eleven syllables, by the aid of which rule he may then make them, according to his whim, of three, five, nine, thirteen, and even of fifteen.

But he will say that he has pursued all the studies of mathematics,
painting, chemistry, medicine, etc., protesting that finally his genius has
forced him to take up poetry, not meaning by this the method of correctly accenting, rhyming, etc., etc., or the terms of poetry, or the fables,
or the histories, but rather, at most, introducing into his works some terms
of the sciences indicated above, or of other sciences which have nothing
to do with poetic training.

He will accordingly call Dante, Petrarch, Ariosto, etc., obscure, harsh,
and tedious poets, and therefore of no account or little to be imitated. But
he will have a stock of various modern poems, from which he will take

sentiments, thoughts, and entire lines, calling the theft praiseworthy imitation.

Before composing his opera the modern poet will seek to obtain from the impresario a precise note of the number and quality of the scenes the latter desires, in order to include them all in his drama, taking care, if there enter into it any elaborate effects of sacrifices or banquets or descending heavens or other spectacles, to come to an understanding with the stage hands as to how many dialogues, soliloquies, ariettas, etc., he must use to prolong the preceding scenes, to enable them to get all ready at their convenience, even at the risk of enfeebling the opera and intolerably boring the audience.

He will write the whole opera without formulating any plot, simply composing it line by line, in order that the public, having no understanding of the intrigue, may remain curious to the very end. Above all, let the good modern poet have a care that all his characters come on very often to no purpose, for then they must necessarily make their exits one by one, singing the customary *canzonetta*.

The poet will never inquire into the merits of the actors, but will rather ask whether the impresario will have a good bear, a good lion, a good nightingale, good thunderbolts, earthquakes, flashes of lightning, etc.

At the end of his opera he will introduce a magnificent scene, of striking appearance, to insure that the public will not walk out in the middle of the performance, and he will conclude with the customary chorus in honor of either the sun or the moon or else of the impresario.

In dedicating his book to some great personage, he will try to find one rather rich than learned, and will make a bargain to reward some good mediator, say the cook or the major domo of the patron himself, with a third of the proceeds of the dedication. From his patron he will ascertain in the first place the number and degree of the titles with which to adorn his name on the title page, augmenting the said titles by affixing "etc., etc., etc., etc." He will exalt the family and glories of his patron's ancestors, using frequently in his dedicatory epistle the terms "liberality," "generous soul," etc., and if (as sometimes happens) he finds in his personage no occasion for praise, he will say that he himself is silent in order not to offend the modesty of his patron, but that Fame with her hundred sonorous trumpets will sound his immortal name from pole to pole. Finally he will conclude by saying, in token of profoundest veneration, that he kisses the jumps of the fleas on the feet of His Excellency's dog.

It will be most useful to the modern poet to protest to the reader that

he composed the opera in his most tender
he did this in a few days (even if he has
a few years), that will be a particularly goo
he has completely renounced the ancient pr

Nonumque prematur in

In such a case he will be able to declare f
for his own amusement, to lighten the bur
tions; that he had no thought of publishing
advice of friends and the command of his pa
do so, and not at all by any desire of fame or
that the distinguished virtuosity of the cast, t
composer of the music, and the dexterity of th
bear will correct the defects of the drama.

In his account of the argument he will disco
precepts of tragedy and the art of poetry, fo
Sophocles, Euripides, Aristotle, Horace, etc. H
that the poet of today must abandon every goo
the genius of the present corrupt age, the licenti
extravagance of the conductor of the orchestra
musicians, the delicacy of the bear, the supernum

But let him be careful not to neglect the custo
three most important points of every drama: the
action, indicating that the place is in *such and such*
eight P.M. until midnight, the action *the bankru*

It is not essential that the subject of the opera be
all the Greek and Latin stories have been treated
and Romans and by the most select Italians of th
the modern poet is to invent a fiction, contriving i
royal shipwrecks, evil auguries from roast oxen, etc
among the dramatis personae some historic name sh
public. All the rest may then be invented at the aut
care, above everything, that the text be not over 1,2
less, including the ariettas.

Then, to give his opera a greater reputation, the n
to name it rather from one of the principal actions th
e.g., instead of "Amadis" or "Buovo" or "Bertha at
call it "The Generous Ingratitude," "Vengeance at th
Bear in the Boat."

2 And keep it back until the ninth year.—Horace, *Ars poetica*, 388

samine," "gillyflower," "saucepan," "cooking pot," "tiger," "lion," "whale," "crayfish," "turkey," "cold capon," etc., etc., etc., for in this way he reveals himself as a good philosopher, distinguishing the properties of animals, plants, flowers, etc., in his similes.

Before the opera is produced, the poet must praise the singers, the impresario, the orchestra, the supernumeraries, etc. If the opera, later, should not be well received, he must inveigh against the actors, "who did not perform it according to his conception, thinking only of singing"; against the composer, "who did not comprehend the force of the scenes, giving all his attention to the ariettas"; against the impresario, "who with excessive economy produced it with an inadequate setting"; and against the musicians and supernumeraries, "who were all drunk every evening, etc."; protesting further that he had composed the drama in another manner; that he consented to make cuts and additions at the whim of those in command and particularly of the insatiable prima donna and the bear; that he will make it possible to read it in the original version; that at present he hardly recognizes it as his own; and if anyone doubts this, let him ask the housemaid or the laundress, who read and considered it before anyone else.

At the rehearsals of the opera he will never disclose his intention to any of the actors, wisely reflecting that they desire to do everything in their own way.

If the requirements of the opera leave any member of the company without a part, he will add one for him as soon as the virtuoso himself or his patron requests it, having always ready to hand a few hundreds of ariettas for use in additions, alterations, etc., and will not neglect to fill the libretto with the customary superfluous verses enclosed between inverted commas.

If a husband and wife should be in prison and one of them should go out to die, the other must inevitably stay behind to sing an arietta. The words of this should be lively, to relieve the sadness of the audience and to make them understand that it is all in fun.

If two characters talk love or plan conspiracies, ambushes, etc., they must always do it in the presence of the pages and supernumeraries.

If any character needs to write, the poet will have the scene changed and a small table and an armchair brought in. After the letter is written, he will have the table taken away, for the said table must no longer be thought of as a part of the setting in which the writing is done. He will follow the same practice with the throne, and with chairs, sofas, grass seats, etc.

He will present dances of gardeners in the halls of the royal palace and dances of courtiers in groves, and will note that the dance of the Piraeus may be presented in a hall, in a courtyard, in Persia, in Egypt, etc.

In case the modern poet discovers that the singer enunciates badly, he must not correct him, because if the singer should remedy his fault and speak distinctly, it might hurt the sale of the libretto.

If members of the cast ask him on which side they should make their entrances and exits or in which direction they should make gestures and what they should wear, he will let them enter, exit, make gestures, and dress in their own way.

If the meters of the arias should not please the composer, the poet will be prompt to change them, introducing into them further, at the latter's caprice, winds, storms, fogs, siroccos, the Levanter, the Tramontane, etc. Many of the arias should be so long that the beginning will be forgotten before the end is reached.

The opera should be presented with only six characters, having due care that two or three parts are so introduced that in case of necessity they may be cut out without detriment to the action.

The part of the father or the tyrant, when it is the principal one, should always be entrusted to *castrati*, reserving tenors and basses for captains of the guard, confidants of the king, shepherds, messengers, etc.

Poets of little credit will have in the course of the year employment in the courts or on estates; they will have charge of accounts, copy parts, correct for the press, speak evil of each other, etc., etc., etc.

The poet will claim a box from the impresario, half of which he will sublet months before the opera is put on and for all the first nights, filling the other half with masks, whom he will bring into the theater free.

He will visit the prima donna frequently, because the success or failure of the opera usually depends upon her, and he will adapt the opera to her genius, lengthening or shortening her role or that of the bear or other characters, etc. But he will not allow himself to confide to her anything relating to the intrigue of the opera, for the modern virtuosa does not need to understand anything of that; giving instead, at the most, some little information on the subject to her mother, father, brother, or protector.

He will call upon the composer and will read the drama to him many times, and will inform him where the recitative is to proceed lento, where presto, where appassionato, etc., as the modern composer is not expected to perceive anything of that sort himself, and will then burden the arias with "very brief ritornelli and passages" (rather, many complete repetitions of the words), that the poetry may be the better enjoyed.

He will be extremely polite to the members of the orchestra, the costumers, the bear, the pages, the supernumeraries, etc., commending his opera to them all, etc., etc., etc., etc.

TO THE COMPOSERS OF MUSIC

The modern composer of music will not need to have any notion of the rules of good composition, apart from a few universal principles of practice.

He will not understand the numerical proportions of music, or the excellent effect of contrary movements, or the false relation of the tritone or of major sixths. He will not know the names and number of the modes or tones, or how they are classified, or what are their properties. Rather, he will say on that subject, "There are only two modes, major and minor; the major, the one which has the major third; the minor, the one which has the minor third," not rightly perceiving what the ancients meant by the major and minor mode.

He will not distinguish one from another the three genera: diatonic, chromatic, and enharmonic, but will confound at his whim the progressions of all three in a single *canzonetta*, to distinguish himself completely by this modern confusion.

He will use the major and minor accidentals at his own free will, confounding their signs at random. Likewise he will use the enharmonic sign in the place of the chromatic, saying that they are the same thing, because each of them adds a small semitone, and in this way he will show himself wholly unaware that the chromatic sign always belongs between tones, to divide them, and the enharmonic only between semitones, its especial property being to divide large semitones and nothing else. For this reason the modern composer, as has been said above, needs to be entirely in the dark as regards these matters and others like them.

Consequently he will have little facility in reading and still less in writing, and therefore will not understand Latin, even though he must compose church music, into which he will introduce sarabands, gigues, courantes, etc., calling them fugues, canons, double counterpoints, etc.

Turning now to our discussion of the theater, the modern master musician will understand nothing of poetry. He will not make out the meaning of the speeches; he will not distinguish the long and short syllables, or the force of the scenes, etc. Likewise he will not observe the special qualities of the stringed or the wind instruments if he plays the harpsichord, and if he is a player of stringed instruments, he will not take the pains to understand the harpsichord, being convinced that he can become a good composer in the modern manner without practical acquaintance with that instrument.

It will do no harm, however, if the modern composer should have been for many years a player of the violin or the viola, and also copyist for some noted composer, and should have kept the original manuscripts of his operas, serenades, etc., stealing from them and still others ideas for ritornelli, overtures, arias, recitatives, variations on "La Folia," choruses, etc.

Therefore, on receiving the opera from the poet, he will prescribe to him the meters and the number of lines of the arias, entreating him, further, to provide him with a fair copy, without omitting any full stops, commas, or question marks, etc., though in setting it to music he will show no regard for full stops, question marks, or commas.

Before putting hand to the opera, he will call upon all the ladies of the company, whom he will offer to serve according to their genius, i.e., with *arie senza bassi*,[3] with *furlanette*, with rigadoons, etc., all with violins, bear, and supernumeraries in unison.

He will take care, after that, never to read the entire opera, to avoid getting confused, but will set it line by line, remembering further to have all the arias quickly changed, using in them, then, motives already prepared in the course of the year, and if, as most often happens, the new words to the said arias fail to fit the notes felicitously, he will again pester the poet until he is wholly satisfied with them.

He will compose all the arias with an accompaniment for the instruments, taking care that each part moves forward with notes or figures of the same value, whether these be quarters, eighths, or sixteenths. For to compose well in the modern manner, one should aim at noise rather than at harmony, which latter consists principally in the different values of the figures, some of them tied over, others not, etc., but to escape harmony of this kind, the modern composer must not use any other suspensions than the usual fourth and third in the cadence, and if in this he still suspects himself of having too great a leaning toward the ancient, he will end his arias with all the instruments in unison.

Let him further see to it that the arias, to the very end of the opera, are alternatively a lively one and a pathetic one, without regard to the words, the modes, or the proprieties of the scene. If substantive nouns,

---

3 See, for example, in Handel's *Agrippina:* I, xviii, "Ho un non sò che nel cor" (Agrippina); III, x, "Bel piacere" (Poppea).

e.g., *padre, impero, amore, arena, regno, beltà, lena, core*, etc., etc., or adverbs, as *no, senza, già*, and others, should occur in the arias, the modern composer should base upon them a long passage; e.g., *paaa . . . impeeee . . . amoooo . . . areeee . . . reeee . . . beltàaaaa . . . lenaaaaa . . .*, etc.; *nooo . . . seeeeen . . . giàaaaaa . . .*, etc. The object is to get away from the ancient style, which did not use passages on substantive nouns or on adverbs, but only on words signifying some passion or movement; e.g., *tormento, affanno, canto, volar, cader*, etc., etc., etc., etc.

In the recitatives the modulation shall be at the composer's fancy, moving the bass with all possible frequency, and as soon as each scene is composed, he will have his wife hear it, in case he is married to a virtuosa; if not, his servant, his copyist, etc., etc., etc., etc.

All the ariettas should be preceded by very long ritornelli with violins in unison, composed ordinarily of eighth and sixteenth notes, and these will be played mezzopiano, to make them more novel and less tedious, having a care that the arias which follow have nothing to do with the said ritornelli.

The ariettas, further, should proceed *senza basso*, and to keep the singer on the pitch, have him accompanied by violins in unison, sounding also a few bass notes on the violas, but this is not essential.

When the musico has a cadenza, the composer will silence all the instruments, leaving it free to the virtuoso or virtuosa to carry on as long as he pleases.

He will not take much pains with duets or choruses, but will contrive to have them cut out.

For the rest, the modern composer will add that he composes with little study and with a vast number of errors in order to satisfy the audience, with this formula condemning the taste of the audience, which in truth now and then enjoys what it hears, even if it is not good, because it has no opportunity of hearing anything better.

He will serve the impresario for the smallest of pay, remembering the thousands of scudi that the virtuosi cost him, and for that reason will be content with less than the lowest of these receives, provided that he is not worse off than the bear and the supernumeraries.

In walking with singers, especially *castrati*, the composer will always place himself at their left and keep one step behind, hat in hand, remembering that the lowest of them is, in the operas, at least a general, a captain of the king's forces, of the queen's forces, etc.

He will quicken or retard the tempo of the arias to suit the genius of the

virtuosi, covering up whatever bad judgment they show with the reflection that his own reputation, credit, and interests are in their hands, and
for that reason, if need be, he will alter arias, recitatives, sharps, flats,
naturals, etc.

All the *canzonette* should be made up of the same things, that is, of
extremely long passages, of syncopation, of chromatic progressions, of
alterations of syllables, of repetitions of meaningless words, e.g., *amore
amore, impero impero, Europa Europa, furori furori, orgoglio orgoglio,*
etc., etc., etc. Consequently, when the modern composer is writing an
opera, he should always have before his eyes, for the sake of this effect,
an inventory of all the aforesaid terms, without some one of which no
aria will ever come to an end, and that in order to ecape as far as possible
from variety, which is no longer in use.

At the end of a recitative in flats, he will suddenly attack an aria with
three or four sharps in the signature and then return to flats in the following recitative; this by way of novelty.

Likewise the modern composer will divide the sentiment or meaning
of the words, making the musico sing the first line, though by itself it has
no meaning at all, and then inserting a long ritornello for violins, violas,
etc., etc.[4]

If the modern composer should give lessons to some virtuosa of the
opera house, let him have a care to charge her to enunciate badly, and
with this object to teach her a great number of divisions and of graces, so
that not a single word will be understood, and by this means the music will
stand out better and be appreciated.

When the musicians play the bass without harpsichords or double
basses, it makes no difference at all that the strings of the said bass (with
regard to the voice and the bowed instrument) should drown out the
singer's part, as usually occurs the more in the arias of the contralti, tenors,
and basses.

The modern composer must also compose *canzonette*, especially for
contralto or mezzo-soprano, which the basses will accompany by playing
the same notes in the octave below and the violins, in the octave above,
writing out all the parts in the score. In so doing he will regard himself
as composing in three parts, though the arietta actually has only a single
part, diversified only by the octave in low and high.[5]

If the modern composer wishes to compose in four parts, two of them
must indispensably proceed in unison or in octaves; at the same time he

---

4 A reference to the so-called "Devisen-Arie" or "Motto-Aria."

5 See, for example, in Handel's *Agrippina:* II, xiv, "Col raggio placido" (Pallante).

will also diversify the movement of the subject; for example, if one part proceeds by half notes or quarter notes, let the other proceed by eighths or sixteenths, etc.

Basses proceeding by quarter notes (*crome*) will be called "chromatic basses" by the modern composer, for it would not be fitting for him to know the meaning of the word "chromatic." He will also take pains to know nothing at all of poetry, because knowledge of this kind was suitable to the ancient musicians, that is, to Pindar, Arion, Orpheus, Hesiod, etc., who according to Pausanias were most excellent poets, no less than musicians, and the modern composer must do his utmost to be unlike them, etc.

He will captivate the public with ariettas accompanied by pizzicati or muted instruments, marine trumpets, cymbals, etc.

The modern composer will claim from the impresario, in addition to his fee, the present of a poet, to make use of as he pleases, and as soon as the latter has written his text, he will read it to his friends, who understand nothing of it, and by their opinion he will regulate ritornelli, passages, appoggiaturas, enharmonic sharps, chromatic flats, etc.

Let the modern composer be careful not to neglect the customary chromatic or accompanied recitative, and to that end let him oblige the poet, presented to him by the impresario as above, to provide him with a scene of a sacrifice, a mad scene, a prison scene, etc.[6]

He will never compose arias with *basso solo obbligato*,[7] bearing in mind that this is out of date and that, further, in the time required to compose one such, he could compose a dozen accompanied by the instruments.

Desiring, then, to compose some arias with basses, he must make up the latter out of two or at most three notes, repeated or else tied together after the fashion of a pedal point, and must see to it, above all things, that all the second parts [8] are made up of secondhand stuff.

If the impresario should later complain about the music, the composer will protest that he is unjust in so doing, as the opera contains a third more than the usual number of notes and took almost fifty hours to compose.

If some aria should fail to please the virtuose or their protectors, he will say that it needs to be heard in the theater with the costumes, the lights, the supernumeraries, etc.

---

6 For accompanied recitatives of this kind see Handel's *Il Pastor fido*, III, vii (sacrifice), *Orlando*, II, xi (mad scene), and *Rodelinda*, III, iii (prison scene); in particular, the treatment of prison scenes in this style had by 1733 become so familiar that the *Beggar's Opera* could ridicule it effectively in the scene of MacHeath's soliloquy, suggested by the prison scene in Ariosti's *Coriolanus*.

7 "When the composer selects and restricts himself to a particular subject in the bass, maintaining it strictly throughout the whole piece without departing from it (unless ever so slightly or by bringing it at the fifth), so that the dominant or melodious part is accommodated to it."— Johann Mattheson, *Das neu-eröffnete Orchestre* (Hamburg, 1713), p. 182.

8 I.e., the middle sections of the da capo arias.

At the end of each ritornello, the conductor must nod to the virtuosi, in order that they may come in at the right time, which they will never know of themselves, because of the customary length and variation of the said ritornello.

He will compose some arias in bass style, for all that they are to be sung by soprani and contralti.

The modern composer will oblige the impresario to provide a great number of violins, oboes, horns, etc., preferring to let him economize on double basses, for these should not be used except in the preliminary tuning.

The Sinfonia will consist of a *tempo francese*, or *prestissimo* of eighth notes in the mode with the major third, which must be followed in the usual fashion by a *piano* in the same mode with the minor third, concluding finally with a minuet, gavotte, or gigue, again in the major mode, in this manner avoiding fugues, suspensions, *soggetti*, etc., as antiquities entirely excluded from modern practice.

The composer will arrange that the best arias fall to the prima donna, and if the opera needs cutting, he will not permit the removal of arias or ritornelli, but rather of entire scenes of recitative, of the bear, of earthquakes, etc.

If the second lady should complain that she has fewer notes in her part than the prima donna, he will manage to console her by making the number equal with the aid of passages in the arias, appoggiaturas, graces in good taste, etc., etc., etc.

The modern composer will make use of old arias composed in other countries, making profound reverences to the protectors of virtuosi, lovers of music, renters of stools, supernumeraries, stage hands, etc., and commending himself to all.

If *canzonette* must be changed, he will never change them for the better, and he will say of any arietta that fails to please that it is a masterpiece, but was ruined by the musicians, not appreciated by the public, taking care to put out the lights which he has at the harpsichord for the *arie senza basso*, to keep his head from getting too hot, and to relight them for the recitatives.

The modern composer will show the greatest attentions to all the virtuose of the operas, presenting them all with old cantatas transposed to fit their voices, in addition saying to each one that the opera owes its success to her talent. The same thing he will say to each man in the cast, to each member of the orchestra, to each supernumerary, bear, earthquake, etc.

Every evening he will bring in masks free of admission fee, whom he will seat near him in the orchestra pit, occasionally giving the cello or the double bass an evening off for the sake of his guests.

All modern composers will have the following words placed under the announcement of the cast:

The music is by the ever most archi-celebrated Signor N. N., conductor of the orchestra, of concerts, of chamber concerts, dancing master, fencing master, etc., etc., etc., etc.

V

The Reformulation of the Theory of Harmony and Counterpoint

18. J. J. Fux

Born in Styria in 1660, Johann Joseph Fux died at Vienna in 1741. He became composer to the Imperial Court in 1698, second choirmaster at the Cathedral of St. Stephen in 1705, and first choirmaster at the Court in 1715. Fux wrote an important quantity of sacred music (including about 50 masses and 3 requiems); 10 oratorios and 18 operas; also a number of orchestral suites, trio-sonatas, etc., of which only a small part was published during his lifetime. Fux is still well remembered today as the author of the theoretical work *Gradus ad Parnassum* (1725), which has served generations as a textbook for strict counterpoint. Its system is based, in an ultra-conservative way, on the church modes.

From the Gradus ad Parnassum [1]

[*1725*]

Book Two

DIALOGUE

(Josephus) I COME TO YOU, revered master, to be instructed in the precepts and laws of music.

(Aloysius) What, you wish to learn musical composition?

(J) That is indeed my wish.

(A) Are you unaware that the study of music is a boundless sea, not to be concluded within the years of Nestor? Truly, you are planning to assume a burden greater than Aetna. For if the choice of a mode of life is universally a matter full of difficulty, since on this choice, rightly or

1 Text: The original edition (Vienna, 1725), pp. 43–81. A complete translation, by Alfred Mann, was published by W. W. Norton & Co., Inc., in 1943. In this dialogue between master and pupil, Fux names the master for Palestrina and modestly gives his own name to the pupil.

wrongly made, the good or bad fortune of all the rest of life depends, how much more cautious foresight must he who thinks of entering upon the path of this discipline use before he can venture to adopt a counsel and decide his own case! For a musician and a poet are born. You must think back, whether from tender years you have felt yourself impelled to this study by a certain natural impulse, and whether it has befallen you to be intensely moved by the delight of harmony.

(J) Yes, most intensely. For, from the time when I hardly had the power of reason, an unknowing child, I have been borne unwillingly onward, carried away by the force of this ardor, directing all my thoughts and cares toward music, and still burning with a wonderful zeal to learn it with full understanding. Day and night my ears seem to be filled with sweet modulation, so that there seems to me to be no ground whatever for doubting the genuineness of my vocation. Nor do I shrink from the severity of the task, which with nature's aid I am confident of mastering without difficulty. For I have heard it said by a certain old man that study is rather a pleasure than a task.

(A) I am wonderfully delighted to perceive how your nature is inclined. I shall raise just one more difficulty; if this can be resolved, I shall inscribe you among my disciples.

(J) Speak freely, honored master. But I am certain that I shall not be deterred from my purpose, either by the cause you have in mind or by any other.

(A) Are you perhaps tickled by the hope of future riches and of abundance of private possessions in wishing to embrace this mode of life? If that is the case, take my advice and change your purpose. For not Plutus but Apollo presides over Parnassus. Those who are inspired by covetousness and seek the way to wealth must follow a different road.

(J) Not at all. I wish you to be persuaded that the compass of my wish is none other than the very love of music, free from any desire of gain. In addition, I recall having been very often admonished by my teacher that if we are content with a modest way of life, we shall wish to be more zealous for virtue, fame, and distinction than for means, for virtue is its own reward.

(A) I am incredibly pleased to have found a youth after my own heart. But do you know all the things concerning intervals, the classification of consonances and dissonances, the varieties of motions, and the four rules,[2] which have been said in the preceding book?

---

2 The four "cardinal" rules are the following: (1) one proceeds from perfect consonance to perfect by contrary or oblique motion; (2) from perfect consonance to imperfect by all three motions (parallel, contrary, or oblique); (3) from imperfect consonance to perfect by contrary or oblique motion; (4) from imperfect consonance to imperfect by all three motions.

(J) So far as I know, I think that not one of them is hidden from me.

(A) Then let us proceed to our work, taking our beginning from God himself, thrice greatest, the fount of all sciences.

(J) Before we begin our lessons, permit me first, revered master, to ask what is to be understood by the name counterpoint, a very common word, which I so frequently hear from the lips not only of the skilled but even of those ignorant of music.

(A) You are right to ask, for this indeed is to be the chief object of our study and labor. You must know that in old times points were set down instead of the modern notes, so that a composition with points set down against points used to be called counterpoint. This term is now used in spite of the change in the notes, and the name of counterpoint is understood to mean a composition elaborated according to the rules of art. Counterpoint as a genus comprises a number of species, which we shall successively examine. Meanwhile, let us begin with the simplest species, namely:

First Exercise—First Lesson

OF NOTE AGAINST NOTE

(J) Through your kindness, my first question has been satisfactorily answered. Now tell me, simply, what this first species of counterpoint is— the species note against note.

(A) I shall tell you. It is the simplest combination of two or more voices and of notes of equal value, consisting wholly of consonances. The species of the notes is immaterial, provided all are of the same value. But inasmuch as the semibreve is the most readily understood, I have thought it advantageous for us to use it in these exercises. With God's help, therefore, let us begin with the combining of two voices, setting down as our foundation some cantus firmus, either freely invented or taken from a choir book. For example:

To each of these notes is to be given, in the cantus above, its particular consonance, observing the considerations of the motions and rules expressed at the end of the preceding book and employing chiefly contrary and oblique motion, through the use of which we shall not easily fall into error. Greater precaution will be necessary in progressing from one note to another in parallel motion, in which case, the danger of error being greater, we must also pay greater attention to the rules.

(J) From the clarity of the motions and rules, all that you have just said seems familiar to me. Yet I recall your making the distinction that, among the consonances, some are perfect, others imperfect; it seems to me, therefore, that I need to know whether some distinction is also to be made in using them.

(A) Have patience; I shall tell you all. There is indeed a great difference between the perfect and the imperfect consonances; here, however, aside from the consideration of motion and that more imperfect than perfect consonances are to be employed, their use is wholly identical, excepting at the beginning and end, both of which ought to consist of perfect consonance.

(J) Are you willing, beloved master, to explain the reasons why more imperfect than perfect consonances are to be employed in this connection and why the beginning and end ought to consist of perfect consonances?

(A) By your eagerness, praiseworthy as it is, I am virtually obliged to discuss certain things out of their turn. I shall discuss them none the less, but not fully, lest, overburdened at the outset by the variety of so many things, your mind be confused. Know, then, that for reasons to be discussed elsewhere, the imperfect consonances are more harmonious than the perfect. Hence, if a combination of this species, in two parts only and in other respects most simple, were to be filled with perfect consonances, it would necessarily appear empty and wholly devoid of harmony. As regards the beginning and end, accept this reasoning. The beginning is the sign of perfection, the end, of repose. Hence, since the imperfect consonances are both devoid of perfection and incapable of concluding an ending, the beginning and end ought to consist of perfect consonances. Observe, finally, that if the cantus firmus is situated in the lower part, a major sixth is to be given to the penultimate note, if in the upper part, a minor third.

(J) Are these things all that is required for this species of counterpoint?

(A) Not all, to be sure, but they suffice to lay the foundation. The rest will be made clear in correction. Make ready for work, therefore, and, having set down your cantus firmus as a foundation, try to erect above it in the soprano clef a counterpoint, following the procedure thus far explained.

(J) I shall do what I can.

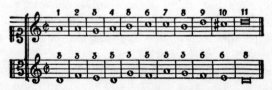

(A) You have hit the nail on the head. I marvel at your perspicacity and attention. But to what end have you placed figures both above the cantus and above the alto?

(J) By the figures placed above the alto I have wished to indicate the consonances employed, in order that, having before my eyes the motions from one consonance to another, I might depart less from the proper way of progressing. And those placed above the cantus, that is, 1, 2, 3, 4, 5, 6, 7, etc., merely indicate the numbering of the notes, to show you, revered master, that, if I hit the mark, I did this not by chance but by design.

You directed me to begin with perfect consonance; this I did, using a fifth. From the first note to the second, that is, from a fifth to a third, or from perfect to imperfect consonance, I progressed in oblique motion, although this might have been done in all three ways. From the second note to the third, namely, from a third to a third, or from imperfect to imperfect consonance, I employed parallel motion, following the rule which says: from imperfect to imperfect consonance in all three motions. From the third note to the fourth, or from a third, an imperfect consonance, to a fifth, a perfect one, I went in contrary motion, according to the rule saying: from imperfect to perfect consonance in contrary motion. From the fourth note to the fifth, or from perfect to imperfect consonance, I progressed in parallel motion, the rule permitting. From the fifth note to the sixth, that is, from imperfect to perfect consonance, the rule so directing, I employed contrary motion. From the sixth note to the seventh the progression was by oblique motion, not subject to any error. From the seventh note to the eighth, or from imperfect to imperfect consonance, I went on in parallel motion. From the eighth note to the ninth, as from imperfect to imperfect consonance, any motion was feasible. From the ninth note to the tenth the case was the same, for the tenth note, that is, the penultimate, forms a major sixth, as you directed, the cantus firmus being in the lower part. From the tenth note to the eleventh I continued by following the rule which teaches that, in proceeding from imperfect to perfect consonance, one uses contrary motion. The eleventh note, as final, is, as you have taught, a perfect consonance.

(A) In this you have proved an excellent judge. So be of good cheer; if you have so implanted the three motions and the four different rules in your memory that, having even a little reflected on them, you do not depart from them, an easy road to further progress lies open to you. Now continue, leaving the cantus firmus in the alto as it is, and set the tenor below as a counterpoint, with the difference, however, that, just as in the previous example you measured the relation of the consonances to the cantus firmus by ascending, you now measure it by descending from the cantus firmus to the bass.

(J) This seems to me more difficult to do.

(A) It seems so. I recall having also observed this same difficulty in other students; it will, however, be less difficult if you observe, as I have said, that the relation of the consonances is to be found by counting from the cantus firmus to the bass.

(J) Why is it, revered master, that you have marked my first and second notes with the sign of error? Have I not begun with a fifth, a perfect consonance? And have I not gone on to the second note, namely, a third, in parallel motion, as permitted by the rule which says: from perfect to imperfect consonance in any motion? Free me at once, I beg you, from the despair with which I am oppressed, for I am thoroughly ashamed!

(A) Do not despair, beloved son, for the first error did not occur through any fault of yours, since you had not yet been given the precept that the counterpoint must be adapted to the same mode in which the cantus firmus is, a rule I would have given to you now. For, in the preceding example, since the cantus firmus is in D la sol re, as evident from its beginning and end, and you have begun in G sol re ut, it is clear that you have led your beginning out of the mode; to correct this I have set, in place of your fifth, an octave, of the same mode as the cantus firmus.

(J) I rejoice that this error, from henceforth to be borne in mind, occurred through inexperience and not through carelessness. But what is the nature of my other error, indicated at the second note?

(A) In this case, the error is not with respect to the first note, but with respect to the third. You have progressed from a third to a fifth in parallel motion, contrary to the rule which says: from imperfect to perfect consonance in contrary motion; the error is easily corrected if the second note stands still below, in oblique motion, on D la sol re and forms a tenth, in which case the progression from the second note to the third, namely, from a tenth to a fifth, or from imperfect to perfect consonance, occurs in contrary motion, as the rule provides. I would not have you discouraged by this little error, for it is scarcely possible for the beginner to be so attentive that he commits no errors at all. Practice is the master of all things. In the meantime, be content that you have done the rest correctly, above all, that, the cantus firmus being in the upper part, you have given to the penultimate note a minor third, as I directed a little while ago.

(J) So that I may in time pay more attention to this rule and bear it more firmly in mind, are you willing to explain the reason why one is forbidden to go from imperfect to perfect consonance in parallel motion?

(A) I shall explain this. It is because in such case two fifths follow immediately on one another, one of them open or evident, the other closed or hidden, this last made manifest by division, as I shall show you now in an example:

The ability to make such divisions is an essential part of the art of singing, especially of solo singing. The same is also to be understood of the progression from the octave to the fifth in parallel motion, in which case two fifths again follow immediately on one another for the same reason, as the example shows:

Here you see how, by dividing the leap of the fifth, two fifths are disclosed, one of which, before the division, was hidden. From this can be concluded that the legislators of any art have ordained nothing needless or not founded on reason.

(J) I see this and am astonished.

(A) Now continue and, repeating this same exercise, go through all the modes contained within the octave, following the natural order step by step. You have begun with D; now there follow E, F, G, A, and C.

(J) Why have you omitted B, the note between A and C?

(A) Because it does not have a consonant fifth and for this reason cannot constitute a mode, as we shall explain more fully in the proper place. Let us look at an example:

Inasmuch as this fifth consists only of two tones and as many semitones, it is a false or dissonant fifth, for the true or consonant fifth, as explained in our first book, consists of three tones and a semitone.

(J) Can I not make a consonant fifth from this false one by adding a flat to the lower note or a sharp to the upper, as in this example:

(A) You can indeed, but in such case, your fifth being foreign to the diatonic genus, you will have no longer a natural mode, the only variety with which we are at present concerned, but a transposed one, regarding which in its proper place.

(J) Do these modes differ from one another?

(A) Indeed they do, and in the highest degree. For the different situation of the semitones of each octave also gives rise to a different species of melody, something which does not at present concern you. Come, therefore, and, resuming your exercise, build a counterpoint above the cantus firmus, which I shall now write out for you in E.

You have done it just right. Now, putting the cantus firmus in the upper part, contrive a counterpoint below in the tenor.

(J) What, have I erred again? If this is what happens to me in two part writing and in the simplest species, what will happen in composition for three, four, and more voices? Tell me, please, what error is indicated by the slur drawn from the sixth note to the seventh, with a cross over it.

(A) Do not be displeased by an error which you could not avoid, having never been warned against it, and do not be tormented in advance by a dread of composition for many voices, for experience will in time make you more careful and more expert by far. I do not doubt that you have often heard the trite proverb, "Mi contra fa est diabolus in musica";

this is what you have done in proceeding from your sixth note, fa, to your seventh, mi, by a leap of an augmented fourth, or tritone, an interval forbidden in counterpoint as difficult to sing and ill-sounding. Be of good cheer and proceed from the E mode to that on F.

Excellent, from beginning to end!

(J) This time, for a change, you wrote out the cantus firmus for me in the tenor clef; has this some significance?

(A) None whatever; I intend only that the different clefs should gradually become more familiar to you. Whereby is to be noted, none the less, that one ought always to combine adjacent clefs, in order that the simple consonances may be more readily distinguished from the composite. Now, form a counterpoint below the cantus firmus, in the bass.

Excellent, to be sure; but why have you crossed over the cantus firmus with your counterpoint from the fourth note to the seventh?

(J) Because I should otherwise have been obliged to proceed this far in parallel motion, a less elegant style of singing.

(A) Most observant, especially in that, considering the cantus firmus, in this case the lower part, as your bass, you measured the relation of the consonances by ascending from it. Let us go on to the G mode.

(J) Though I fashioned this counterpoint with the greatest possible attention, I remark again two signs indicating errors, namely, from the ninth note to the tenth, and from the tenth note to the eleventh.

(A) You seem to me impatient; at the same time I am highly delighted with this eagerness of yours not to depart from the rules. How do you expect to avoid these minutiae, regarding which you have never been taught? From the ninth note to the tenth you have employed a leap of a major sixth, forbidden in counterpoint, in which variety of composition all things ought to be most easy to sing. Then, from the tenth note to the eleventh, you have progressed from a tenth to an octave in conjunct motion, that is, ascending by step in the lower part and descending by step in the upper; this sort of octave, occurring at the beginning of the measure, is called *ottava battuta* in Italian, *thesis* in Greek, and is prohibited. Nevertheless, though I have repeatedly reflected at length on the reason for this prohibition, I have never been able to discover the cause of the fault or any difference that could explain why the octave is approved in this example:

but rejected in this one:

the octave being in either case the product of contrary motion. The case is different when a unison is produced in this way, namely, in a progression from a third to a unison, for example:

for the unison, resulting from equal proportion, is barely audible here and seems, as it were, absorbed and lost, for which reason it ought never to be used in this species of counterpoint excepting at the beginning and end. But to return to the so-called *ottava battuta* mentioned above, I leave it to you to avoid or employ it as you please, for it is of little consequence. But if, as in this example, a descent to the octave, taken conjunctly, is made by a leap from some more remote consonance, I regard it as intolerable, even in composition for many voices.

bad   bad

The same applies also, and with more force, to the unison, for example:

bad   bad

In composition for eight voices, as will be explained in the proper place, such leaps are scarcely to be avoided, especially in the basses or in those parts which serve in their stead. You have still to put the counterpoint of the last example in the lower part.

(J) What is the meaning of the N.B. placed above the first note of the counterpoint?

(A) It indicates that, in any other case, the progression by leap from a unison to another consonance would be improper, as is also the similar progression from another consonance to a unison, as we said a moment ago. But inasmuch as, in this case, the leap is part of the cantus firmus, which cannot be altered, it may be tolerated here. The case would be different if, not hampered by consideration for a plainsong, you could do as you pleased, working of your free will. But why have you added a sharp, not usually employed in the diatonic genus, to your eleventh note?

(J) Here it was my aim to use a sixth. But when I learned the art of singing I was told that fa tends to descend, mi to ascend; accordingly, since the progression from this sixth to the following third was an ascending one, I added a sharp in order that this ascent might be made more valid. Aside from this, if the eleventh note, F, were taken without a sharp, there would result a somewhat unfavorable relation to the thirteenth note, F, taken with a sharp.

(A) You have been most observant. I believe that every stumbling block has been removed. Go on, therefore, to A and C, the two remaining modes.

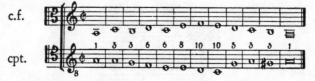

From these last two examples it is apparent that you have now noted everything one needs to know about this species. Therefore let us pursue the second species.

First Exercise—Second Lesson
OF THE SECOND SPECIES OF COUNTERPOINT

Before I undertake to explain this second species of counterpoint, know first that we are at present concerned with duple time, whose beat or measure is made up of two equal parts, one consisting in a lowering, the other in a raising of the hand. In Greek, the lowering of the hand is called *thesis,* the raising *arsis,* and for our greater convenience I propose that we use these two words alternately in the present exercise. This second species arises when against one semibreve are taken two minims, of which the one, occurring in the thesis, must always be consonant, while the other, in the arsis, may be dissonant if it moves by step from the preceding note to the following, but must be consonant if it results from a leap. Dissonance, then, is admitted in this species of counterpoint only by division, that is, when it fills the space intervening between two notes separated by a leap of a third. For example:

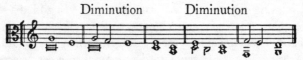

Nor need one consider whether this note of division is consonant or dissonant; it is sufficient that it fills the empty space between two notes separated by a leap of a third.

(J) Aside from this, is not what was taught in the first species of counterpoint about motion and progressions to be observed here also?

(A) Most strictly; except for the penultimate measure, which, in this species, should have first a fifth and then a major sixth, if the cantus firmus or plainsong is in the lower part, or first a fifth and then a minor third, if the cantus firmus is in the upper part. An example will show this clearly.

It will facilitate matters if you will consider the end before you begin to write. Now do you take the work in hand, employing the same cantus firmi as before.

(J) I shall do so. But I beg your indulgence should I fall into errors, for I have only a highly confused idea of this matter.

(A) Do what you can; I shall take nothing ill, and correction will readily dispel the darkness of obscurity.

(J) Not unwarranted was my dread of erring, for I remark two signs of rebuke, neither of which I understand, the first at the first note of the ninth measure, the second at the first note of the tenth measure, although I have progressed throughout from imperfect to imperfect consonance in contrary motion.

(A) You reason correctly, for the cause of these two errors is one and the same, and I do not wonder at your not knowing it, never having been thus taught. Note, therefore, that a leap of a third can save neither two fifths nor two octaves, for the intervening note, occurring in the arsis, is regarded as nonexistent, its small value and narrow interval preventing its so modifying the sound that the relation of the two fifths or octaves will not be perceived by the ear. Let us look at the last example, beginning at the eighth measure.

Now, if the note intervening, or occurring in the arsis, is regarded as nonessential, the situation stands thus revealed:

The same applies also to the octave.

idem

With a leap of a wider interval, for example, a fourth, fifth, or sixth, the case is different, for here the distance from the first note to the second seems to make the ear as it were oblivious to the sound of the notes occurring in the first and second theses. Let us look at the octaves of the last example, whose succession may be saved by a leap of a fourth.

good

For the same reason, it is because of this leap of a fourth that in your last exercise I marked the third to fourth measure with no sign of error, for leaving this note out of account, the situation stands thus:

This progression is contrary to the rule which says: from imperfect to perfect consonance in contrary motion; your leap of a fourth removes the error in this manner:

good

Let your preceding exercise be now corrected.

I see now that you have sufficiently in mind what has been said thus far. But before you take up the composition of this exercise with the counterpoint in the lower part, I shall propose to you certain things most useful to know, whose observance will greatly facilitate matters. First, in place of the first note of all you may put a rest of the value of half a measure; second, if it chance that the two parts are so close and so conjunct that you scarcely know which way to go and cannot possibly progress in contrary motion, you may manage by a leap of a minor sixth (which is permitted) or of an octave, as in the following examples:

Now continue, and build up the counterpoint of the preceding exercise in the lower part.

Now, again taking up all the cantus firmi set down in the first species of counterpoint, run through the remaining five modes, forming your counterpoint above and below.

(J) I recall your having said a little while ago that when a counterpoint of this species is in the lower part, the first note of the penultimate measure ought to be given a fifth; it appears, however, that in this variety of mode the fifth is not admitted, the relation *mi contra fa* making it a dissonance. For this reason I thought it wise to use the sixth in its place.

(A) Your observation pleases me exceedingly. Now continue, and pursue the same exercise through the remaining four modes.

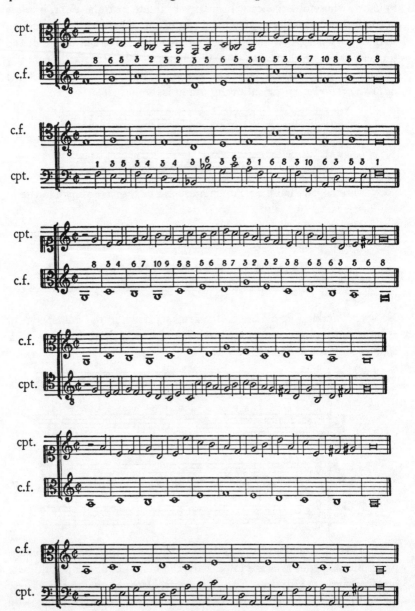

You have managed this quite well enough. Thus the gods bestow all things on the industrious; bear also this saying in mind: "The drop of water wears away the stone, not by its force, but by its constant falling," which teaches that untiring application to study is required for the attainment of the sciences, so that (as the saying goes) we should "allow no day to pass without its line." Aside from this, I have sought to teach you here to consider not only the measure in which you are working, but also those that follow.

(J) So you have indeed, revered master. For in composing the preceding exercises in counterpoint I should scarcely have known what to do if, considering one measure or another before deciding to write, I had not anticipated what was fitting there.

(A) Seeing you so wise, I rejoice marvelously and urge you again and again to overcome the great difficulty at the beginning by zealous and constant attention, not suffering yourself to be oppressed by the severity of your burden or to be enticed away from the assiduity of your study by flattery, as though you already understood a great deal. Do this, and little by little you will perceive the darkness giving place to light and the veil of obscurity being raised before you to some extent, and you will rejoice.

Here we ought also to speak of triple time, in which three notes are taken against one. Because of its facility, however, the matter is of little moment, and I do not think it worth while to devote a special lesson to it. You will find that a few examples only are sufficient for its understanding.

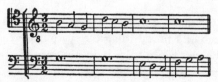

Here, since all three notes move by step, the intermediate one may be dissonant; it would be otherwise if one or other of the three were to leap, for in this case it is evident from what has already been said that all three should be consonant.

First Exercise—Third Lesson
OF THE THIRD SPECIES OF COUNTERPOINT

The third species of counterpoint is the combination of four semiminims against one semibreve. Note here, to begin with, that when five semiminims follow one another by step, ascending or descending, the first should be consonant while the second may be dissonant, the third must again be consonant while the fourth may be dissonant if the fifth is consonant, as in the examples:

The first situation suspending this rule is one in which the second and fourth notes chance to be consonant, in which case the third may be dissonant, as in the following examples:

Here, in each example, the third note is dissonant; we call it a division of the leap of a third. To lay bare the truth of this matter, let us reduce these examples to their essentials in this manner:

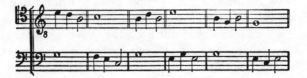

From this it is clear that the dissonant third note is nothing more than a division of the leap of a third, filling the space intervening between the second and third notes, which space is always open to division, that is, to being filled by the intervening note.

The second case in which we depart from the general rule is the changing note, in Italian *nota cambiata*, by means of which we progress by leap from a dissonant second note to a consonance, as seen in the following examples:

Strictly speaking, this leap of a third from the second note to the third ought to be made from the first note to the second, in which case the second note would form the consonance of the sixth in this manner:

In this situation, if a division were made from the first note to the second, the matter would stand thus:

But since in this species of counterpoint the quaver is not admitted, men of great authority have been pleased to approve the first example, in which the second note has the seventh, perhaps because of the greater elegance of the melody.

Finally it remains to show how the penultimate measure is to be contrived, for this measure presents much greater difficulty than the others. When the cantus firmus is in the lower part, it should be constituted in this manner:

But when the cantus firmus is in the upper part, it is to be made in the following way:

Now that you understand these things, together with those of which we have spoken previously in connection with the other species, I hope that this species of composition will be easy for you; at the same time, if you would avoid obstacles as you go along, I would admonish you again and again to have a special consideration for the measures that follow. Take up your work, then, pursuing in order all the cantus firmi set down in the first lesson.

Why have you sometimes used a b-flat, a sign scarcely usual in the diatonic genus with which we are concerned?

(J) It seemed to me that some harshness would otherwise proceed from the relation *mi contra fa*. Nor did I think it prejudicial to the diatonic genus, since it was introduced, not essentially, but accidentally and from necessity.

(A) Well noted; for the same reason, even sharps are sometimes to be employed, though one must use special judgment in considering when and where. From the preceding examples it appears that you have what is required for this species sufficiently in mind. To keep our discussion within bounds I leave the three modes still remaining, G, A, and C, for you to pursue on your own account. Let us go on, then, to the

First Exercise—Fourth Lesson
OF THE FOURTH SPECIES OF COUNTERPOINT

This species arises when against one semibreve are taken two minims, these placed on one and the same degree and bound together by a tie; the first must occur in the arsis, the second in the thesis. It is usually called *ligature* or *syncope* and has two varieties—the consonant and the dissonant.

A consonant ligature is one whose two minims, in the arsis and in the thesis, are both consonant. Examples will make the matter clear.

Consonant Ligatures

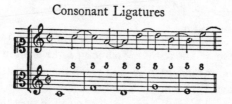

A dissonant ligature is one whose first note, in the arsis, is indeed consonant (an invariable rule), but whose second, in the thesis, is dissonant, as may be seen in the following examples:

Dissonant Ligatures

Further, since the dissonances here are not accidental or by division, as in the preceding species, but essential, occurring in the arsis; and since, as disagreeable to the ear, they are unable to cause any pleasure of themselves and must derive their charm from the consonances immediately following, in which they are resolved; for these reasons we must now speak

OF THE RESOLUTION OF DISSONANCES

Before I undertake to say how dissonances should be resolved, it will be useful to know that tied notes, bound as it were in chains, are nothing more than retardations of notes that follow, and that afterwards, as though liberated from their servitude, they are seen to enter into the free state. For this reason, dissonances should always be resolved in the nearest consonances, descending by step, as clearly seen in the following example:

Removing the retardation, the example stands thus:

From this may be concluded that it is easy to know in what consonance each dissonance should be resolved: namely, in the one found in the thesis of the measure immediately following when the retardation is removed. Whence it follows that, when the cantus firmus is in the lower part, the second must be resolved in the unison, the fourth in the third, the seventh in the sixth, and the ninth in the octave. This reasoning holds good to such an extent that it forbids a progression in ligature from a unison to a second or from a ninth to an octave, as seen in the following examples:

Removing the retardation in this manner, you will see a succession of two
unisons in the first example, of two octaves in the second:

The opposite occurs when the progression is from a third to a second or
from a tenth to a ninth, in this way:

These situations are correctly constituted, for they are valid even when
the retardation or ligature is removed in the following manner:

Having shown what dissonances may be employed and how they should
be resolved when the cantus firmus is in the lower part, we have now to
say what dissonances are admitted and by what means they should be
resolved when the cantus firmus is in the upper part. I say, therefore,
that one may here employ the second resolved in the third, the fourth
in the fifth, and the ninth in the tenth. For example:

(J) Why do you omit the seventh here? Is it because it cannot be employed when the cantus firmus is in the upper part? May it please you to tell me the cause of this.

(A) I confess that I omitted the seventh here deliberately. But I can give scarcely any reason for this but the great authority of the classical authors, to whom much is to be conceded in practice and of whom barely one is to be found who used the seventh resolved in this manner in the octave.

One might say perhaps that the seventh resolved in this manner was avoided as resolving in a perfect consonance, the octave, from which it could derive very little harmony, were it not that one frequently finds in these same authors the second, which is the inversion of the seventh, resolved in the unison, from which, as the most perfect of the consonances, a dissonance can derive still less harmony. In this particular, then, I think that the usage introduced by the great masters should be taken into consideration. Let us look at an example of the inverted seventh, or second, resolved in the unison.

(J) Before I go on to the lesson, have I your leave to inquire whether the retardation or ligature of the dissonance is also admitted in ascending? Is not the nature of the following examples the same:

(A) You raise a question more difficult to disentangle than the Gordian knot, which you cannot now understand without being taken beyond the boundary of this discipline and which is therefore to be answered at another time. Even though, when you remove the retardation, the nature of the thirds appears the same, there none the less remains a certain difference, which, as I have said, I shall explain in the proper place. In the mean-time, speaking ex cathedra, I tell you that all dissonances should be re-solved by descending in the nearest consonance. Aside from this, when the cantus firmus is in the lower part, the penultimate measure in this species is to be concluded by a seventh resolved in a sixth, when the cantus firmus is in the upper part, by a second resolved in a minor third, which will progress at the end to a unison.

(J) Is each measure to be given its ligature?

(A) Generally speaking, wherever possible. But you will sometimes happen on a measure in which no ligature is admissible, in which case it will have to be filled with single minims until an opportunity of making ligatures again presents itself. Come, apply yourself to your ligatures.

You have indeed done well; but why did you omit the ligature in your fifth measure? There would have been one if, after your third, you had used the fifth; this would have been the first note of your ligature, and, keeping it on the same degree, you would have had the second note, namely, the sixth, in the thesis of the following measure. I have said, you know, that no opportunity is to be overlooked.

(J) To be sure, I could have made one; but I omitted it deliberately in order not to fall into an odious repetition, for immediately before, in the third and fourth measures, I had used the same ligatures.

(A) A sufficiently prudent observation, for one must yield not a little to the nature of the melody and to the elegance of the progression. Con-tinue.

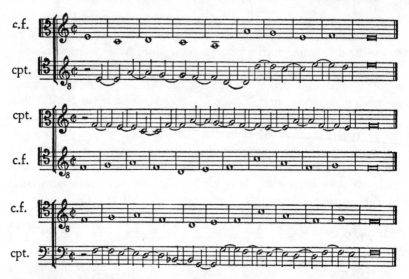

Let these examples suffice for the present. But since the ligatures contribute in no inconsiderable way to the seasoning of musical harmony, I
recommend to you not only that you pursue in this manner the cantus
firmi of the three remaining modes, but also that you invent others and
give yourself further exercise in this species, in which you will never have
exercise enough.

As a refinement belonging to the next species, I shall explain here in
advance that the ligatures of which we have spoken thus far may also be
made in another way; so made, they lose little of their essential character,
yet bring to the harmony a means of a more lively movement. For example:

From these examples it is quite clear that the first and third situations are
essential; those that follow, marked "idem," are variations, used for the
sake of the melody or of the movement. It is also usual to break the ligature in the following way:

Aside from this, one may in the next species occasionally interpolate two

quavers; these, however, are to be taken in the second and fourth parts
of the measure, never in the first and third.

These things being understood, let us go on to the

First Exercise—Fifth Lesson

OF THE FIFTH SPECIES OF COUNTERPOINT

This species is called florid counterpoint, because it should bloom like a
garden of little flowers with ornament of every kind, pleasant melody,
graceful easy movement, and an elegant variety of figures. For just as
in division we use all the other common species of arithmetic, such as
counting, addition, subtraction, and multiplication, so this species is
nothing more than an amassing and combining of the preceding species
of counterpoint, nor is there about it anything new to be taught, aside from
the elegance of the melody, with which I exhort and entreat you to take
the utmost care and pains, never losing sight of it.

(J) As far as within my power, I shall take pains, but I scarcely trust
myself to take up my pen, having no example before my eyes.

(A) Be of good cheer; I shall form the first example for you.

The counterpoints of the remaining cantus firmi I leave to you to be pat-
terned after this model.

Your work is industrious enough, and what pleases me not inconsiderably is that you have paid no little attention to writing a good melodic line and that at the beginning of the thesis you have frequently employed oblique motion or syncope, a labor which I would have further commended to you, since it brings the utmost grace to the counterpoint.

(J) I am immeasurably delighted to learn that the result of my application and effort does not altogether displease you, and, encouraged by your flattery, I believe myself on the point of making no inconsiderable progress in little time. Am I to pursue the remaining three modes in your presence or on my own account?

(A) Inasmuch as this species is more useful than I can say, I shall indeed ask you to complete the aforesaid three modes in my presence; at the same time I would admonish you to exercise yourself unceasingly more and more in this variety of composition.

(J) I shall always observe your counsel as a law.

What is indicated by the N.B. placed above the cantus in the fifth
measure of the last example?

(A) Do not distress yourself, for you have thus far heard nothing
about this from me. I tell you now, not indeed as a rule, but rather as a
counsel, that, when two semiminims are placed at the beginning of the
measure without a ligature immediately following, the melody takes on
the character of an ending. For this reason it will be advisable for you to
employ two semiminims at the beginning of the measure only in connection with a following ligature or to make easier a continuation with two
further semiminims as in the following example:

better

Now praise be to God, we have completed two-part writing, running
through all five species with an underlying cantus firmus. Now we are
to return to the beginning, namely to note against note in three parts, and
to see what is to be observed in each species and in what manner the combining of three parts ought to be arranged.

19. J. P. Rameau

Rameau was both the founder of the theory of harmony, in the modern sense of the term, and the most important French composer of the eighteenth century. He was born in 1683 at Dijon and occupied, at the beginning of the eighteenth century, the post of organist at the Cathedral of Clermont in the Auvergne. He soon abandoned this post, however, and went to Paris, where he published in 1706 his first book of pieces for the harpsichord. Later Rameau changed his residence several times, but in 1732 he settled down in Paris and lived there until his death in 1764.

With Rameau's return to the capital, the series of his great operatic successes began: in 1733, *Hippolyte et Aricie;* in 1735, *Les Indes galantes;* in 1737, *Castor et Pollux;* in 1739, *Les Fêtes d'Hébé* and *Dardanus,* etc. Aside from operas Rameau wrote a number of cantatas and motets, also pieces for the harpsichord, alone and in conjunction with other instruments.

As a theorist, Rameau published in 1722 his epoch-making *Traité de l'harmonie.* It was the first in a long list of writings that appeared between 1722 and 1760.

From the Traité de l'harmonie [1]

[*1722*]

Preface

IN WHATEVER progress music has made thus far, it appears that the more sensible the ear becomes of its marvelous effects, the less curious the mind is to fathom its true principles, so that one may say that, while experience has here acquired a certain authority, reason has lost its rights.

Such writings as have come down to us from the ancients make it very clear that reason alone enabled them to discover the greater part of music's properties; yet, though experience still obliges us to approve most of the

1 Text: The original edition (Paris, 1722), preliminary leaves 2–3, pp. 125–128, 138–143.

rules which they passed on, we neglect today all the advantages we might derive from reason in favor of the experience of ordinary practice.

If experience can apprise us of the different properties of music, it is in other respects not capable alone of permitting us to discover the principle of these properties with all the precision that belongs to reason; the consequences we derive from it are often false, or leave us at least with a certain doubt that only reason can dispel. How, for example, shall we be able to prove that our music is more perfect than that of the ancients, when it no longer seems to us capable of the effects which they attributed to theirs? Will it be by saying that the more familiar things become, the less surprise they cause, and that the rapture into which they could throw us when they were new degenerates insensibly as we accustom ourselves to it, becoming in the end mere amusement? This would at most presume its equality, not its superiority. But if, by the statement of a self-evident principle, from which we subsequently derived the due and certain consequences, we could make it clear that our music had reached a final stage of perfection which the ancients were far from realizing (the reader may refer on this point to Chapter 21 of Book 2),[2] we would in that case know what to believe, we would better perceive the force of the previous reflection, and, knowing by these means the limits of the art, we would abide by them the more willingly; persons of superior taste and genius would no longer be fearful of lacking the knowledge necessary for proficiency; in a word, the light of reason, thus dispelling the doubts into which experience may plunge us at any moment, would be a sure guarantee of the success we could promise ourselves.

If modern musicians (that is to say, musicians since Zarlino [a]) had applied themselves as the ancients did to giving reasons for what they practiced, they would have abandoned many preconceived ideas which are not to their advantage, and this would even have led them to give up those with which they are still too much occupied and of which they are having great difficulty in ridding themselves. Experience, then, is too much in favor with them, it somehow seduces them until it is the cause of the little pains they take to inform themselves properly about the beauties which it leads them to discover daily; their knowledge is not common property, they have not the gift of communicating it, and, since they do not at all

---

a Zarlino, a celebrated writer on music who wrote nearly one hundred and fifty years ago and of whom one finds very feeble imitations in the works on this subject that have appeared since his.

["More than with anyone else we ought to occupy ourselves with this author, for he has served posterity as a model and in practical matters we are constantly being referred to him as to one who for some musicians is still the oracle and whom M. de Brossard himself calls the 'Prince of modern musicians.' "—*Traité*, p. 18.]

2 "On the modes."

perceive this, they are often more astonished at one's not understanding them than they are at their not making themselves understood. This reproach is somewhat harsh, I admit, but I include it here because I perhaps still deserve it myself, despite all I have done to avoid it. However this may be, I have always wished that it might make on others the effect it has made on me. It is, then, for this reason, and above all to revive that noble rivalry which formerly flourished, that I have risked communicating to the public my recent researches in an art to which I have sought to give all the simplicity which is natural to it in order that the mind may comprehend its properties as easily as the ear is sensible of them.

No one man is capable of exhausting a subject as profound as this one; it is almost impossible for him not to be constantly overlooking something, despite all his pains; but at least the new discoveries which he may join to those already made known on the subject are so many paths marked out for those who may be able to pursue them further.

Music is a science which ought to have certain rules; these rules ought to be derived from a self-evident principle; and this principle can scarcely be known to us without the help of mathematics. I ought, too, to admit that, notwithstanding all the experience I may have been able to acquire for myself in music through having practiced it during a considerable period of time, it was only with the help of mathematics that my ideas disentangled themselves and that light replaced an obscurity that I had not previously recognized as such. If I did not know how to distinguish the principle from the rule, the principle soon offered itself to me in a way at once simple and convincing; the consequences with which it next supplied me led me to recognize in them as many rules, related through them to the principle. The true sense of these rules, their proper application, their relation to one another, and the order they ought to observe among themselves (the simplest serving as introduction to the less simple, and so on by degrees), finally the choice of terms; all this, I say, of which I had formerly been ignorant, developed in my mind with so much clarity and precision that I could not avoid concluding that it would be desirable (as someone said to me one day when I was applauding the perfections of our modern music) if the knowledge of the musicians of this century were to correspond to the beauties of their compositions. It is, then, not enough to be sensible of the effects of a science or of an art; it is necessary beyond this to comprehend them in such a way that one may make them intelligible; and it is to this end that I have chiefly applied myself in the body of this work.

. . . . . .

Book Two—Chapter 18

Observations on the Establishment of Rules, in Which is Taught
the Method of Composing a Fundamental Bass

ARTICLE I

ON THE ESTABLISHMENT OF RULES

We may judge of music only through the intervention of hearing, and reason has authority in it only in so far as it agrees with the ear; at the same time, nothing can be more convincing to us than their union in our judgments. Our nature is satisfied by the ear, our mind by reason; let us then judge of nothing excepting through their co-operation.

Experience offers us a number of harmonies, capable of an infinite diversity, by which we should always be confused, did we not look to another cause for their principle; this diversity sows doubts everywhere, and each of us, imagining that his ear cannot be deceived, wishes to be himself the sole judge. Reason, quite the other way, sets before us a single harmony, whose properties it easily determines if experience assist. Once experience confirms what reason authorizes, the latter ought to be given the upper hand, for nothing is more convincing than its decisions, especially when they are drawn from a principle as simple as the one it offers us. Let us rely, then, on reason alone, if this is possible, calling experience to its aid only to corroborate its proofs.

The first musicians—in a word, all those who confined themselves solely to speculation—admitted only the triad as universal principle. If Zarlino, joining practice to theory, spoke of sixth chords and six-four chords, we know already that these arise from it also. Beyond this, it is only a question of determining whether the dissonances cannot similarly be reduced to it, something easily proved, for all of them are generated by a new sound added to the primary harmony, which is always present in its full perfection. Thus reason alone still suffices to authorize this addition and to determine its use, the addition being naturally made by a *rule of three* or (as pointed out in Book I, Chapter 7, page 29) [3] by a new multiplication of the numbers which gave us our primary harmony. Hence—the rules of music being concerned only with the consonances and feasible dissonances, these consonances being all of them contained in the triad, these dissonances in the same harmony and in the seventh added to it—it is evident that our rules ought to be based chiefly on the primary harmony and that which is formed by the added seventh. And if, after having derived the

---

8 "On harmonic division or the origin of the harmonies."

consequences of a principle so simple and so natural, we follow step by step that which has been taught and practiced, especially where this has been skillfully done, accommodating ourselves always to that which experience leads us to approve, who can doubt for a moment that this principle is not the true object of our rules?

See to this end what Zarlino says on the subject of the fundamental bass and its progression, the progression it imposes on the other parts, and the progression of the thirds, the consonances in general, and the dissonances; note that he has omitted those dissonances which we call *major*,[4] that he has not properly defined the *interrupted cadence*,[5] that he does not speak at all of the *irregular cadence*[6] or of the inversion of harmonies (although he teaches its use by those of the sixth, second, etc.), that he cites without qualification the chord of the ninth (which we treat as inadmissible except *by supposition*),[7] that he is not on solid ground with his *modes*, that (as we shall see in Chapter 21) his music can accordingly not profit by the perfections with which ours is graced, and finally that his examples do not agree with his text. Examine his reasons, whether they be reasons or words and whence he derives them; examine his explanations, his comparisons, and the sources of his knowledge; after this, draw proper conclusions from them and you will actually discover that all harmony and all melody must turn on the two harmonies we have proposed and, what is more, on their lowest sound (which is in either case the same) and, as we have maintained to this point, on its progression. Then hear the music of the most skillful masters, examine it, and put it to the test by means of a fundamental bass, following the explanation we shall give at the end of this chapter; you will find only the triad and the chord of the seventh—you will find, I say, only the tonic note and its dominant, provided you are well acquainted with *modulation* and able to distinguish all the changes of key, it being further noted that the sixth step often replaces the dominant,[8] though only in minor keys.

---

4 "Dissonances are either major or minor, like the thirds from which they are derived and whose properties they share. The major are derived from the leading tone and become such only when combined with the minor dissonances, which are derived from the seventh."—*Table des termes.*

5 "A cadence is called 'broken' [or 'interrupted'] when the dominant, in the bass or in one of the other parts, ascends one step."—*Table des termes.*

6 "A cadence is called 'irregular' when the bass ascends a fifth. This succession results in a dissonance which proceeds irregularly but which can always be suppressed."—*Table des termes.* The dissonance to which Rameau refers is that of the "added sixth," as in the succession II $\frac{6}{5}$—I. In later writings Rameau also calls this succession the "imperfect" cadence.

7 " 'Supposition,' a term . . . applied to sounds which alter the perfection of harmonies in that by their addition the harmonies exceed the compass of an octave. There are only two harmonies 'by supposition' and from these are derived two others."—*Table des termes.* The two harmonies "by supposition" are those of the ninth and eleventh; derived from them are those of the "augmented fifth" (III $\frac{9}{5}$) and "augmented seventh" (I $\frac{11}{7}$), as Rameau calls them. In his *Génération harmonique* (1737) Rameau explains "supposition" more precisely as resulting in "a dissonant harmony arranged by thirds, below which is added a third or a fifth." "Harmonies by supposition" are incapable of inversion.

8 Rameau first uses the term "subdominant" in his *Nouveau système* (1726).

The principle of harmony is present not only in the triad and in the chord of the seventh formed from it, but still more precisely in the lowest sound of these two harmonies, which is, so to speak, the *harmonic center* to which all other sounds must be related. This also is one of the reasons why we have found it necessary to base our system on the division of a single string, inasmuch as such a string, giving us our lowest sound, is the principle of all those that arise from its division, just as the unit with which it is compared is the principle of all the numbers.

To perceive that all the harmonies and their different properties originate in the triad and the chord of the seventh is not enough; beyond this it is necessary to note that all the properties of these two primary harmonies depend absolutely on the *harmonic center* and its progression. The intervals of which they are composed are intervals only in relation to this *center,* which makes use of the same intervals to form its progression, on which progression the order and progression of the two primary harmonies alone depend. These intervals are all comprised in the third, fifth, and seventh, for if others occur they are either inversions (like the sixth, fourth, and second), or extensions of one or the other (like the ninth and eleventh), or alterations (like the tritone and false fifth)—we make no mention of the octave, knowing that it is a mere duplication. This reduction of the intervals has yet another exact relation to that of the harmonies: the inverted intervals form inverted harmonies, the extended intervals form harmonies "by supposition," the altered intervals form harmonies "by borrowing," [9] the whole arising from our three primary intervals, from which the fundamental harmonies are formed, and related solely to our *harmonic center.*

Even this is not enough; the ear not only sanctions these fundamental harmonies but—once their progression has been determined by that of their lowest and fundamental sound—finds always agreeable and never otherwise everything that conforms to this fundamental, whether it be understood, inverted, "supposed," or "borrowed," reason and hearing agreeing in this to such an extent that not one exception is to be found.

How marvelous this principle is in its simplicity! So many harmonies, so many beautiful melodies, this infinite diversity, these expressions, so beautiful and so proper, these sentiments, so well contrived—all this arises from two or three intervals arranged in thirds whose principle is summed up in a single sound:

---

[9] " 'Borrowing' is a new term, used to distinguish a particular class of harmonies which can occur only in minor keys."—*Table des termes.* "We call these harmonies 'borrowed' in that they borrow their perfection from a sound which they do not contain."—*Traité,* p. 43. The chief "borrowed" harmony is that of the diminished seventh; from this Rameau derives "by supposition" III $\frac{5}{4}$ and 1 $\frac{7}{6}$

Fundamen-	Third	Fifth	Seventh
tal sound			
I	3	5	7

The reader ought already to be persuaded by the foregoing remarks, and the rules which we shall establish on our principle will serve to convince him.

. . . . . .

Chapter 19

CONTINUATION OF THE PRECEDING CHAPTER, IN
WHICH IT APPEARS THAT MELODY ARISES FROM HARMONY

At first sight it would seem that harmony arises from melody, inasmuch as the melodies which the single voices produce become harmony when they are combined; it has, however, been necessary to determine in advance a path for each of these voices in order that they may agree together. No matter, then, what order of melody we may observe in the individual parts, taken together they will scarcely form a tolerable harmony (not to say that it is impossible that they should do so) unless this order has been dictated to them by the rules of harmony. Nevertheless, to make the whole theory of harmony more intelligible, we begin by teaching the method of constructing a melody, and supposing that we have made some progress with this, whatever ideas we may have formed concerning it are set aside the moment it is a question of joining to it another part; we are no longer masters of the melody, and while we are occupied in seeking out the path which one part should follow in relation to another, we often lose sight of the one we proposed to ourselves, or are at least obliged to change it, lest the restraint this first part imposes on us prevent our always giving to the others a melody as perfect as we might wish. It is, then, harmony that guides us, not melody. A learned musician may indeed propose to himself a beautiful melody suitable for harmonization. But whence has he this happy faculty? Cannot nature have provided it? Assuredly. And if, on the other hand, nature has refused him this gift, how may he succeed? Only by means of the rules. But whence are we to derive these? This is what we must determine.

Does the first division of a string offer us at once two intervals from which we might form a melody? Surely not, for a man who sings only a given note and its octave can construct no very acceptable melody. The second and third divisions, from which arise the whole of harmony, do

not furnish us with sounds more suitable for melody, for a melody composed only of thirds, fourths, fifths, sixths, and octaves would still be far
from perfect. It is harmony, then, that is generated first; it is accordingly
from harmony that we must necessarily derive our rules of melody, and
we shall be doing just this if we single out the harmonic intervals of which
we have spoken in order to form from them a fundamental progression.
And although this is not yet melody, when these intervals are taken in succession above one of their number, following a natural diatonic course laid
down for them by their very progression as they serve one another as
mutual foundation, we derive from their consonant and diatonic progression all the melody we need. Hence we must know the harmonic intervals
before the melodic ones, and all the melody one can teach a beginner (if
we may call this melody) consists in these consonant intervals. We shall
see in Chapter 21 that, although it arises from harmony, the ancients still
derived their *modulation* from melody alone.

Once we are familiar with this consonant progression, it takes but little
more effort to add three sounds above the sound which serves as bass than
to add only one. This is how we account for the two procedures. Above a
given bass you may place the third, fifth, or octave—or you may place
the third, fifth, and octave; to make use of any one of these intervals you
must know them all, and if you know them all it is no more difficult to
use them together than to use them separately. Furthermore, if the bass
descends a third, the part which had the third before now has the fifth—
we can account for the matter in no other way. But if, in these different
progressions of the bass, we find the third here, the fifth there, and the
octave in a third place, we must always know what ought to follow, according to the momentary progression of the bass. Hence, without realizing it, we teach composition in four parts while we explain it only in two.
Then, since I must know what follows each consonance, according to the
momentary progression of the bass, each of the consonances occurring in
turn, it is no more difficult to use them together than to use them individually. The more so since, if I am unable to distinguish them when they
are together, I can only confine myself to each one individually. Thus,
by one means or another, I find a way of composing a harmony perfect in
its four parts, from which I then derive all the knowledge necessary for
arriving at perfection. Besides, the explanation which we add makes mis-
takes impossible, if we may rely on the experience which various persons
who knew only the notes have had in this, and who, after a second reading
of our rules, have composed a harmony as perfect as one could wish.

Finally, if the composer can give himself the satisfaction of hearing his productions,[b] his ear will form itself little by little, and, once he has become sensible of the perfect harmony toward which his beginnings lead him, he may be certain of a success which depends without qualification on these primary principles alone.

After this, there can be no doubt that, when four parts are once familiar to us, we shall be able to reduce them to three and to two. But what rule can teach us to compose in two parts, even when we have thoroughly mastered it, something which is nearly impossible, seeing that we are guided in this by no foundation and that everything that can be taught about it is sterile, either because our memory is incapable of retaining it or because it is only with difficulty that everything is included, it being necessary to add at the end the words *Caetera docebit usus?* [10] Would we progress from two to three and four parts? What is taught about this is so little that we shall need genius and taste as consummate as that of the great masters themselves if we are to understand their teachings. On the subject of four-part writing, Zarlino [c] says that it can scarcely be taught on paper and that he leaves it to the discretion of the composers, who can form themselves on his previously stated rules for two and three parts. Our ideas are exactly opposite, for we have just said that harmony can only be taught in four parts, where all its properties are summed up (as we have maintained all along) in two harmonies, and that it is very easy to reduce these four parts to three and to two; whereas Zarlino, who does not even define his two and three parts precisely, admits his inability to define four, after having agreed that perfect harmony consists in four parts, which he compares (Chapter 58, fol. 281) [11] to the four elements. In conclusion we shall say that, if the reader has failed to obtain a perfect understanding of the rules of harmony which we have given thus far, the principle which we have adopted is a sure means of attaining such an understanding and will permit nothing to escape.

Chapter 20

OF THE PROPERTIES OF HARMONIES

It is certain that harmony can arouse in us different passions, depending on the particular harmonies that are employed. There are harmonies that are sad, languishing, tender, agreeable, gay, and striking; there are also

---

b It is partly with this in mind that we give rules for accompanying.

c *Istituzioni armoniche,* Part 3, Chapter 65, fol. 310. ["Necessary observations on compositions for four and more voices."—Ed.]

10 Experience will teach the rest.

11 "The method to be followed in composing music for more than two voices, and the names of the parts."

certain successions of harmonies for the expression of these passions; and although it is quite foreign to my purpose I shall give of this as full an explanation as experience has given me.

Consonant harmonies are to be found everywhere but should be employed most frequently in music expressing gaiety and magnificence; and, since we cannot avoid intermingling some dissonant harmonies, we must contrive that these arise naturally, that they are as far as possible prepared, and that the most prominent parts, the soprano and bass, are always consonant with respect to one another.

Sweetness and tenderness are sometimes well enough expressed by prepared minor dissonances.

Tender complaints sometimes require dissonances "by borrowing" and "by supposition," rather minor than major, such major dissonances as may occur being confined rather to the inner parts than to the outer.

Languishings and sufferings are perfectly expressed by dissonances "by supposition" and especially by chromatic progressions, regarding which we shall speak in our next book.

Despair and all passions having to do with anger or which have anything striking about them require unprepared dissonances of every kind; above all, the major dissonances should be situated in the soprano. In certain expressions of this nature it is even effective to pass from one key to another by means of unprepared major dissonances, yet in such a way that the ear is not offended by too great a disproportion; like all other such procedures, this can accordingly be carried out only with considerable discretion, for if we do nothing but pile dissonance on dissonance wherever there is place for it, it will be a much greater fault than allowing only consonance to be heard. Dissonance, then, is to be employed with considerable discretion, and, when we feel that its harshness is not in agreement with the expression, we ought even to avoid allowing it to be heard, in those harmonies that cannot do without it, by suppressing it adroitly, dispersing the consonances which make up the rest of the harmony through all the parts; for one ought always to bear in mind that the seventh, from which all the dissonances arise, is simply a sound added to the triad which does not at all destroy the basis of the harmony and may always be suppressed when we think it appropriate.

Melody has not less force than harmony in expression, but it is almost impossible to give certain rules for it, since good taste is here more influential than other considerations. Hence we leave to happy geniuses the pleasure of distinguishing themselves in this particular, the source of almost all the force of the sentiments, and hope that skillful persons, for whom we have said nothing new, will not resent our having revealed secrets of which they have wished, perhaps, to be the sole proprietors, for our limited intelligence does not permit us to rival them in this last degree of perfection, without which the most beautiful harmony becomes insipid and through which they are always in a position to excel. As we shall see in what follows, it is only when we know how to arrange a series of harmonies appropriately that we can derive from them a melody suited to the subject, but taste is, in this, always the prime mover.

It is here that the ancients would appear to have excelled, if we may believe their accounts: one by his melody made Ulysses weep, another obliged Alexander to take up arms, still another rendered a furious young man mild and gentle. In a word, one sees on every hand the astonishing effects of their music, regarding which Zarlino is most plausible when he says that with them the word "harmony" often signified nothing more than simple melody and that all these effects arose more from an energetic discourse whose force was intensified by their manner of reciting or singing it and which can certainly not have enjoyed all the diversity which perfect harmony, of which they were ignorant, has obtained for us today. Their harmony, he says further,[d] consisted only in a triad, which he calls a "symphony," above which they sang all sorts of melodies indifferently, very much like what is played on our musettes and vielles.

For the rest, a good musician ought to surrender himself to all the characters he wishes to depict and, like a skillful actor, put himself in the place of the speaker, imagine himself in the localities where the different events he wishes to represent occur, and take in these the same interest as those most concerned; he ought to be a good speaker, at least by nature; and he ought to know when the voice should be raised or lowered, by more or by less, in order to adapt to this his melody, his harmony, his modulation, and his movement.

---

d *Ibid.*, Chapter 79, fol. 356. ["Of the things which contribute to the composition of the genera." —Ed.]

Index

Acciajoli, Cavaliere Filippo, 128
Addison, Joseph, 151–57
Agazzari, Agostino, 64–71
Alexander the Great, 48, 214
Alsace, 83
Amphion, 162
Archilei, Vittoria, 11, 15
Arigoni, Cardinal Pompeo, 33
Arion, 73, 169
Ariosti, Attilio, Il Coriolano, 169n.
Ariosto, 159
Aristotle, 53n., 161
Aristoxenus, 14n., 42, 53n.
Artusi, G. M., 33–44, 45n., 46–52
Athens, 139
Augsburg, 85, 89, 90
Austria, 83

Bacilly, Benigne de, 141
Bardi, Giovanni de', 3, 10–11, 12, 18, 48
Bardi, Pietro de', 3–6
Bassani, G. B., 121
Bavaria, 83
Beauchamps, Pierre, 116
Boësset, Antoine, 144
Boethius, 42, 53
Bohemia, 83
Boileau, Nicolas, 131n., 153
Bologna, 121
Bonnet, Jacques, 120n., 129n.
Bononcini, G. B., 121
  "Mai non si vidde ancor" (Camilla), 119
Bottrigari, Ercole, 49
Brandi, Antonio, 15
Brossard, Sébastien de, 205n.

Caccini, Giulio, 4, 5, 8n., 10–12, 16, 17–32, 48
  Aria di romanesca, 28, 31

"Deh, dove son fuggiti," 19n., 29–30, 31
"Dovrò dunque morire," 11, 19
Euridice, 10–12, 16
"Itene all'ombra," 10, 19
"Perfidissimo volto," 11, 19
"Vedrò il mio sol," 11, 19
Campra, André:
  Hésione, 140
  Tancrède, 128n.
Carissimi, Giacomo, 121, 135n.
Cassani (singer), 153
Cavaliere, Emilio del, 13, 48
Charpentier, Marc Antoine, 135
Chiabrera, Gabriello, 19
Christian IV of Denmark, 74n., 79
Christian, Prince (son of Christian IV), 74–76, 77
Cicero, 153
Cini, Francesco, 15
Clemens non Papa, 48
Cleonides, 14n.
Colasse, Pascal, Thétis et Pélée, 132
Corelli, Arcangelo, 89, 121, 127, 146
Corneille, 132
Corsi, Jacopo, 5, 8, 13, 15
Crecquillon, Thomas, 48

Dante, 4, 8, 159
Demodocus, 162
Descouteaux, Philibert, 115n.
Doni, G. B., 3, 5–6
Dryden, John, 152n.
Dumény (singer), 125

England, 16n., 153, 154, 157
Euripides, 161

Ferinni (singer), 126
Ferrara, 33n., 34n.
Ferrara, Benedetto, 78n.

Ficino, Marsilio, 47n., 50n.
Fiorini, Hippolito, 34
Florence, 3, 4, 5, 11, 18, 19, 121
Fontanella, Count Alfonso, 15, 48
Fontenelle, Bernard Le Bovier de, 131n.
France, 51, 82–83, 89, 113–29, 131n., 136, 138–39, 142, 144n., 145–47
Freneuse, Le Cerf de La Viéville, Seigneur de, 120n., 124n., 128n., 129–47
Fux, Johann Joseph, 175–203

Gabrieli, Andrea, 40
Gabrieli, Giovanni, 73
Gaetani (lutenist), 127
Gagliano, Marco da, 5n.
Galen, 48
Galilei, Galileo, 3
Galilei, Vincenzo, 3–4
Galliard, J. E., 113n.
Gastoldi, Giovanni Giacomo, 40
Germany, 76–77, 79, 82–83, 84, 87, 88, 89, 97, 99, 109–10
Gesualdo, Carlo, Prince of Venosa, 48
Giacomelli (Jacomelli), G. B., 15
Giovanelli, Ruggiero, 40
Giusti, Jacopo, 16
Gogava, Antonius, 42n.
Gombert, Nicolas, 48
Goretti, Antonio, 34
Goths, 4
Greece, 3, 7, 11, 14, 15, 49, 159, 161
Guarino Veronese, 41

Handel, George Frederick, 153
  Agrippina, 166n., 168n.
  Amadigi, 151n.
  Il Pastor fido, 169n.
  Rinaldo, 151n., 152–53, 154
  Rodelinda, 169n.
Hawkins, Sir John, 113n.
Hesiod, 169
Hill, Aaron, 153n.
Hippocrates, 48
Homer, 8
Horace, 39, 41, 43, 46, 86, 151, 161
Hotteterre family, 115n.

Ingegneri, Marc' Antonio, 48
Italy, 16n., 51, 76, 79, 80–82, 84, 89, 91–92, 109, 113–29, 131n., 135n., 142, 145–47, 153, 157

Johann Georg I, Elector of Saxony, 72, 74n.
Johann Georg II, Elector of Saxony, 72–74, 78–80
Josquin Desprez, 48
  Missa Faisant regrets, 52

Krünner, Christian Leopold, 86

La Barre, J. C., 146
La Bruyère, Jean de, 135, 144n.
La Fosse, Antoine de, 143n.
Lambert, Michel, 144
Lapi, Giovanni, 15
La Rochoix (singer), 125
La Rue, Pierre de, 48
Lasso, Orlando di, 40
Legrenzi, Giovanni, 121
Leopold I, Emperor, 85, 128n.
Lorenzani, Paolo, 146
Louis XIV, 145
Lully, Jean Baptiste, 83, 87, 89, 116, 120, 121, 122, 129n., 131n., 132–35, 138, 144, 145–46
  Acis et Galatée, 132–33, 136
  "Amour que veux-tu" (Amadis), 136, 138
  Armide, 136, 139, 147
  Atys, 116
  "Bois épais" (Amadis), 135, 136
  Cadmus, 146
  Isis, 116, 138n.
  Persée, 116, 134, 139–40
  Phaëton, 134
  Proserpine, 138
  Roland, 138n.
  Thésée, 137–38
Luzzaschi, Luzzasco, 34, 48

Malvezzi, Cristofano, 4
Mancini, Francesco, L'Idaspe fedele, 154n.
Marcello, Benedetto, 158–71
Marchand, Jean Baptiste, 146
Marenzio, Luca, 48
Maria Medici, Queen of France, 7, 16
Martial, 154
Masson, Charles, 132n.
Mattheson, Johann, 169n.
Melani, Jacopo, 121
Ménage, Gilles, 144
Merula, Tarquinio, 78n.

Merulo, Claudio, 40
Milan, 121
Mocenigo, Girolamo, 54
Molière, 133n., 137n., 144n.
Montalvo, Don Grazia, 15
Montausier, Charles de Sainte-Maure, duc de, 132
Monte, Philippe de, 40
Monteverdi, Claudio, 5, 34–44, 45–65, 76
   "Anima mia perdona," 34n., 35
   Arianna, 5n.
   "Armato il cor," 77, 78n.
   "Cruda Amarilli," 34n., 35, 36–38, 41–44, 46, 47
   "O Mirtillo," 51
   "Zefiro torna," 78n.
Montèverdi, G. C., 45–52
Morales, Cristóbal:
   Magnificat in Tone V, 43
Moritz, Landgrave of Hesse-Cassel, 73n.
Mouton, Jean, 48
Muffat, Georg, 82–92
Munich, 90, 136

Nanino, G. M., 40
Naples, 121
Neri, Nero, 19
Netherlands, 136
Nicolini, 151, 154–57
Niedt, Friedrich Erhardt, 93–110

Ockeghem, Joannes, 48
Orpheus, 8, 153, 155, 169

Paciani (singer), 126n.
Palantrotti, Melchior, 15
Palestrina, Giovanni Pierluigi da, 40, 70, 175n.
Palle, Scipione del, 17
Paris, 83, 139, 146n.
Pasquini, Bernardo, 89, 127
Passau, 82, 83, 85, 89, 90
Pausanias, 169
Pecci, Tomaso, 48
Pepusch, John Christopher, *The Beggar's Opera*, 169n.
Peri, Jacopo, 4, 5, 11n., 13–16, 48
   Dafne, 5, 8, 13
   Euridice, 8, 11n., 13–16
Perrault, Charles, 131n.
Perrault, Claude, 131
Petrarch, 159

Philammon, 162
Philbert (flutist), 115n.
Philidor, Anne, 115n.
Pindar, 169
Plato, 18, 46–47, 49, 50, 53, 54n.
Playford, John, 17–32
Pliny, 162
Plutarch, 162
Porta, Costanzo, 40
Ptolemy, 42

Quinault, Philippe, 114, 134

Racine, 145n.
Raguenet, François, 113–28, 131, 144
Rameau, Jean Philippe, 139n., 204–14
Rasi, Francesco, 15
Rich, Christopher, 154
Rinuccini, Ottavio, 5, 7–9, 13
Rome:
   Ancient, 4, 7, 14, 15, 49, 159, 161
   Modern, 5, 19, 61, 70, 71, 89, 121, 126, 127, 128, 135, 137
Rore, Cipriano de, 40, 47, 48, 49
   "Crudel acerba," 47
   "Dalle belle contrade," 47
   "Et se pur mi mantieni amor," 47
   "Non gemme, non fin'oro," 43
   "Poichè m'invita amore," 47
   "Quando signor lasciaste," 52
   "Se bene il duolo," 47
   "Un altra volta la Germania stride," 47
Rossi, Giacomo, 153n.
Rossi, Luigi, 121, 146n.
Rousseau, Jean Jacques, 139n.

Saint Real, Abbé de, 135
Salzburg, 82, 83, 90
Sannazaro, Jacopo, 10, 19
Sartorio, Antonio, *Orfeo*, 128n.
Schütz, Heinrich, 72–81
   "Es steh Gott auf," 77
Segrais, Jean Regnauld de, 145
Sophocles, 8, 161
Strabo, 162
Striggio, Alessandro, "Nasce la pena mia," 52
Strozzi, Leone, 19
Strozzi, Pietro, 15
Stuck, Jean Baptiste, 146n.
Swift, Jonathan, 131n.

Tasso, 54, 153n.
Temple, Sir William, 131n.
Terpander, 162
Timotheus, 48
Turco, Giovanni del, 48
Turin, 121, 128

Vecchi, Orazio, 15
Venice, 54, 73, 76, 121, 127, 128
Vergil, 153
Vespasian, 127
Viadana, Lodovico Grossi da, 59–63
  "O sacrum convivium," 62n.

Vienna, 90, 128n.
Vitello, Erasmus, 36

Watzdorff, Volrad von, 74
Wert, Giaches de, 40, 48
Willaert, Adrian, 40, 48, 49
  "Ne projicias nos," 52
Wotton, Sir Henry, 131n.

Zannettini, Antonio, Temistocle in
  bando, 126n.
Zarlino, Gioseffe, 48, 49, 50, 52, 205,
  207, 208, 212, 214